THE POLITICS OF HUMANITY
The Reality of Relief Aid

John Holmes has been Director of the Ditchley Foundation in Oxfordshire since 2010. Prior to this, he spent three and a half years as UN Under-Secretary-General for Humanitarian Affairs and Emergency Relief Coordinator. John Holmes served in the Foreign and Commonwealth Office for over 30 years, including spells as Ambassador in both Paris and Lisbon, and was Overseas Affairs Adviser to prime ministers Tony Blair and John Major.

THE POLITICS OF HUMANITY

The Reality of Relief Aid

JOHN HOLMES

First published in 2013 by Head of Zeus Ltd.

Copyright © John Holmes 2013

1 3 5 7 9 10 8 6 4 2

A CIP catalogue record for this book is available
from the British Library.

ISBN (HB) 9781781850916
ISBN (XTPB) 9781781850923
ISBN (PB) 9781781850947
ISBN (E) 9781781852088

Printed in Germany.

Head of Zeus Ltd
Clerkenwell House
45–47, Clerkenwell Green
London EC1R OHT

www.headofzeus.com

Dedication

To Penny, for all her patience and support; and Sarah, Lucy and Emilie for their interest and enthusiasm.

To all the staff of OCHA for their commitment, and particularly to the members of my private office for their dedication to my welfare and performance. Special thanks to Andrew Cox and Shani Harris for their encouragement and comments.

Finally to all those working for and supporting humanitarian organisations throughout the world, who do so much to help others at their time of greatest need.

Maps

All maps are used courtesy of the United Nations Office for the Coordination of Humanitarian Affairs (OCHA).

The publishers would like to express their thanks to Akiko Harayama of the Communications and Information Services Branch (CISB)/OCHA/United Nations, for her assistance in the making of this book.

The boundaries and names shown and the designations used on the maps do not imply official endorsement or acceptance by the United Nations.

The designations employed and the presentation of material on the map of the Occupied Palestinian Territories do not imply the expression of any opinion whatsoever on the part of the Secretariat of the United Nations concerning the legal status of any country, territory, city or area or of its authorities or concerning the delimitation of its frontiers or boundaries.

Contents

INTRODUCTION

An accidental humanitarian   1

CHAPTER ONE

The Secret Life of an Emergency Relief Coordinator   13

CHAPTER TWO

Darfur: how not to solve a crisis   25

CHAPTER THREE

South Sudan: the (unmade) road to independence   63

CHAPTER FOUR

Sri Lanka: the end of the LTTE   85

CHAPTER FIVE

The Democratic Republic of Congo: not losing hope   131

CHAPTER SIX

Somalia: endless night   163

CHAPTER SEVEN

Myanmar: cyclone strike and government obstruction   189

CHAPTER EIGHT

Gaza: collective punishment, conflict and controversy   219

CHAPTER NINE
Afghanistan and Pakistan: safeguarding humanitarian space   253

CHAPTER TEN
Earthquake horrors in Haiti   285

CHAPTER ELEVEN
Food Insecurity: country lessons and the 2008 food crisis   313

CHAPTER TWELVE
Prevention is better than cure: acting before disasters happen   341

CHAPTER THIRTEEN
Humanitarian Intervention, and protecting civilians in
armed conflict   363

CHAPTER FOURTEEN
Humanitarianism in the twenty-first century: rising needs
and declining security   393

GLOSSARY   407
INDEX   410

An accidental humanitarian

Standing on Clermont-Ferrand TGV station in early December 2006, I took a call from Prime Minister Tony Blair. After thirty-three years in the Foreign Office, and more than five as ambassador in Paris, there were no obvious diplomatic jobs available for me at that moment. I guessed the prime minister was a little embarrassed about this, since I had worked as his diplomatic adviser for two years after his 1997 election victory.

He came quickly to the point. He wanted someone 'good' to take a senior job in the UN Secretariat. The UK had had no one at under-secretary-general (USG) level for more than a year. Kieran Prendergast, USG for political affairs for ten years (the latest in a line of distinguished Britons holding that post since the legendary Brian Urquhart), had been eased out in 2005. Now the British government wanted the post back and were hoping that the new secretary-general-elect, South Korean Ban ki-Moon, would oblige.

I was not at all sure I wanted to go abroad again after eight years in Lisbon and Paris. And although I had enjoyed a short spell in New York thirty years before, the UN did not have a great reputation as a place to get things done. But when the prime minister asks, particularly one as persuasive as Tony Blair, saying no is not easy. I agreed to think about it. He stressed that Ban

1

was putting his senior management team together and that other countries were also pressing hard for the top spots. I needed to get out to New York in person quickly.

When I saw him, Ban ki-Moon surprised me almost as much as Tony Blair had by making clear that the job of USG for political affairs was not, in fact, available. He did not say so, but he had already promised it to the Americans in exchange for their support for his candidacy. He offered me instead the job of USG for humanitarian affairs and Emergency Relief Coordinator (ERC), then most recently held by Norwegian Jan Egeland – a distinguished humanitarian, though perhaps best known to press and public for supposedly calling the Americans stingy in the immediate aftermath of the Indian Ocean tsunami of 2004.

I explained that I knew nothing of humanitarian affairs. Moreover, I was not sure that, being British, I had the right nationality for the job. We were seen by many as military interveners, particularly after Iraq – not the best recommendation, even if the UK was a generous aid contributor. Ban was unimpressed by these arguments. In his persistent way, he made clear that he liked British fairness and common sense, and was sure I could do the job well.

I took advice from those who knew the UN. Most were positive. Not only was the task obviously worthwhile, but as ERC you had more freedom of action and scope to make a difference than most USGs. The UK Department for International Development, the givers of British humanitarian aid, swallowed their reservations about my non-existent humanitarian credentials and encouraged me. My long-suffering wife reluctantly gave a green light. So in the end, not without misgivings, I agreed. This was the start of a fascinating and exhausting three and a half years as ERC, and head of the excitingly named UN Office for the Coordination of Humanitarian Affairs (OCHA).

I had two months to resign from the Foreign Office, leave Paris in an orderly fashion, become an instant expert on humanitarian issues, and get to New York in order to start work in earnest on 1 March 2007. Meanwhile, some humanitarian non-governmental organizations (NGOs) had not taken well the appointment of a diplomatic type as ERC and had voiced their disapproval publicly, including in the correspondence columns of the *Financial Times*. I had to grin and bear it, having nothing much to offer in my defence at that stage. I simply hoped that I would do a good enough job in practice to win them over.

The humanitarian 'system'

What was I supposed to be coordinating? The international humanitarian set-up is not a 'system' in any recognizable sense. Rather, it is a collection of organizations and groups which have, over the years, been morally impelled to alleviate the world's misery.

Humanitarianism as we know it today was founded by a Swiss businessman called Henri Dunant, inspired by the desperate plight of the wounded after the Battle of Solferino between the French and the Austrians in 1859. The International Committee of the Red Cross (ICRC) which resulted was the first organized group dedicated to helping victims internationally. They drafted the First Geneva Convention in 1863, articulating the basic tenets of humanitarian relief: humanity, independence, neutrality, and impartiality.

These principles have remained the guidelines for humanitarians ever since. Their essence is that the unique driving force of humanitarian aid must be the needs of the suffering, based on objective criteria, irrespective of the political, ethnic or religious affiliation of either the people in need or those providing the aid.

3

Humanitarian relief must not be used for political or security purposes, still less withheld for such reasons, or manipulated in other ways. Humanitarian aid is a moral imperative, not part of anyone's stabilization strategy. If I emphasize this now, it is because so many of the issues raised in what follows cannot be understood except in the light of these principles.

The ICRC was followed into the field by many other organizations: the International Federation of the Red Cross/ Red Crescent (IFRC), bringing together all the national Red Cross and Red Crescent Societies; the United Nations High Commissioner for Refugees (UNHCR); the United Nations Children's Fund (UNICEF); the World Food Programme (WFP); the humanitarian arms of the Food and Agriculture Organization (FAO), the World Health Organization (WHO), the UN Population Fund (UNFPA), and so on; the increasingly numerous international NGOs, i.e. independent charitable groups not answerable to anyone other than their own governing structures and those who give them money – OXFAM, Save the Children, Médecins Sans Frontières, World Vision, the International Rescue Committee, Care, Concern, Action Contre la Faim, Islamic Relief, and many others; and a further largely unknown and under-appreciated universe of local NGOs and civil society organizations. To call this community fragmented is an understatement, even by British standards. And its fragmentation is if anything increasing, even though there is a more positive side of diversity too.

The aim of humanitarian aid is simple: to keep alive those worst affected by natural disasters and conflict, and allow them some human dignity and a modicum of hope for the future. It is about emergency relief, not longer-term development or encouraging good governance in other countries, however much we want these things. It can involve urgent rescue from danger, for example after an earthquake, but mostly means making sure the bare necessities of life are available: food, clean water and sanitation, medical care and shelter.

However it does not stop there. Protection of the vulnerable from abuse, particularly but not only women, children, the elderly, and the sick, is increasingly important. Emergency education for children traumatized by having been stuck in camps for months on end can be hugely important psychologically, restoring some sense of normality to them. Urgent help to enable people to restart their livelihoods quickly is vital, particularly seeds and tools for local farmers, to make sure more than one harvest is not missed. Sometimes cash is part of the answer, to help get people back on their own feet and reduce their dependence.

The amount of international humanitarian aid made available in any one year varies according to the number of major disasters, but from 2005 to 2010 it averaged around $12 billion. Where exactly does this money come from and where does it go to? It comes mostly from a few generous Western governments, but also from the private sector, and, to some extent, from individuals.

Governments who give money to humanitarian causes usually set aside a certain proportion of their overall development aid budgets for this purpose, often around 10 per cent of the total. They then allocate this money through the year to the main crises, and sometimes smaller ones too, in response to appeals for help, usually from the UN acting on behalf of the rest of the system. These countries are often collectively referred to as the 'donors'. They can and often do have strong views on how and where their money is spent, and there is a constant dialogue between them and the organizations to which they are giving money. Their motives in giving humanitarian aid are essentially altruistic, to respond to glaring need and to demand from their publics to do something when disaster strikes. But there can also be other

5

factors at work, such as historical links with particular countries or political or other motives for wanting to be sure that a certain population group does not suffer.

For their part, private-sector companies become involved for a variety of reasons, often to do with the views of a particular company leader. Individuals give usually because they see something which touches or scandalizes them on television, though many also subscribe on a regular basis to the charity/NGO of their choice.

Around 70 per cent of humanitarian aid normally goes to the victims of conflict, with the rest going to those affected by natural disasters. Two thirds goes to Africa, with Asia and Latin America next, but some way behind.

The destination of the money is most often humanitarian organizations of one kind or another – the Red Cross, UN agencies or the major NGOs – though it can in some cases be given directly to the government of the country affected. Some money is given as core annual financing for the humanitarian organization concerned, not tied to any one crisis. But for the most part, the organizations put forward specific requests to fund specific needs and are expected to account carefully for how the money they are given is spent. They will often themselves subcontract local organizations in the country in question to implement the projects for them, under close supervision. In their turn, they insist on close accountability from them for where the money actually goes, all without falling into the trap of too much bureaucracy when people are at risk of dying. Because of these precautions, and particularly because humanitarian aid does not generally pass through the hands of the governments of affected countries but is channelled straight to those in need, the risks of diversion or corruption are relatively low.

But there is a constant struggle to get everyone working

together, to keep the overhead costs down, to make sure the aid is effective and what people actually need, and to be sensitive to local cultures. Humanitarian efforts have improved out of all recognition in the last twenty years – financing, speed of response, professionalism, and coordination. However, humanitarians themselves, a self-critical bunch, are only too aware of how much further there is to go.

The UN's Office for the Coordination of Humanitarian Affairs and the ERC are needed precisely because the system is so fragmented. Without central coordination, the risks of gaps in coverage of relief aid, whether in terms of geographical areas or sectors, or of duplication of coverage, and more widely of a lack of overall coherence are unacceptably high. The problem was recognized more than twenty years ago, in 1991, when the UN created the Department of Humanitarian Affairs, renamed the Office for the Coordination of Humanitarian Affairs in 2001.

OCHA has over time become centrally involved not only in coordination, but also in areas such as policy development, standards, advocacy, training, early warning, and fund-raising. It runs the collective appeals on behalf of all humanitarian organizations, with detailed projects in the key sectors: so-called 'consolidated appeals' for continuing crises and 'flash appeals' for new catastrophes. It currently has a staff of some 1900. Four hundred and fifty are divided between the New York headquarters and Geneva and the rest, mostly local staff, are scattered around the world.

Global policy coordination is assured through a body called the Inter-Agency Standing Committee, chaired by the Emergency Relief Coordinator. This brings together the heads of the main UN agencies, NGOs and the Red Cross family to agree on policies and on the issues thrown up by the crises of the day, as well as on wider standards.

But most coordination is done at local level (where it is most needed) through the OCHA country office and a country-level humanitarian coordinator. The latter is a senior international official with an aid background and lots of experience, appointed by the ERC and given specific responsibilities and accountabilities for the delivery of humanitarian aid in the country concerned. He or she is often, for coherence reasons, the same individual as the UN resident coordinator, who brings together the activities of all the different UN agencies and organizations in the country, mostly on the development side. In certain circumstances, however, it can be a separate appointment to ensure that he or she can concentrate on, and speak out freely about, humanitarian issues without either worrying about other responsibilities or having to stick unduly close to the views of the local government. This is a controversial area, as we shall see.

Neither the ERC, nor the local humanitarian coordinator, nor OCHA more generally, has the power to issue instructions to the many organizations involved. They can only recommend, encourage, and exhort. The Red Cross is completely independent, and the UN agencies and NGOs are also fiercely protective of their own brand of independence. All concerned recognize the need to be coordinated, even if they find it irritating at times, and do their best to cooperate. But this kind of voluntary arrangement has obvious drawbacks.

As a result of weaknesses shown up by the 2004 Indian Ocean tsunami and the Darfur crisis, my predecessor set in motion a process of reform, with the strong support of key government donors. The main change was the appointment of a lead agency within each of the main sectors (rechristened 'clusters'), with the responsibility of ensuring needs were met and proper coordination was guaranteed in that sector, at both a global and a local level. For example, the World Health Organization leads the health cluster, the World Food Programme leads on food, and UNICEF on protection of civilians. OCHA's task is to ensure that all this is working and to provide overall coordination between these clusters.

A new financing mechanism was also established, the UN Central Emergency Response Fund (CERF), financed annually by governments to the tune of some $400 million, to kick-start the response immediately after a new crisis appears and ensure fair funding between different crises. Under the direct control of the ERC, this is a hugely helpful tool.

Other changes were designed to improve the quality of humanitarian coordinators on the ground (for example, by widening the pool from which they are recruited) and to drive much closer partnership between UN and non-UN actors, particularly NGOs.

These reforms have been a success overall, though implementation has been patchy. But there are still many questions about whether the 'system' is fit for purpose, as we shall see.

The ERC is responsible not only for overall coordination of aid operations and fund-raising for the system, but also for ensuring common policy approaches, and drawing attention to neglected crises. He or she is expected to be the voice of the voiceless and the spokesman for humanitarianism in general (without actually presuming to speak specifically on behalf of the independent organizations which make up the system), and to be the collective negotiator with reluctant or actively unhelpful governments and non-state actors, in order to achieve access to those in need. The ERC has to denounce breaches of accepted principles and uphold the rights of those affected by conflict or disaster, without straying too far into politics or the domain of human rights. It is often a high-wire act.

From March 2007 to August 2010, I made eighty-five overseas trips, covering almost 300,000 miles, and visited forty-three countries, many several times. I saw suffering humanity in every conceivable setting, and talked to leaders, humanitarians and as many as possible of the affected people themselves. I battled to be non-political in situations which were highly politicized. I tried to speak out about abuses by governments or rebel movements, or both, without destroying our standing with either, so that humanitarian organizations could continue their work on the ground. I endeavoured to avoid exaggeration, and to stick to saying what we knew, even at the expense of easy headlines. I worked to raise awareness of humanitarian needs around the world, and to reassure those providing the money that it was being well spent.

My aim in this book is not to give an account of what I did for its own sake, but to use experiences of specific crises in which I was involved to show the difficulties and complexities of humanitarian policy and practice, particularly in conflict settings, and to promote better understanding between humanitarians and governments. The objective is also to relate humanitarian issues to broader international questions, drawing on my previous experience in the FCO and as adviser to two prime ministers. Seeing crises from both ends – the field reality in some of the bleakest places on earth, as well as the strategic view from a comfortable diplomatic chair – made me think in new ways about the world. The observations in this book are the fruits of those reflections.

There is a lot of 'I' in the previous paragraphs and in the book as a whole. This is shorthand. It was not, of course, 'I' at all. The dedicated staff of OCHA and many other humanitarian organizations were the ones doing the hard grind. I have not often mentioned the names of others in what follows in order not to confuse the reader. But my dependence on them was total, and this book is about their work, not mine.

I have aimed to be dispassionate about the events I describe. But behind the occasionally dry-seeming policy issues were always individuals suffering in dire and deadly circumstances. Helping them was always the priority.

I have tried not to shy away from the weaknesses which exist, or from admitting mistakes. My main concern is to help ensure that humanitarian issues are better understood, that humanitarian needs are never overlooked or subordinated to political ends, and that the right policies and resources continue to be found to reduce suffering.

CHAPTER ONE

The Secret Life of an Emergency Relief Coordinator

It may be easier to understand the chapters about individual crises which follow, and relate to the issues raised, if I give a little more background on how the UN works from a humanitarian point of view, and how the ERC fits into the system, both in the UN and more widely. For example, what is working life like in New York, and what does a field trip to see a crisis on the ground actually consist of?

To start with New York, as ERC and under-secretary-general for humanitarian affairs, I was one of the senior members of the UN Secretariat, the body of international officials under the secretary-general who serve the UN membership in the various fields of its activity. This central secretariat is separate from, but works closely with, the UN specialized agencies, which deal on an operational level with individual issues such as economic development (UNDP), agriculture (FAO), or food (WFP). I had an office on the thirty-sixth floor of the main UN building (the iconic skyscraper on the East River in Manhattan), two floors below the secretary-general, and therefore in close proximity to him, alongside my political and peacekeeping colleagues. This reflected the ERC's position as one of Ban ki-Moon's key advisers. This was true not only in my own area of humanitarian operations, which was important to him and the organization, because we could make a visible and popular difference in an area which was on the whole not politically contentious between the different UN groupings, but also more broadly on the wider political challenges facing the UN. My experience and background gave me a breadth of view which I think had a certain value. I was also in a position where I could express my views with total independence and freedom, since I was not engaged in the political or peacekeeping operations myself, and was in no way beholden to the British or any other government, for my future career or anything else.

This readiness to say what I thought about issues which were outside the strict purview of my own department did not always endear me to my closest UN colleagues, particularly the heads of the Departments of Political Affairs and of Peacekeeping, and occasionally those on the development side too. But I tried to ensure that any differences were always kept private, and that working relationships overall remained good.

My association with Ban ki-Moon and his key staff was also close and positive. Whatever criticisms there may be of Ban, I always found him supportive of me and of humanitarian concerns, anxious to do the right thing, and genuinely moved by the suffering of the victims of disasters or conflicts, partly based on his own tough and humble upbringing in the aftermath of the Korean War. In my experience he was hardworking to a fault, totally honest, absolutely committed to the UN and its role, and determined to make a difference where he could. His political instincts were usually sound and his readiness to tell his frequent senior visitors what they did not want to hear much greater than often supposed from the outside.

He has weaker points, of which he is well aware himself. He is not charismatic or a great strategic thinker. Like his predecessors, he is not in a position to tell the big powers what to do nor to fix their disagreements (of course they themselves do not really want a strong secretary-general, whatever they claim in public). But the UN and the international community could have done a good deal worse, especially at a very difficult time of many simultaneous political and economic crises (and long-term climate challenge, on which he has been particularly outspoken). Ban has also been a notable victim of the usual media tendency to confuse the UN as an institution with its member states, blaming the former for the failings and disagreements of the latter.

In any case, I worked closely and well with Ban ki-Moon on some of the key issues I faced in Myanmar, Haiti, and elsewhere, and was grateful to him for his readiness to back me up against obstructive or critical local governments when necessary. I am not, therefore, among those who blame him for the world's ills or look back to a presumed golden age when the UN secretary-general was supposedly a real world leader.

Although I was away from New York a good deal, when I was there I was a frequent participant in the secretary-general's formal policy committee meetings, looking at the big issues we faced, and also in the rather more important and operational informal meetings he called on a frequent basis to deal with tricky problems like Darfur, peacekeeping issues in the Congo, Middle East dilemmas, or how to address the aftermath of the Haiti earthquake of 2010.

But I also had my own humanitarian policy responsibilities to tackle and my own constituencies to coordinate and, where necessary, lead. There were various bodies which helped me to stay in touch with the big issues and coordinate policy approaches. I chaired a monthly meeting of the UN Executive Committee on Humanitarian Affairs, which brought together the heads of the main UN humanitarian organizations – UNHCR, UNICEF,

WFP, and so on – together with representatives from the political, economic, and human rights parts of the UN Secretariat. We looked regularly at the main crises, to ensure we were all pointing in the same direction, and at big cross-cutting issues, and tried to make sure that our debates were not just theoretical, but as practical as possible with hard conclusions and recommendations which the participants were supposed to implement.

There was also a parallel humanitarian policy and coordination structure, under the broad umbrella of the so-called Inter-Agency Standing Committee (IASC), which involved not only the UN humanitarian organizations, but also the main humanitarian NGOs and the Red Cross/Red Crescent bodies. This met formally from time to time, but more importantly could be convened immediately in person or by video/teleconference whenever a new crisis struck to make sure that information about needs and problems was instantly and fully shared, and any policy issues identified and dealt with – for example, about free access to the affected area or how to raise sufficient funding for an effective operation to be mounted.

As always, these formal bodies had their uses, but the real work was done through personal contacts outside them, at all levels. I spent a good deal of time on the phone to the heads of the main humanitarian organizations, within and outside the UN, and to the main donors, to make sure the fragmented system was as joined up as we could make it in the circumstances.

Much of my time was also obviously devoted to running OCHA itself, trying to ensure it was administratively and financially sound (unlike other parts of the UN Secretariat, we were mostly dependent on voluntary funding from governments), and that it was contributing effectively to humanitarian relief efforts around the world. This meant a lot of internal management and coordination in New York and Geneva, as well as much time spent liaising with and talking to our field offices and the humanitarian coordinators on the ground, especially in the hottest spots of the day.

Although many people are scathing about the effectiveness of UN bureaucracy, I considered myself fortunate in OCHA for the most part, since the staff there were relatively young, and were dedicated humanitarians, not office-bound time-servers. Many had previously worked in NGOs and brought to the UN that can-do operational spirit so desperately needed in crises. I was hugely grateful for their knowledge, support, and energy.

I was particularly fortunate in my personal office, with totally committed staff ready to work all hours if necessary, notably Andrew Cox, chief of staff for most of my time, and Shani Harris, my special assistant for nearly all of it. They kept me up to speed not only with what was going on around the world, but also the inside story of developments within the UN and OCHA itself. They also kept me on the right road, metaphorically and literally, on the frequent field trips.

A lot of my time in New York was also spent dealing with the press, particularly when a new and media-attractive crisis struck. I was a frequent guest briefer at the UN Press Office's daily press conference, as well as giving apparently endless interviews to the radio, TV and newspapers from around the world. Trying to make sure that the right messages got through about what was happening on the ground, that major needs were not going unmet because of ignorance, and that abuses by governments or others were being exposed, was a crucial part of my role. Being available to the press more or less all the time was, therefore, essential.

Consequently, working days in New York were long and packed with meetings and encounters of all kinds. However, it was clear to me from my first day in office that the job could not be done properly just from New York – or indeed Geneva, the other major international humanitarian centre. In order to understand what was really happening in any emergency, and to be able to talk about it and the associated problems with any credibility and conviction, I had to go to see for myself. This was why I spent so much time on the road, despite the demands of headquarters in New York, and the valuable work to be done there.

The number of crises needing my attention meant that the time available for visits was never sufficient. It was therefore necessary to cram as much as possible into short periods, even when the destinations were distant and the travelling time at the other end long and tiring. I was lucky in some respects – I was often able to call on the UN's resources to get me to remote areas quickly, for example using peacekeeping helicopters. Nevertheless, in many places there was no avoiding long trips over rough roads or tracks to get to the people in need. And there was no substitute for this: I had to meet those we were trying to help, to understand exactly why they were where they were, and what they really thought and needed. I also had to talk to the humanitarian staff on the ground – again, in order to have a clear picture of what they and we were really up against and how I could best contribute to resolving some of the problems they faced. I needed to experience a little of what they were experiencing on a daily basis, by staying in the places they had to stay in – often so-called guest houses. These were basic buildings in remote locations, with rudimentary facilities, put up by a UN organization or NGO to ensure their staff had at least somewhere to rest their heads at night, and some kind of office with communications back to headquarters.

A typical field visit would involve arriving in an African or Asian capital on an overnight flight from New York via Europe.

After a rapid briefing from the UN resident/humanitarian coordinator and the head of the OCHA country office (if one existed in the country we were visiting), I would plunge straight into initial meetings with senior representatives from the local government, the heads of the main local humanitarian organizations (UN, Red Cross and NGOs, sometimes separately, sometimes together) and often a group of local ambassadors from the main countries too. I would be both learning from them how they saw the local situation, and giving them my overall approach based on what I knew already.

Then it would be straight to the airport to catch an internal plane or helicopter flight to the affected area and/or a car journey to the site of the action. After supper with the local humanitarians and a short night's sleep, we would be off the next morning to the camps or the disaster location, to get round as many of the key points as possible. At each place I would need to meet the local authority representatives first, as a courtesy and to get their point of view, but also to ensure that they did not control my visit, so that I would see the reality, not just what they wanted me to see. I would then visit the people we were trying to help, meeting as many of them – individually or collectively – as possible, without the presence of the local police or army, so they could speak freely. To complement whatever I was hearing from the local male leaders, separate meetings with the women were always an important feature, giving me a more grounded and less political view.

I would be accompanied by staff from my own local OCHA office, as well as from other agencies and NGOs, to explain what I was seeing and to act as interpreters as necessary. I usually travelled in the car between meetings with the representative of a particular humanitarian agency or NGO to allow them to bend my ear on their own preoccupations, partly for my own edification, but also to give them the sense that we were listening to all points of view.

The meetings with those affected were often harrowing and distressing. They were anxious to tell me their stories and their sufferings, and to make sure I understood exactly what they needed. Tears and anger were not uncommon, but extraordinary calm and dignity in the face of unimaginable tragedy and violence were more usual. My minders were always anxious to move me on, since we were usually behind schedule, with many more people and places to see before the day was done. But I never felt I could leave without hearing people out. I could do little enough to help them in all conscience, and the least I could do was to listen and understand, so as to equip myself to represent them to the outside world.

After each stop, there was usually a gathering of the press – local or international – to allow me to talk for a few minutes about what I had seen and heard, and individual interviews to give in addition. I typically had to steer a careful course between emotional outbursts concerning the horrors I had just seen or heard about, and the need to maintain some kind of working relationship either with the local government or armed group in question or both. I was often walking on eggshells, and choosing my language very carefully. My diplomatic background certainly came in useful at these moments, though some humanitarian colleagues would have preferred me to be less diplomatic and more emotional at times.

After finally arriving at our destination for the night, my day would be far from done. I would eat with another group of aid workers, to give them their chance to ensure I understood what they were dealing with – and there were invariably a few who could not wait to give me a piece of their minds about the iniquities of UN policy – before facing a further round of interviews, often down a crackly mobile phone line to the BBC World Service or their French equivalent.

My final acts before collapsing into bed after a couple of glasses of whisky, if I could find some, would be to catch up on emails and messages from New York and take any decisions needed on them, and then approve a report back to New York about what we had seen and done that day, and agree a written press release for wider publicity purposes. The next morning would see us up and on the road early to repeat the process in a different part of the crisis area, often with more helicopter or road journeys taking a significant proportion of time, as well as energy.

Following two or three days of this kind of field trip, I would return to the capital. This generally meant further high-level calls on the government, including if possible the president or prime minister, to make them aware of the reality of what was going on in a remote part of their country they might never have visited themselves, and to ask for their help in facilitating our work and changing unacceptable parts of their own policies. This entailed more tightrope walking with senior politicians who were proud and sensitive to interference in their affairs from outsiders (particularly from someone from a former colonial power), but who needed to be brought to face the facts of what was actually happening on the ground, and the problems being caused by parts of their own governments or themselves.

I also had to report back on what I had seen and on my policy conclusions to the local humanitarian teams in the capital and to the ambassadors, as well as hold a final press conference with a combination of the local media (usually anxious to protect the reputation of their country) and the international correspondents (looking for a headline and a row between me and the local government, if they could find one). Then it was back to the airport to catch a plane out, normally by the skin of my teeth, just grateful when the flight back was long enough to catch up on a little sleep.

Once back in New York, the last part of any such trip was the private reports to Ban ki-Moon and to the heads of other international agencies and NGOs about my impressions and conclusions. I often gave a more public report to the Security Council, which was an important opportunity to bring home to them the severity and requirements of the situation, and to try to influence their thinking about some of the key issues. There was also usually a New York press conference and related interviews.

Of course, the visits were not just work. They were fascinating, and often fun too, in their own special way – or at least enlivened by lighter moments of particularly ludicrous behaviour by my hosts or colleagues, or surreal experiences which only those with me could really understand or appreciate. Take, for example, an unexpected local medal handed out in the full heat of the African sun by the president in one capital, to the accompaniment of an execrably played national anthem; or landing literally in the middle of nowhere (having cleared the goats off the dirt runway first by a low-level pass), only to be met by a keen local UN representative giving us a battery-fuelled PowerPoint presentation on the glorious future of the country we were in. Moments like these helped keep us going through the more harrowing visits and meetings where man's inhumanity to man was all too starkly on show.

I record all this not to say that I had an impossibly hard life – though it was certainly busy enough, which was why most of my predecessors as ERC had not lasted more than a couple of years – but to illustrate what lies behind the process of understanding humanitarian affairs and policy-making about them. I hope this will help bring to life what I have to say about the particular crises, without needing to explain on each occasion what a visit to the country concerned actually meant.

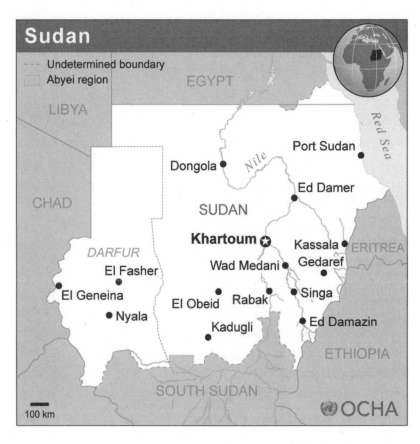

Sudan

- - - Undetermined boundary

Abyei region

EGYPT

LIBYA

Red Sea

Port Sudan

Dongola   Nile

CHAD

Ed Damer

SUDAN

Khartoum ✪

Kassala   ERITREA

DARFUR

El Fasher

Wad Medani   Gedaref

El Geneina

Singa

Nyala

El Obeid   Rabak

Kadugli   Ed Damazin

ETHIOPIA

SOUTH SUDAN

⊛OCHA

100 km

Map Sources: UNCS, SIM, Natural Earth. Map created in Jan 2012.
Final boundary between the Republic of Sudan and the republic of South Sudan has not yet been determined. Final status of the Abyei area is not yet determined.

CHAPTER TWO

Darfur: how not to solve a crisis

The first place I visited in my capacity as ERC was Sudan in March 2007. It was a gruelling trip during which I also travelled to Chad and the Central African Republic – a real baptism of fire.

Darfur was the biggest humanitarian operation in the world, and I spent much of my time as ERC grappling with the Khartoum government to keep the operation there going, and prevent harassment of those on the ground. The government were unprincipled, and determined to keep the whip hand over a community who were providing vital aid, but who were also witness to the terrible things the government were doing in Darfur. I learned at first hand the difficulties of sticking to humanitarian principles in such a context, as well as the dilemmas which flow from the tension between peace and justice.

The background

Darfur (land of the Fur, one of the main tribes) is a large, arid region in western Sudan, bordering mainly on Chad, with a population of around 6 million people. It became a household name in 2003 when fighting broke out between mainly African rebels and the Sudanese army. The causes included demands for greater autonomy, and for more money from Khartoum for development and infrastructure, but also strong feelings among Africans of being discriminated against by the Arabs, in charge in Khartoum and locally. The Africans are mostly sedentary and the Arabs mostly nomads, and conflict over water and grazing land is an important part of the story, against a background of advancing desertification. But the groups overlap more than is usually understood. Both are black and largely Muslim, and both speak mostly Arabic.

Everything about Darfur is controversial, including the nature and origins of the conflict. But the core of the problem is poor governance in Khartoum, and marginalization of the peripheral regions, the east and the south, as well as the west. Decisions are concentrated in the hands of a small minority, and the benefits from oil revenues have not spread much beyond the capital. The resulting resentment has fuelled conflicts across the country. Sudan's limited sources of oil are likely to dry up soon, which will exacerbate the issues of underdevelopment around the country, but also put new pressure on the governing military elite – if the contagion of the Arab spring has not radically changed the situation before then.

The armed revolt in Darfur was led by two main rebel groups: the Sudan Liberation Movement/Army (SLM/A) and the Justice and Equality Movement (JEM). The government enlisted on their side local militias drawn principally from the Arab nomadic tribes, who became known as the 'janjaweed' – the men on horseback. Their interest was partly the money they were paid by the government, but also the prospect of loot and grazing land. The direct fighting between the rebels and the government quickly stagnated, but the janjaweed were unleashed in a reign of terror, burning villages and driving out the inhabitants. Murder and rape were commonplace, and vast numbers of mainly African villagers fled to safer parts of Darfur or, in the case of almost

250,000 of them, across the western border into Chad. The janjaweed have never been disarmed or disbanded, despite international demands, though they have become disillusioned themselves by the failure of the government to reward them properly for their crimes.

The international community was slow to realize the scale of what was happening and reluctant to react when it did. There is still controversy over how far killing in Darfur was deliberately played down in New York in the early stages for fear of jeopardizing the simultaneous talks on a peace agreement in the south. However, by late 2003 the humanitarian aid agencies were waking up to the fact that there was a major crisis in Darfur. They set in motion what became a huge operation to establish camps for the displaced and provide the necessary food, water, and medical care. But it was poorly organized. Awareness of this helped drive the wider reform of the international humanitarian community described in the introduction, particularly much stronger coordination within the main 'clusters' of assistance.

By early 2004, more than 2 million people had fled their homes and villages, and more than 1 million were in a network of camps all over Darfur. The struggle to keep them alive, costing around 1 billion US dollars per year, continues as I write in mid-2012. Almost two thirds of the population depend to some extent on international aid, and however laudable the intentions of the humanitarian community, and however necessary the aid, this has, over time, raised some fundamental questions. Was it right for the international community to take on almost the entire burden of the displaced, leaving the government (and rebels) free to pursue the conflict, safe in the knowledge that the victims would be taken care of by someone else? What will be the long-term consequences of the huge camps for the economic and social fabric of Darfur, let alone its fragile environment – many camps are well on the way to becoming suburbs of the main towns, and the number of those likely ever to return home is steadily diminishing. Should the international community go on with its humanitarian assistance programme while the government continues to make life for the agencies providing it so difficult?

Darfur saw a major controversy over casualties – a pattern in many crises. On the basis of a morbidity study by the International Rescue Committee, my predecessor Jan Egeland suggested in 2006 that some 200,000 people had died because of the conflict. The media have constantly and wilfully taken this to mean that 200,000 people had been killed violently, whereas the figure referred mostly to premature deaths as a result of the stresses of conflict and displacement. The true figure of violent deaths is unknown, but is probably in the low tens of thousands. In 2008, I told the Security Council that an extrapolation of the figures given by Jan Egeland would suggest extra deaths had by then reached 300,000, though this could only be a rough estimate. The figure was again taken by many to refer to violent deaths, and the Sudanese government reacted with predictable fury, claiming that only some 9000 people had been killed in Darfur altogether since the beginning of the conflict in 2003 – a figure that is certainly too low, even for those violently killed. This controversy continues.

The important wider point here is that we too often reduce the casualty figures of conflict to those who die by violence. The indirect effects are often much more deadly, if also more difficult to calculate. The gulf between the two kinds of figures is even more striking in the case of Congo, as we shall see in Chapter Five.

By 2006, as janjaweed attacks continued, and displacement increased, the war was settling into a nasty stalemate. That year saw the first serious effort by the international community to settle the conflict. Internationally mediated negotiations between the government and the two main rebel movements (the SLM/A and the JEM) resulted in the Darfur Peace Agreement (DPA), finalized in the Nigerian capital, Abuja, in May 2006. It set out power- and wealth-sharing arrangements, and created a Transitional Darfur Regional Authority, in advance of a final referendum on Darfur's status.

But the finalization of this agreement was rushed by the international mediators and only the Sudan Liberation Movement (SLM/A) signed it in the end. The Justice and Equality Movement (JEM), then led by the nationally ambitious Khalil Ibrahim, refused to do so, then or later. The DPA has remained largely stillborn as a result. Its provisions are not unreasonable in themselves, and much of it will no doubt need to be incorporated into any final peace settlement. Nevertheless, it was simply not able to attract sufficient support either from the rebel leaders or from the displaced themselves. It certainly did not stop the violence.

Peace efforts since, led by various joint UN and African Union mediators, with support from international envoys, have gone through many phases. But it has never been clear that either the authorities or the rebels are really ready to make the necessary compromises for a new, more effective agreement. There was a tendency in the early days of the conflict, particularly in the Western media, to see the rebels as heroic freedom fighters. Over time, there has been greater recognition that, whatever their original genuine grievances, their own actions often bear little scrutiny. Their lack of military effectiveness, inability to bridge their own internal divisions, and chronic liability to split into ever more fragmented groups, have reduced their credibility and made them particularly frustrating interlocutors. At one stage there were no fewer than twenty different groups or factions, some without much if any fighting ability, and most without clear leadership or a discernible political platform. Granted, Khartoum has cynically encouraged these divisions, through bribes and fifth columnists. But the absence of a unified and credible negotiating partner on the other side has always provided the government with a pretext for lack of progress in peace efforts, and spared them from the real effort of making the necessary compromises.

Darfur peacekeeping

Peace efforts have included the deployment of international forces. The African Mission in Sudan (AMIS) was an African Union force mandated and supported by the UN Security Council, which deployed in 2004. In theory, it had some 10,000 troops but it was never at full strength, and remained ill equipped and unable to impose its will in such a huge territory. It was replaced in 2007 by a joint UN/AU force, UNAMID. Led by a joint special representative appointed by the AU and the UN, and commanded by African generals, in practice it relied heavily on UN direction and support.

Headquarters discussions of Darfur during my first eighteen months were dominated by the attempt to bring UNAMID up to its full strength of 26,000 troops. It was the main subject of Ban ki-Moon's regular Policy Committee meetings at the time, and of a special group of senior officials looking at Sudan issues, which I also attended. Under heavy pressure from events and Western member states, he was constantly insisting to my peacekeeping colleagues that this process move faster. They were doing their best. But the fact was that obtaining suitably trained and equipped forces, and providing the logistical support they needed, was a mammoth task. It would have been so even with a helpful host government. But the Khartoum government had opposed the deployment of international forces from the start and only accepted UNAMID under great international pressure. They did everything in their power to slow down its deployment, complicate its task, and weaken its capacity.

The government had many levers at their disposal to achieve this: insistence that they had to agree which countries would provide the forces, and that these should be exclusively African; bureaucratic measures to slow down the movement of materiel and men on the long route through Port Sudan to Darfur; arguments over use of local airfields, including blocks on their use at night, even in case of emergency; refusal to provide visas for officers from countries they did not like; demands that their sovereignty be respected in every area conceivable, from water to troop movements. And so on. These obstacles could be and were overcome, but this all took time and huge political effort.

The almost fatal handicap was a combination of Sudanese insistence on African troops (who were not necessarily sufficiently trained or equipped for such operations and therefore needed extra time and money to reach the required readiness) and the reluctance by Western and other countries to put at the UN's disposal crucial force multipliers: lift and attack helicopters and other aircraft. This was in spite of multiple, desperate appeals from Ban ki-Moon. Ironically, the countries who refused practical help with this key equipment were often the very same ones who were most critical of UN HQ for its slowness and the weaknesses of UNAMID. This caused deep frustration in New York.

Darfur was, in fact, a classic case of a peacekeeping force being inserted into a situation where there was no effective peace to keep and without adequate soldiers or weapons to perform the alternative task of peace enforcement properly. It was also saddled with a so-called 'Christmas tree' mandate, meaning that it has had every conceivable extra requirement hung on to its basic purpose: from stabilization through protection of civilians to the promotion of women's rights.

The underlying reality was that the international community was not willing to intervene with coercive military force, divided as it was between Western powers exercised about so-called genocide and others worried about interfering in another country's sovereign rights. But it was also intensely frustrated about the situation, and under pressure from Western public opinion to act. It therefore called on the UN to 'do something'. That something was not only vaguely defined, but also virtually impossible to enforce, even with well-armed and trained troops – hence the unsatisfactory mess.

None of this excuses the inadequate performance on the ground by UNAMID. Hampered not only by its lack of mobility and firepower, but also by poor leadership, reluctance by the troop-contributing countries to put their troops at risk, and divisions between the UN and AU, it has been mostly weak and ineffective. The AU leadership have often seemed vulnerable to Sudanese attempts to invoke African solidarity against real or supposed UN/Western arrogance, while the UN did not always respect AU sensitivities. The result has been a force that has done occasional good work in patrolling camps, but has also managed the considerable feat of having neither a constructive relationship with the Sudanese authorities, nor credibility with the rebels and the displaced population, who have seen it as complicit with the government. It has been regularly humiliated, the target of rebel attacks when it has scarcely fired back, and the victim of hostage-taking by armed groups who have appeared on examination to be suspiciously close to the government.

First visit

By the time of my initial visit in March 2007, there was little major fighting between rebels and government. On the other hand, there was a background of almost daily violent incidents: janjaweed attacks on African villages, bloody clashes between Arab tribes over grazing rights, and a pervasive state of insecurity and lawlessness in which civilians were the principal victims. The aid operation had saved many lives and improved countless others. It was meeting most basic needs. But it already faced serious questions about its longer-term viability, and was constantly struggling with obstruction by the government. The necessary humanitarian access to the affected areas and people was often absent, through a combination of lack of security and bureaucratic restrictions. Humanitarian workers were being regularly attacked and abused.

Shortly before my visit, an NGO residential compound in Darfur had been raided by government officials. The staff had been abused, verbally and physically. To add insult to injury, they had then been charged with criminal offences. Their 'crime' seemed to be looking into abuses of civilians, and speaking out about them, rather than sticking to giving out food and medical help. Insisting to the government that protection work aimed at stopping the trampling of civilians' basic rights was as much a part of modern humanitarianism as providing basic services became an all-too-regular feature of my discussions with the Sudanese authorities.

One of my aims was nevertheless to make a fresh start with the Sudanese government. My predecessor Jan Egeland had become so frustrated with them that the relationship had become openly confrontational. I wanted to establish better cooperation, without compromising humanitarian principles or letting the government off the hook. This was a tricky line to walk.

Confrontation could easily put vulnerable players on the ground – civilians and aid workers, as well as the people themselves – at greater risk for little practical reward. But a more conciliatory approach brought the danger of appearing to be conned by government soft soap, and not putting them under enough public pressure.

I quickly had my own experience of what government obstruction could mean. A visit to a sensitive camp in North Darfur had been arranged. But when we arrived, we were unable to get through the final official military checkpoint – in reality, a single soldier sitting under a tree with his gun. He insisted he had no authority to let us through, and telephone discussions with his security bosses proved fruitless. We had to turn round. Unluckily for the government, there were journalists in my convoy, not least the BBC.

The incident quickly became headline news all over the world, and the authorities rapidly realized the own goal they had scored. When I returned to the North Darfur capital of El Fasher that evening, the governor turned up to apologize in person for the mix-up between different security agencies – an unprecedented abasement. I accepted the apology. But the damage was done for the government: if I, as the VIP face of humanitarianism, faced such problems, despite all the advance preparation of my trip, what hope did ordinary humanitarian workers have? The governor, incidentally, never forgot the humiliation of this apology. On future visits he was usually unavailable, except on one memorable occasion when what I had expected to be a private meeting with him turned out to be an occasion for him to harangue me in front of the local press and TV. Not a nice man.

On this first trip to Darfur, I found a humanitarian community already under severe pressure. There were around 13,000 relief workers in place. The vast majority were local Sudanese staff, either trained experts in relief aid or support staff of different kinds, but over 1000 were expatriates. Intimidation of both local and international staff by official security agencies had already become a way of life, though it was to get worse later. NGO workers were particularly vulnerable for a variety of reasons: they lacked the protection of the UN as a universal international organization of which Sudan was, of course, itself a member; they were often physically isolated, working closely with local communities in the remote areas of the 'deep field'; and, in the case of international NGO staff, they depended on the goodwill of the authorities for exit visas – if they faced a family emergency at home, for example.

These problems were not new. In mid-2004, the then UN Secretary-General Kofi Annan had concluded an agreement with the Khartoum government known as the Moratorium, which had the effect of waiving or reducing some of the bureaucratic requirements for obtaining visas and other permits needed for travel and work in Sudan. This had helped, but implementation had been patchy at best. Its annual renewal also meant a period of great anxiety for the humanitarian community, particularly NGO staff, while negotiations went on with the government. The latter clearly enjoyed holding this sword of Damocles over humanitarian heads, extracting the greatest price possible before renewing the administrative fast-track arrangements at the last moment.

During my visit, perhaps partly because the government themselves had recognized the need to reduce confrontation with the humanitarian community and therefore to respond to my overtures, we agreed a new 'Joint Communiqué'. This was supposed to speed up further procedures over visas, travel permits, customs and so on, particularly for the NGOs. It worked well for a period and was a valuable reference point to use for putting pressure on the government. But the pattern was one of constant backsliding, and arguments that then took huge efforts to resolve. These government tactics were well developed. There was, no doubt, an element of genuine bureaucratic inadequacy involved, which we tried to overcome through training for the officials concerned. However, the basic problem lay deeper: the control the government wanted to exert, and the use of administrative methods to do so.

My discussions with the government followed a pattern which was to become frustratingly familiar – a reasonably friendly reception in Khartoum, accompanied by a general air of injured innocence about our complaints; promises of readiness to cooperate more closely and of better performance on issues like NGO visas; but an underlying attitude that this was their country and they were going to dictate at the end of the day what happened in it. Lack of trust was all-pervasive.

The Sudanese government's intelligence agencies clearly thought some of the humanitarians were too close to the rebels, or deliberately out to make trouble for the government for political reasons. There was a constant drumbeat of officially inspired articles in the press about the incompetence and venality of humanitarians, and accusations that they were not neutral or were even working for foreign intelligence. All this was designed to keep the humanitarian community off-balance and less able to protect the civilian population by documenting and speaking out about what was happening. Unfortunately, while this did little for the government's wider reputation, and fed the perception that they had a lot to hide, these tactics were partly effective. Those humanitarian staff sitting in vulnerable and remote locations in Darfur were often intimidated, despite all our push-back and complaints.

Visits like mine were therefore important in reassuring the humanitarian community that their concerns were being taken seriously in New York, in keeping up the pressure on the government, and in shining a light on what was actually happening on the ground. Visits by the ERC, for example, provided the opportunity for reports to the Security Council to make sure the truth was getting out and being reported back to the key capitals. But they could also occasionally open up new possibilities. For example, on this visit I was able to get to a community in the mountainous Jebel Marra region which the government had cut off from outside assistance for several months. It was an extraordinary experience. As our helicopter landed, it was clear that the whole population of the area had turned out to greet me, with children singing, and people holding banners saying 'Welcome Mr Holmes', 'UN for ever' and the like.

Visiting the village of Deribat, while carefully avoiding too much fraternization with the local gun-toting rebels, the plight of the people was all too evident, with stocks of food and medical supplies low or non-existent and wells suffering from lack of maintenance. The visit culminated in an insistence from the local elders that I speak to the thousands gathered around the main square of the village. A microphone was thrust into my hand, feeding a ropey-looking, crackly but somehow functioning PA system. Speeches in the elegant salons of Paris had not quite prepared me for this, but I did my best to get across that we would do all we could to help and to lift the government siege, while making clear that I could not promise miracles or solve all their problems.

This kind of address to the crowd was a ritual with which I was to become only too familiar. I became better at it, I hope, but was uncomfortably aware that people were usually anticipating miracles. I always tried not to raise expectations that we could not fulfil, but too often this left little to say beyond platitudes. Nevertheless, as in Deribat on this occasion, the sight of a senior official from New York usually seemed to be enough in itself. They certainly cheered my every word with great enthusiasm.

Another surreal moment on the same visit came in neighbouring Chad, where I was visiting the Darfur refugees in the camps strung out along the border. Word reached me in Abeche that the leadership of the Sudanese rebel Justice and Equality Movement (JEM), camped out in a nearby wadi (the Arabic name for the bed of a river or stream that is dry except in the rainy season), would like to see me. They were based in Chad at the time, with clear (but officially denied) support from the Chadian government. Despite my non-political role, this was an opportunity to hear where they stood on the then peace process, in which they had been refusing to engage. I also had humanitarian messages to deliver to them. We therefore gave our accompanying press party the slip, and drove out to the wadi that night, crossing our fingers for our own security.

We found the JEM leadership, including Khalil Ibrahim, sitting in a circle, by the headlights of a military 4x4. They offered us cold Cokes, and we talked for well over an hour. I stressed the need for them to respect international humanitarian law in their activities. They spent most of their time denouncing Khartoum. But they did also usefully make clear their readiness to join peace talks at the right moment, saying that they saw no prospect of an outright military victory by any side. What surprised me most, however, was not what they had to say, but the people saying it. Several had impeccable British accents. It turned out that no fewer than three of the leaders had, until relatively recently, been National Health Service doctors in Britain. I forbore to ask whether they had found better working conditions in the hostile desert of eastern Chad.

I found myself back in Sudan again in December 2007. The aim was partly to keep up the pressure on the government over the implementation of the March agreement, but mainly to look at the rapidly deteriorating situation on the ground: 130 humanitarian vehicles had been hijacked, often at gunpoint, 60 staff members had been physically or sexually abused, 75 convoys ambushed and looted, and at least 12 workers killed – all in a context of almost total impunity. Establishing which armed men were responsible was difficult. Rebel groups or criminal gangs linked to them seemed to be the main perpetrators, but many incidents also took place in towns that were clearly under government control. I strongly urged the government to increase security in such areas.

For their part, the government had stepped up their accusations that humanitarian staff in Darfur were engaged in inappropriate activities, without providing convincing evidence. They had just effectively expelled the OCHA representative in South Darfur, on the pretext that he had been inciting the local leaders of the biggest camp there (in a place called Kalma) to resist the government. This huge camp would remain a flashpoint throughout my time as ERC. The almost 100,000 people there had fled from the government and janjaweed attacks against their towns and villages of origin, and taken refuge in Kalma, becoming in the process what are known in the humanitarian jargon as internally displaced persons (IDPs) – in other words, people who have fled from their homes and need help, but have not crossed an international border.

The IDPs in Kalma were strongly resistant to any government presence in and around the camp, and were highly politicized, in the sense that they were sympathetic to the rebels – particularly the SLM/A, led by Abdul Wahid from his comfortable exile in Paris – and tended to reflect rebel positions in what they said and did. An attack on the camp by government forces in 2008, supposedly to flush out rebels with weapons there, resulted in at least thirty-five deaths and many more injuries. The government are still desperate to close it today.

Nevertheless, the accusations against the OCHA representative were nonsense: he had simply been doing his job in keeping in touch with all parties, which included advising the IDPs of their rights in the face of government threats.

I protested strongly to the government in Khartoum and the local South Darfur administration about this expulsion and other attacks on the humanitarian community. The basic point was that the government were responsible not only for the protection of civilians in Darfur, but also for the protection of the humanitarian workers who were there to help those civilians. It was fundamentally unacceptable that the government seemed to regard those looking after a significant part of their population not as a precious asset to be facilitated and helped, but as a source of danger to be blocked and discouraged at every turn.

Returns

The issue of when IDPs should go home was also becoming increasingly controversial. The government argued that peace had returned to Darfur, despite occasional incidents, and that there were two reasons why people were not returning to their homes: we were giving them too much aid; and the rebel groups were actively preventing them from returning, because they saw them as a weapon to use against the government. The grip of the rebels over some of the camps was certainly strong – it became more and more difficult for visitors to the camps like me to hear the authentic voice of the IDPs because the rebels had scripted in advance what everyone was supposed to say.

However, there was also little doubt that the conditions for safe returns were simply not there. Most IDPs were simply not ready or willing to go back to their villages, not only because these had in many cases been burned, and the grazing land taken over by others, but because they strongly believed that the janjaweed were still around, ready to renew their assault as soon as any would-be returnees showed their faces. This was the one point on which those I met in the camps, men and women, would usually insist. They often described in tragic detail how they had been driven out of their villages, losing many family and friends in the process, and why, despite their hatred of camp life itself, they simply could not go back there until the situation had fundamentally changed.

Our constant response to the government was therefore that, while we too wanted the return of the IDPs as soon as conditions allowed, this had to be voluntary and involve proper consultations with those concerned. Moreover, the security conditions had to be right, or the returns would not be sustainable.

There were nevertheless legitimate concerns on the part of some donors about growing dependency on outside aid among the IDPs and the constantly diminishing chances of their successful return to their homes. There was also an understandable desire to start to spend money on lasting development rather than endless humanitarian relief. I had increasing sympathy for these arguments as time went on and I visited Darfur more. The problem was that every time such considerations were raised, for example during a 2006 international study on putting Darfur back together after the conflict, the government seized on the debate, using it as backing for their contention that the conflict was already over and that the IDPs should be forced back home. This remained unacceptable.

My own insistence was that the problems of the humanitarian relief operation and the risks of 'aid-dependency syndrome' demonstrated not a case for forcing the IDPs to return against their will, but the need to get on with a definitive peace settlement. However, the sad reality was that peace efforts at that stage were going nowhere, despite manful efforts by the UN/ African Union mediators, Jan Eliasson and Salim Salim. The government were not really serious, while the rebels remained hopelessly divided, unable to agree any common position or even the composition of a joint negotiating team.

Festering among all this were government claims that the humanitarians were deliberately keeping the IDPs in the camps just to maintain their operations and keep contributions flowing. It was suggested for example, by government spokesmen and media outlets, that many humanitarian workers were young Americans or Europeans who were only in Darfur for a bit of gap-year fun, or because they were unemployed at home, and that they were also taking the opportunity to enjoy wild alcohol-fuelled parties. This kind of loose allegation made me furious, whether made by Sudanese authorities or cynical journalists. In reality, the majority of humanitarian workers are of local origin, while the international staff who are there are mostly experienced and dedicated relief actors. They live in rough and sometimes dangerous conditions, often in remote places with few if any facilities, and risk their lives and the cohesion of their families at home to help others. They would be only too happy to declare the operation over and go back to something easier. They are idealistic, but have no hidden political agenda, and no built-in anti-government bias, despite all the problems governments create for them.

Stagnation and deterioration

In 2008 the situation in Darfur gradually deteriorated further, as the numbers of displaced or redisplaced crept up. Attacks on humanitarian workers rose again, with almost 300 vehicles hijacked. Again, rebel movements or their criminal hangers-on seemed to be mostly responsible – but a significant number of incidents still took place in government-controlled areas. Sexual violence was also on the rise, despite official attempts to deny its existence (President Bashir claimed at one stage that rape was impossible in Sudan because it was against the national culture). As in other places, its true prevalence was hard to demonstrate publicly without putting at risk those victims brave enough to register cases, and the organizations trying to help them.

When I went to Darfur and Khartoum again in December 2008, the emphasis was therefore once again on access, protection of civilians, and the security of humanitarian workers. Discussions with the government had a distinctly 'Groundhog Day' feel, as they assured me of their willingness to cooperate further without convincing me that they meant it.

What also struck me on this visit was the fragility of the situation in many of the camps, as frustrations grew and rival groups clashed. It did not help that the government were not allowing key agencies like the office of the UN High Commissioner for Refugees (UNHCR) to perform their usual functions in areas like camp management. Ostensibly, the government did not accept that UNHCR should deal with IDPs as well as refugees, whose official definition is that they have crossed an international border. This was manifest nonsense when UNHCR were dealing with IDPs in many other crises, including Pakistan and Sri Lanka.

Visiting the huge camp in Kalma in South Darfur also brought home to me the long-term damage to the environment from the presence of so many people in such a small area. Kalma had been a forest area, but by then virtually every tree had been chopped down for firewood or to make bricks – a common and valuable source of income for IDPs in such circumstances, and almost impossible to stop, but a major consumer of precious water as well as wood. This could only hasten desertification, and intensify conflict, in the longer run.

Those I met in Kalma, in addition to requests for more aid and better education facilities for their children, were particularly virulent about the government and the unacceptability of their attempts to force them to go back home when conditions were still so intolerable. What they really wanted me to do was to promise them that the international community would intervene to depose President Bashir and put him on trial for his crimes. I had to explain that my role was strictly non-political, while also making clear that their hopes of international intervention of this kind were almost certainly in vain, and they needed to promote local political solutions. This was not a welcome message, though they usually remained polite about it.

Darfur and the ICC

The main issue hanging over Darfur by 2008 was the likelihood that the International Criminal Court (ICC) would decide to extend the war-crimes charges already laid against two key actors in the original Darfur violence (former interior minister Ahmed Haroun, and janjaweed leader Ali Kushayb) to major political figures in Khartoum, particularly the president. The government had taken no action to hand over the two already indicted, and had indeed thumbed their noses at the Court by making Haroun minister of state for humanitarian affairs!

The then ICC prosecutor Luis Ocampo duly filed ten charges against Bashir in July 2008 – five for crimes against humanity, three for genocide, and two for murder. While few in the international community disputed that such charges might be well deserved, there was less certainty about the wisdom of moving the legal attack straight to the president himself, and the effects this might have on the prospects for a peace settlement, and indeed on the UN presence in Sudan.

The ICC is an independent non-UN body, but its mandate in this particular case came from the Security Council and there was little disposition in Khartoum to draw fine distinctions between the member states and the UN as an institution. This ICC sword of Damocles had an increasingly pernicious effect on all the actors – the government were making dire threats about what they would do if any action were taken against the president; the rebels saw no reason to make political moves while they waited to see what effect further ICC indictments might have on the situation; and the UN and others were focussed on battening down the hatches to ensure they could cope with whatever revenge action might be taken against them.

An ICC arrest warrant against President Bashir was finally announced on 4 March 2009. The Court accepted the crimes against humanity and murder charges, but rejected those of genocide (the prosecutor appealed and the genocide charges were eventually also accepted in July 2010). The predictable government reaction was one of complete rejection of the charges. But retaliation came in a less expected way, and one which was very damaging. The government announced that sixteen NGOs working in Darfur would be expelled, thirteen of them international and three local. It was claimed that these NGOs had been working with the ICC against the interests of Sudan, had been engaged in espionage, were collaborating with unnamed foreign powers, and had in any case not been delivering anything useful for the people of Darfur, despite the very high cost.

This was a devastating blow to the humanitarian operation: the organizations chosen were among the most effective and heavily involved, including Oxfam, Save the Children, Care, the International Rescue Committee, Médecins Sans Frontières, and Action Contre la Faim. Six and a half thousand staff were affected, mostly local Sudanese, representing about half the capacity on the ground. The criteria for the government's choices were not obvious, except that some of those expelled had been particularly involved in the protection of civilian activities the government most disliked. What was clear was that the action had been carefully prepared by the intelligence and security services, and that there had been absolutely no use of the agreed consultation mechanisms. It was claimed by some that Bashir himself had wanted to expel the UN and some Western embassies, but had been persuaded that moving against NGOs would have fewer international consequences, with the bonus of getting rid of organizations that had long been a thorn in the government's side.

The expulsions were unacceptable from every point of view. The position of principle was clear: they should be reversed, and the NGOs allowed to continue their vital relief work. We pressed this hard, including in the Security Council. But in reality everyone knew that once the government had taken such a political decision and the president himself had backed it publicly a Sudanese volte-face was unlikely. The expulsions were, in fact, accompanied by a lot of talk about the need to get rid of international humanitarian organizations altogether, and to 'Sudanize' relief efforts as quickly as possible. For example, President Bashir made a speech a few days later suggesting that all foreign aid agencies would be expelled within a year. This always looked more like an empty threat than a real plan, but it deepened uncertainty and fear among the humanitarian community.

The fact of the expulsions was bad enough. Even worse was the manner in which they were carried out. Vehicles, computers and other assets belonging to the NGOs were summarily seized in threatening raids by the security services. Staff were told to leave immediately, with no time to hand over their life-saving programmes. Bank accounts were frozen. Some staff were arrested, at least temporarily. Many more were humiliated and harassed. The NGOs were told to pay severance compensation to their local staff well above the normal rate, sums they could hardly afford. The money was also supposed to be paid to the government, not to the individuals themselves, arousing suspicion as to where it might finish up. The atmosphere of intimidation was deeply unpleasant.

OCHA did all it could to stop these abuses and protect the NGOs. The humanitarian coordinator, Ameerah Haq, an experienced and able UN official, devoted herself to this task. But the bigger issue was this: should the humanitarian community accept this government action, albeit under the strongest protest we could manage, and carry on helping the people of Darfur through those organizations that remained? Or were the expulsions a step too far which should, as such, trigger a withdrawal from Darfur or other more drastic action?

The government certainly deserved a tough response. Withdrawal would have obliged them to take on their responsibility to the people of Darfur – our intervention was, after all, saving them the equivalent of a billion dollars a year. But the government would not suffer the main consequences; the displaced people of Darfur would be the real victims, left alone to face the wrath and neglect of their government, without a significant international presence on the ground to act as witnesses or provide the kind of services they had a right to expect. But the bottom line was that we had little leverage. We could only be there, as in any other country, with the government's agreement. And the government would have been happy to see us all go.

Our decision, after much agonized debate, was therefore to stay engaged. We adopted a three-track approach: Track One was the campaign to allow the NGOs to stay, or to be let back in later; Track Two was to fill the most urgent life-saving gaps left by the departing NGOs; Track Three was an attempt to agree a more stable basis for the humanitarian presence for the long term – we could not go on as we had been, always at risk of arbitrary action by the government.

This approach was agreed by all the humanitarian organizations concerned, both those which had been expelled, and those which were left. However, some NGOs were clearly uneasy that we were letting the government off too lightly, and that Track One was mostly for show. They also feared the precedent that was being set by such action against NGOs, which some other sensitive governments might be only too ready to follow. I shared these concerns, and their frustration. At the same time, however, I believed that maintaining some kind of working relationship with the government would help the NGOs get out in decent order, and at least keep the humanitarian show on the road for the sake of the millions of people who needed crucial supplies of food, clean water and medical care.

To maintain the pressure on the Sudanese government to reverse the decision, we enlisted the help not only of Western governments, but also of other Arab and African countries and the Arab League and African Union too. While these countries and organizations believed that Sudan had the right to say who worked on their territory, they recognized the dangers of a further humanitarian crisis in Darfur, and did not believe that the government had had real grounds for the action they had taken. In fact, the Sudanese government had produced no evidence for its claims of espionage or other wrongdoing on the part of the expelled NGOs, and never did. A government dossier released a few weeks after the expulsions contained no convincing evidence that NGO staff had been doing anything other than what they were there for.

Meanwhile, the top priority was to establish exactly what operational capacity had been lost, and to find ways of replacing it. We did not expect an immediate catastrophe: humanitarian food distributions were not the exclusive source of food for most, and people could survive with reduced food intake for some time, if necessary. But the effects over time threatened to be much more serious as nutritional levels declined, especially for children, water pumps and filters in the camps stopped working through lack of fuel and maintenance, sanitation facilities were no longer maintained, and lack of medical care took its toll. The disappearance of so many projects designed to protect the civilian population against abuses by the authorities and the rebels would also greatly reduce our ability to prevent or even document abuses.

All this was hugely disheartening for the Darfur humanitarian community, which had spent the previous five years bringing down rates of malnutrition and establishing an effective network of basic services. Replacing the capacity of the NGOs who had been expelled was complicated by the anger of the remaining NGOs and agencies at what had happened, and by their instinctive solidarity with those who had been expelled. They were unwilling simply to fill the gaps as if this was just a technical question. They also lacked resources and ability to fill gaps immediately, and feared that, if they did make the huge effort and investment required, they could easily be expelled in their turn.

In any case we decided that the proper field-based assessment of exactly how much humanitarian capacity had been removed by the expulsions, and the impact of this, would be best achieved through a joint study with the government. Though somewhat counter-intuitive in the circumstances, this would at least confront the government directly with the reality of what it had done.

The results of the study were clear – for example, there were now over one million people left without food aid who had been receiving it before. The government did all they could to cast doubt on such conclusions, but finally accepted not only that there were serious problems, but that they would have to play a part in providing replacement capacity. They would have had difficulty arguing anything else, given the emphasis at the time on 'Sudanization'. We insisted, for example, that the health ministry had to man clinics formerly run by NGOs. In the end they did so, up to a point, but our well-justified fear was that they would not maintain this over time, given the central government's notorious reluctance to provide resources for Darfur.

UN agencies, other NGOs and the International Committee of the Red Cross also agreed to help out where they could while the battle to reverse the expulsions continued. This went against the grain for them, given the unreasonableness of the government's original decision. But as so often, the humanitarian imperative prevailed: the expulsions were certainly not the fault of the displaced population of Darfur, and they should not be the ones to suffer the consequences.

These combined efforts managed to avert a renewed humanitarian crisis over the following weeks and months, in quantitative terms. But it was clear that the quality of what had been there before could not be replaced in the same way. The expulsions and increased intimidation from the security services had significantly reduced the humanitarian presence in the so-called 'deep field', where the biggest problems were, and the likelihood of abuses by government forces and rebels alike was now at its highest. International staff were particularly thin on the ground, which increased the risks: deterrence against abuses can be maintained by presence on the ground to witness what is going on, with the strong likelihood of publicity if unacceptable behaviour or atrocities are seen. But this is inevitably less effective when local employees alone are involved, since they are so much more vulnerable to government intimidation – of their families, as well as themselves.

Progress was at best slow on Track Three of our response to the expulsions, the attempt to build a more effective architecture between the government and the humanitarian community, to prevent future crises. But it was at least agreed to set up a new high-level body to consult on all these issues, involving this time not only the government and the humanitarian organizations but also the African Union and Arab League, and major bilateral actors including Russia, China, and the US.

The Americans had, in fact, recently appointed a new special envoy for Sudan, General Scott Gration, a friend of President Obama with personal knowledge of Africa and a fresh commitment to making a difference. From the start, he took a different line from his US predecessors, making clear that he wanted to develop a more productive relationship with the government and was ready to reciprocate, including even lifting sanctions, if the Sudanese government were ready to behave better.

This shift was the subject of much division within the US government. An influential group of Democrats believed, like the Republican administration before them, that the only language the Sudanese government understood was that of pressure. This went along with denouncing the Sudanese government for responsibility for a true genocide in Darfur, and with pressing for tougher sanctions. Unfortunately, this position had failed to deliver results. The problem was that the implicit threat of sharper intervention from outside that accompanied it carried little conviction. It was clear to all, in the aftermath of Iraq, that the likelihood of a further US-led invasion of a Muslim country was minimal, and that there would be no international support for such an adventure, even if the US were interested.

The Gration approach was therefore a conscious attempt to try something else. He was vulnerable to charges of naivety, setting tight timetables for a solution in Darfur which looked – and proved to be – impossible, on the basis of vague promises from the government and the rebels. He gave the government the benefit of the doubt when others saw only empty words. However, it was worth a try. And he was very helpful to the humanitarian community in the post-expulsions environment, once we had convinced him that there was little prospect of political movement in Darfur if a new humanitarian disaster were to hit. Together, therefore, we pressed hard for more time and better conditions for the expelled NGOs, for rapid clearance of approvals allowing remaining NGOs to work, and for other long-sought concessions (such as multi-entry visas for NGO staff).

Gration even managed to persuade the government to contemplate allowing some of the expelled NGOs to return, beginning with the US-based ones. This was an odd business. The government could not go back publicly on their decision, and we were not allowed to say that they had. But suddenly, some expelled organizations could get back in as long as they changed their names, even marginally (for example – hypothetically – from Care US to Care Switzerland), and reapplied for official registration. Some did eventually receive agreement to restart work; others did not want their ability to work in Sudan to be the subject of political negotiation, especially by a US envoy, since this only tended to reinforce the impression that they were part of a Western political agenda. In the event, even those organizations which did get back in were reluctant to invest too much for fear of a repeat performance from the government down the line.

As part of the attempt to deal with the expulsions I visited Sudan and Darfur again in May 2009, and joined the first meeting of the new high-level joint committee set up to discuss problems frankly and avoid future nasty surprises. It passed off well enough in principle. Government representatives made clear that whatever might have been said in the heat of the moment during the expulsions, international NGOs were welcome as long as they behaved. Talk of rapid 'Sudanization' largely disappeared. We agreed to set up new troubleshooting mechanisms in the three Darfur states.

But none of this could disguise the unpleasant realities on the ground. Discussions with the local humanitarian workers, and a visit to Zam Zam, one of the big camps in North Darfur, brought home the effects of the expulsions. Health coverage was much less good than it had been, increasing the risks of diseases such as measles and meningitis, especially in the rainy season. Food and water supplies were fragile. And there was little visibility of what was going on in the more remote areas. Once again, the women and men I met, individually or in groups, vented the depth of their anger and frustration at the government and the janjaweed. In particular, they pressed for greater protection for women around the camps at times of greatest vulnerability, such as when collecting firewood. This was always an issue, often raised by the men as well as the women, and was certainly a real problem with which we tried to help. But there never seemed to be any inclination on the part of the men to protect their women through their own efforts, still less go to collect the firewood themselves!

New problems had meanwhile been added, in the shape of a wave of kidnappings of international personnel, some from UNAMID, but the majority from NGOs. The motives were apparently mercenary, involving ransom demands from tribal militias, often former janjaweed fighters. But those responsible had suspiciously close ties to the government. This meant that the government were well placed to get hostages released, usually after a few months of tortuous talks, but also that they were widely suspected of complicity.

UN policy was firmly against ransom payments, for the usual reason of discouraging repeat kidnappings. However, it was far from clear that the member states whose nationals had been kidnapped, or the NGOs from which they came, were really prepared to stick to such a no-ransom policy, in their understandable anxiety to get their people back safely. And whatever their initial role in encouraging some of these kidnappings, the government were usually keen to resolve them peacefully in the end, and were certainly ready to make payments (usually described as 'expenses'). The effect of all this on the morale of humanitarian workers further reduced the chances of an effective presence in remote locations. This may well have been the intention.

The reality is that the expulsions were a cynical and calculated act by a government content to use their own population as pawns in political games, and with no interest in their welfare. They did result in a long-term diminution of international humanitarian capacity in Darfur, with significant negative consequences for the vulnerable. Government promises to replace the NGO contribution with their own efforts and contributions from elsewhere in the Arab world came to very little in practice. The effects of this disastrous and unjustified government decision are still being felt.

The aftermath

Although the huge effort put into stopping the expulsions from triggering a new humanitarian disaster averted the worst, the mess they caused created lasting problems for everyone. The government's image was badly dented even among their own natural international supporters. Our efforts to create a new climate of trust and a new architecture under which humanitarian organizations could operate more effectively did not in the end bear significant fruit. American policy shifted back in a more threatening, less conciliatory direction a few months after the expulsions, since the opposite tack under Gration had achieved few tangible results. While we believed we had no good alternative to working with the government in order to undo the worst effects, some in the NGO world continued to think that the UN should have taken a tougher line with the government, rather than, in effect, turning the other cheek.

All this also brings into focus the broader issue of the ICC, and how peace and justice go together. How can you negotiate effectively with someone whom you are at the same time indicting for war crimes, which involves seeking his arrest in order to send him for trial in The Hague? In the Sudan case, was the indictment of President Bashir helpful to peace in Darfur? The evidence suggests that, in fact, it hardened attitudes on both sides, and made an accommodation less likely, though it was not the decisive factor in preventing a peace deal either.

In the short term, it also contributed to increased suffering in Darfur. That is not meant to suggest that the government reaction to the indictment, which reduced humanitarian assistance, was remotely justified. Nevertheless the decision to go straight from the previous mid-level indictments all the way up the command chain to the president, however justified the accusations against him, seemed to reflect a view by the prosecutor that this was what the political situation now demanded, rather than particular new evidence. The later decision to indict some rebel leaders too, to show balance, also looked more political than judicial.

Any thought that the indictment would provoke those around the president to ditch him because of the embarrassment of such a charge against the country's head of state and the restrictions it would impose was naive at best. The immediate Sudanese political reaction was predictably the opposite – to close ranks around the president at home, to exploit unease about the ICC role abroad (particularly elsewhere in Africa and the Middle East), and to show their contempt for the ICC by trying to ensure that the president continued to travel internationally as much as possible, either to places which did not accept ICC jurisdiction anyway or to other African countries which could be bullied into promising not to arrest him while he was on their territory.

Will the indictment nevertheless decrease the culture of impunity in Sudan or more widely in the longer term, by showing that even a head of state of a major country will have to answer for his crimes? I profoundly hope so. For the moment, the fact that – short of a revolution taking place in Sudan – Bashir does not look likely to be handed over for trial tends to undermine the credibility of the Court, rather than the opposite.

I will come back to these issues in a later chapter. Meanwhile, one of the effects of the ICC charges was extreme reluctance on the part of Western governments to have any dealings with President Bashir, for fear of appearing either to legitimize him or to minimize the seriousness of the accusations against him. This was understandable, but it imposed obvious handicaps when it came to trying to influence Sudanese policy, which we desperately needed to do. For example, it made senior UN officials extremely cautious about any contact with Bashir, lest they be accused by the media and some member states of softness towards him and of undermining the ICC. Ban ki-Moon in particular had virtually no contact with Bashir after 2009. Is this sensible when the UN has had such a huge stake in Sudan, including two peacekeeping forces, and when the fate of so many people in the region depends on UN influence? Clearly, social hobnobbing with Bashir would be inappropriate, but I argued strongly at the time, and still believe, that where there is serious business to transact, as there almost always is between the UN and Sudan, there should be no inhibition on the UN secretary-general dealing with Bashir to achieve vital international objectives.

Farewell to Darfur

Paying my fifth and final visit to Sudan in May 2010, I found a Darfur which had changed very little. While key humanitarian indicators in areas like nutrition and health had not worsened as much as feared, the quality and coverage of assistance had not recovered. Renewed fighting in areas like the Jebel Marra mountains had reduced access further, and the kidnapping cases and other attacks on humanitarians had continued to have their insidious effect on presence in remote rural areas. The mechanisms set up after the expulsions were not really working as intended.

There was also increased tension between the humanitarian community and the peacekeeping force UNAMID, now under the leadership of the Nigerian former UN under-secretary-general for political affairs, Ibrahim Gambari. The humanitarians felt that UNAMID, while still not doing its basic job of providing security properly, was seeking to interfere well beyond its mandate in areas such as returns of the displaced, and tending to take the government's side too much. Politically, the prospects for a peace settlement looked no better despite much apparent activity around an initiative sponsored by the Qataris. Government and rebel willingness to make the compromises necessary for a deal was still not there, and the rebels were as fragmented and divided as ever.

This was depressing. Every year without peace reduced the chances of the displaced being able to return to their homes and resume anything resembling normal lives, as well as aggravating the damage to Darfur's economic, social and environmental fabric. Rising aid dependency had strengthened the need to encourage people to take more responsibility for their own lives. But the government gave little appearance of caring, while the international community was frankly losing interest.

I left Darfur and Sudan for the last time as ERC, more convinced than ever that the only way forward was a durable ceasefire and political peace agreement, and less confident than ever that there was an imminent prospect of any such thing. As I write, nothing that has happened since has changed this grim prognosis.

The truth is that Darfur has been a failure for everyone. It is above all a failure for the government of Sudan, who have destroyed the region's old economy and political system while putting nothing in its place. They are investing virtually nothing in the region's future and seem content to ensure that neither the rebels nor the international community can achieve anything worthwhile either. This is a terrible indictment of a government containing many intelligent and perceptive individuals, but with no vision or strategy for the future other than their own survival.

The rebels have also failed: not only to achieve whatever military objectives they set themselves when they set off down this road in 2003, but also to unite around any kind of political platform from which to negotiate effectively. The result is that they have made no political progress either.

The international community have prevented the worst from happening militarily, politically, and in humanitarian terms, but have neither wanted to intervene on the ground nor been able to find ways of engaging productively with the government and the rebels to move the situation on. The West has failed to devote enough continuous high-level attention to the problem to resolve it, and has often seemed content to condemn the government and hide behind lazy and highly emotive terms like 'genocide' to describe the attacks of Arabs on African communities without wanting to understand the more complex reality underneath, where the issues are at least as much political, economic and environmental as ethnic. The Darfur lobby groups and their equally simplistic narrative have, at times, succeeded in keeping the issue in front of the Western public, but they have failed to realize that they were not going to provoke the kind of Western intervention that some of them would have liked. In the process, they have raised false hopes and expectations among the population of Darfur, and ultimately have not helped them achieve any of their goals. Their blindness to the weaknesses of the rebels has also been counterproductive.

So this is not a story from which anyone comes out well. I include even the humanitarian community in that, in one sense. That may seem unfair, given the huge effort put into the humanitarian operation and its success in keeping people alive. It is certainly not meant to denigrate that effort or the instincts of those involved. But we have to accept that our very success in mitigating the consequences of a conflict like this, and allowing the protagonists to avoid their responsibilities, can in some ways serve to prolong the conflict. This is a very uncomfortable conclusion, which does not change the humanitarian imperative to help those in need. But we need to recognise that it can be an issue. In any event, cases like this provide the most vivid illustration possible that humanitarian efforts alone cannot solve problems, and that the political will to find a solution is the indispensable ingredient for success. It was absent in Darfur.

The international community needs to look long and hard at why it failed the people of Darfur. But let responsibility rest where it should. The political and military leaders in Sudan who have been and are still content to watch the people of Darfur suffer while they play their games have by far the most to answer for. Whatever my reservations about the ICC, I trust those leaders will in the end be held accountable.

Meanwhile, the international community needs to go back to taking notice of what is happening in Darfur and to making a real and concerted effort to promote a lasting settlement. This has to involve a determined attempt to re-engage with the government, despite the reservations about Bashir and his ICC indictment. Without them no progress will be made. The rebels also have to be confronted anew with their own failures and brought to the table. The death of Khalil Ibrahim in mid-2012 may even help with this. But the time has also come to get Abdul Wahid, the SLA leader in exile in Paris, out of his comfort zone once and for all, and back around the negotiating table. A united approach from the international community – including China and Russia – is vital to achieve this. This may have proved impossible over Syria until now, but Sudan could be potentially easier. There is no excuse for not making the effort, and no guarantee that the Arab spring will reach Khartoum in time to make the necessary difference, or that it will have the desired effect in the short term, even if the current regime is overturned.

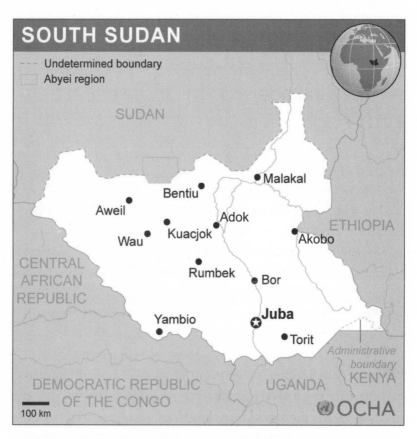

Map Sources: UNCS, SIM, Natural Earth. Map created in Jan 2012.
Final boundary between the Republic of Sudan and the republic of South Sudan has not yet been determined. Final status of the Abyei area is not yet determined.

CHAPTER THREE

South Sudan:
the (unmade) road to independence

South Sudan is an extraordinary place – huge, beautiful, and, in recent years, tragic. Each time I went I marvelled at the vast empty spaces we flew over, usually on the way to the capital, Juba, from Khartoum or Darfur. Long minutes would pass without any sign of human habitation. The population is only 8 million or so, for a country the size of both France and Germany combined. But these are not uninhabitable tracts – far from it. South Sudan has a vast amount of cultivable land and plenty of water to go with it.

There are certainly problems which are consonant in size with the scale of the country – a lack of roads and indeed most infrastructure, endemic diseases, a hostile and disaster-prone climate and geography, and deep tribal divisions. None of these is insurmountable. Indeed, South Sudan is already a tempting target for international land-grabbers looking for places to grow crops for their own populations. But its history over the last fifty years has been truly terrible, with almost constant conflict destroying and degrading whatever there was in the way of development. Its present remains highly uncertain and fraught with every kind of risk.

My involvement spanned a period from 2007 to 2010 that began when OCHA and the humanitarian community were first of all trying to withdraw from a situation we thought was no longer an acute humanitarian crisis. We then struggled to build it back up again as it became clear that humanitarian needs were once more huge and rising. It is a story that illustrates clearly the problems the international system faces in trying to build nations once the fighting has stopped. The issues are mostly political and developmental, but the humanitarian community cannot escape its share of responsibility too.

The legacy of civil war

Conflict between 1955 and 1972 had already done untold damage to south Sudan. But it was the more than twenty years of brutal fighting after 1983 between the mainly Muslim north and the mainly Christian south which really wrecked the country. The war started when the Sudan People's Liberation Movement/Army (SPLM/A) established itself in the south to lead the struggle for independence. It led to over 2 million deaths and 5 million displaced, both within the country and south to Kenya and beyond. It spawned the extraordinary phenomenon of the 'Lost Boys' of south Sudan, as well as huge camps like Kakuma in Kenya, where hundreds of thousands spent long years awaiting an end to the war while desperately trying to be resettled elsewhere, preferably in the US. A huge humanitarian effort – Operation Lifeline Sudan – had to be mounted to keep people in the south alive.

The legacy of bitterness among those who fought the war weighs very heavily on both north and south, as well as on relationships within the south between those who went with the northern side at various times, and those who never wavered from the liberation struggle. The conflict left the country and its people, always poor, at the bottom of international tables for almost everything. South Sudan still has some genuinely scary statistics in areas like maternal and infant mortality, much worse than those in Darfur: one child in every seven in the south dies under the age of five, and a girl has more chance of dying in childbirth than finishing secondary school. The position of women is particularly distressing: in a country where polygamy and forced marriage at early ages are still widely practised, wives are bought with cattle and often treated as possessions afterwards, and sexual violence has become endemic, not least in domestic settings.

After intensive international mediation, the fighting was finally brought to an end by the Comprehensive Peace Agreement (CPA), signed in January 2005 between the Khartoum government and the SPLM/A, led at the time by the charismatic John Garang. The CPA allowed the south the option of independence or continued association with the north, a choice which they exercised in 2011 with an overwhelming and joyous vote for independence.

At the end of the war, there was said to be less than one kilometre of tarmac road in the whole of the country, and virtually no infrastructure of any kind still standing. The autonomous southern government set up in 2006 started with virtually nothing. Even now, as I write six years later, it has not yet established an effective administration. Local conflicts between warlords and the southern government, no doubt with encouragement from the divide-and-rule experts from the north, continue to displace and impoverish too many of the population. Drought, flood, and disease take regular tolls, with transport of supplies a logistician's nightmare, especially in the rainy season when most roads are impassable. Along the southern border with the DRC, the continuing presence of elements of the Lord's Resistance Army (LRA), a brutal armed group responsible for killings, rape, and abductions on a terrifying scale, only intensified the problems.

They had been driven out from their original operational areas in Uganda and scattered around neighbouring countries, but continued their reign of terror wherever they were found – in the case of south Sudan there was a constant question mark over the extent to which Khartoum had at times been helping the LRA, just to keep the south off balance.

In March 2007, at the insistence of my advisers, I added a quick trip to Juba on to a scheduled visit to Khartoum and Darfur. International attention was not on the south at the time. Darfur had come to dominate virtually all reporting and thinking about Sudan. I had no time to see much, but I was able to talk to President Salva Kiir and his deputy, Riek Machar, as well as local aid representatives. I quickly began to understand why my advisers had been so keen for me to take an interest. Salva Kiir had none of the charisma of Garang, who had died in a helicopter crash shortly after the conclusion of the CPA, but he was nevertheless impressive in his own way. His slow and quiet delivery, from under the cowboy-style hat he invariably wears, showed real understanding of the scale and nature of the challenges he faced. While he did not bother to conceal his distrust of the leadership in the north, he recognized the imperative of working with them if independence was to be achieved.

But above all, there was no doubt that independence was the objective. The northern leaders were supposed to be showing that unity could be attractive, but in practice their actions did exactly the opposite, constantly demonstrating why the only choice for the south was to go their own way. There was certainly no question, even then, that the people of the south, if allowed a free vote, would vote for independence. It was clear, therefore, that whatever position of neutrality the UN had to adopt publicly, we should be preparing for the south to become an independent country.

What was already well understood by the experts became abundantly clear to me too: however much international attention was at the time focussed on the problems of Darfur, the north–south issue was more fundamental for the future of Sudan. If the north and south could not find a way forward, there was no hope of solving Darfur's problems because they would be swept up in the mess and the renewed war that would result. Per contra, a solution to Darfur would help the dynamics between north and south and increase the chances of peace, which was why the southern leaders constantly offered their help in mediating a Darfur deal.

The transition gap

The immediate problem for the humanitarian community was how to manage the post-war move from a humanitarian crisis to a period of construction and development. The issue was a familiar one in post-conflict situations. The humanitarians wanted to reduce their presence and move on to other situations of huge need. I was keen to cut the large amount of resources OCHA had been putting in over many years, start to end aid dependency, and hand over the leadership and coordination of the international effort to the development agencies. However, the local authorities, as well as the NGOs and others working on the spot, were desperately urging OCHA to stay, partly because of continuing needs, but mainly for fear that once we had left there would be effectively no central coordination to take our place.

The underlying point was this: OCHA had been created because of the international community's recognition that central coordination was essential if chaos among humanitarian agencies was to be avoided. The humanitarian agencies had never really liked this, but had acknowledged the necessity and logic of such an arrangement. They had been prepared to work with OCHA because OCHA had no operational role itself, and was therefore not in competition with them. It could be trusted to raise and allocate funds without favour, and was regarded as essentially neutral. On the whole this worked. It meant that there was an organization responsible for making sure that the overall effort was effective, and one to which the local authorities and the donor community could turn for advice on needs and priorities across sectors.

But there was and is no OCHA on the development side. While the UN Development Programme (UNDP) is supposed to fill the coordination and leadership role, it is itself a huge operational agency, one unfortunately not trusted by the other agencies to act neutrally, and therefore not able to fulfil the kind of role played by OCHA. While the UN resident coordinator in a particular country has the job of bringing together the development effort of the UN, reporting to UNDP, he or she often has insufficient credibility and authority – the local UN agency heads are often higher in rank, have their own authorities, funds, and objectives, and are little inclined to take notice of a supposed coordinator.

The problem is being tackled to some extent by a so-called 'One UN' initiative aimed at bringing together once and for all – politically, administratively and financially – the disparate efforts of the many UN agencies in a country. But this is struggling to make headway outside a few pilot countries, and the fundamental issue of the reluctance of the other agencies to accept the leadership of UNDP is largely unresolved. One way to go would be the creation of a new body, a sort of development OCHA, but UNDP is reluctant to give up its central role, and the other agencies also seem to prefer the inconveniences of the present system to any arrangement which might trammel their own freedom of manoeuvre.

In the particular case of south Sudan, while we recognized the need to retain a presence in Juba, we wanted to close the outlying OCHA offices in the various states which make up the south, and also stop running central facilities, such as a tented camp for the international aid community. We were generally keen to hand over responsibility for overall coordination to someone else, preferably UNDP. But UNDP did not really have the will or the resources to take over as we would have wanted, and we were unable to identify a viable alternative. The resulting partial transfer to UNDP of coordination responsibility was a recipe for muddle – and muddle was what duly followed.

Meanwhile, the reconstruction effort was hampered by another all-too-common problem: the rivalry between the UN and the World Bank. While both organizations have long professed the desire to work closely with each other, and occasionally even meant it, in practice they have usually found it difficult to do so. Institutional mistrust and competition have been the result, to the detriment of the overall aid effort.

The Bank has excellent people, and is well resourced. They produce good, well-written papers, and finance many major projects. Bank representatives tend to look down on the UN as disorganized and ineffective, and moreover without the money to put where their collective mouth is. There is some truth in this. But for their part, UN representatives, particularly those on the ground, while looking at the Bank's money with envy, also regard the Bank's efforts as too often unproductive. They see Bank representatives as being more at home in the offices of the ministers they are dealing with than at the sharp and dirty end of development work.

I saw an example of this when I visited Uganda in 2008 to look at the efforts to help the north recover from the massive displacement problem caused by the LRA in the 1990s. There too, as the emergency receded, transition efforts were struggling, and were being hampered by lack of cooperation between the UN and the Bank. The local OCHA representative suggested that the new Bank representative in Kampala come with us to look at the camps. To her credit, she did so, and found the experience extraordinarily valuable. The point was that she and her predecessors had not previously made a practice of such visits, or talked to the local players without the filter of central-government views. She began to understand why several Bank projects in the area had never worked.

In the case of south Sudan, the Bank had set up a post-war Multilateral Trust Fund for development projects, but was unwilling to give the UN agencies on the ground any say in how it operated, or any access to its funding. The result was a long period when very little money was spent. While good progress was made in areas like demining of rural roads, rehabilitation of wells, and return of refugees, in development sectors project proposals took an inordinately long time to be studied and approved. The people of south Sudan, desperate for signs that life was improving, waited in vain for new schools or clinics to appear, or jobs to be created. Everyone, including the donors, became extremely frustrated. Things only began to improve in 2009/10 when a second and more flexible 'window' for funding was opened, to which direct access was possible for aid organizations.

Why are such problems in the transition from emergency relief to development so common? Part of the problem is the different funding pockets, as well as the fact that development experts and humanitarians have different mindsets and timescales.

Humanitarians want and need to act fast, or people will die. There is little or no time for detailed planning or comprehensive strategies. Mistakes are bound to be made, and often are, but the process is one of trying whatever might work. Errors can be corrected as the effort moves along.

The development approach is one of greater deliberation and careful planning, in close consultation with the local government. A minimum five- or ten-year time frame is normal. Big mistakes at the beginning can too easily undermine longer-term progress, and priorities need to be set with appropriate care. This is understandable. However, if applied too mechanically, this kind of approach ignores the human aspects of a post-crisis situation. Quick wins and swift change are needed, to give people hope and confidence that things are improving, and to reduce, as far as possible, the chances of a rapid relapse into conflict, always a high risk.

It cannot be beyond the wit of man to devise a system which combines short-term action, including the necessary quick wins and visible improvements, with a longer-term development plan, with both being worked on simultaneously. Mistakes would no doubt still be made – they always are – but the results should fit better with what is needed on the ground. The transition has been done better in other places (for example, in Sierra Leone and Liberia), but the problems I have described are still too common.

This is all part of the wider issue of making a success of nation-building, over which the UN and the donor community have been agonizing for many years. There is no simple answer. The issues are complex and understanding local dynamics tough. But reducing the gap between humanitarian and development experts has to be part of the answer, as are good leadership and a more integrated approach between the various international actors.

The importance of agriculture

Whatever the truth of these complicated institutional issues, progress on the ground in south Sudan was painfully slow. Basic educational and health services were still largely lacking, and economic development patchy at best, leaving aside a property boom in Juba itself. Jobs were not being created – for example, to give the hundreds of thousands of refugees returning from the north some economic future.

Perhaps worst of all was the lack of movement in the key area of agriculture. If the population is to survive and prosper, most will have to live off the land for the foreseeable future. As already noted, good land and water are not lacking. However, what I saw as I went around the south on various trips was discouraging. Little or no investment seemed to be going in. Techniques were rudimentary at best. Yields were poor and extremely vulnerable to the vagaries of the weather. One worrying sign was that, as Juba's population exploded, nearly all its food was being imported from neighbouring Kenya and Uganda. This was good for producers there, and even better for the middlemen making a fortune out of the new trade. But it was a missed opportunity for the local economy, which needed every boost it could get. When I returned for a short visit in early 2012, this time under the auspices of an NGO, the International Rescue Committee, nothing had changed in this respect. The government still seemed uninterested.

There is a cultural issue here. By far the greatest effort from many south Sudanese goes into livestock, particularly cattle, rather than crops. Cattle are the main form of wealth, indeed perhaps the only way of holding wealth for many, and are also vital as a dowry for young men looking to marry. They provide benefits for the owners in terms of milk, meat, and leather products. But they are not farmed intensively for these products, neither to feed local families better nor to sell on wider markets. Meanwhile, little effort goes into arable crops – regarded largely as women's work. The risks of food insecurity are correspondingly high.

I saw the same phenomenon in other nomadic societies in parts of Kenya and in Karamoja in Uganda. In the particular context of conflict-ridden south Sudan, it had helped embed over the years of civil war an unhealthy degree of reliance on outside food aid. Communities had come to see the World Food Programme's decades-long provision of the basic necessities – grain, oil, sugar and so on – as normal. They had had little real incentive to step up their own food-production efforts, even when the war had stopped.

WFP were well aware of this and were by 2009 trying hard to reduce rations, target them only towards the neediest, and encourage greater local production. But this was a hard struggle for a number of reasons: the population was extremely poor and the food aid still vital for many families; drought and flood frequently set back all efforts; and there was little availability of new seeds, tools, and fertilizer. Moreover, the local chiefs had become accustomed to using their power to distribute international food aid as they saw fit, creaming off part of it for themselves in the process. I visited several communities where WFP agents were facing opposition (including the threat of violence) from locals fearful of change, encouraged by the chiefs.

The people I met were immensely dignified, but desperate for a better life. This meant not only more reliable supplies of food and clean water, but basic provision of health and education facilities for their children, and opportunities for jobs outside subsistence agriculture. They were patient – probably too patient – but wanted at least to see some improvement in their daily existence. They supported their leaders in the struggle with the north, but had little trust in them otherwise. I always left south Sudan feeling that I had met people who deserved so much better, but were not likely to get it for many years, if ever.

Whatever the truth of this, reducing food aid to south Sudan, except for new localized emergencies, is certainly vital to ensure that habits of self-reliance are rebuilt, and local agriculture and the broader local economy established on a sustainable basis. In the same way, it is essential that locally financed and run clinics and schools take the place of the services that have hitherto been provided by NGOs and UN agencies. Aid dependency is dangerous from many points of view. But in south Sudan we had to accept that none of this could be rushed since the population was still so weak in so many ways, the administration so poor, and the overall situation so unstable.

Arrested development

Overall, our instinct in 2007 that, with the conflict over, we should start pulling back and leaving it to the development agencies, may have been right in principle. But the new institutions were too fragile to take over much responsibility, and the international development community was not well placed to do so either, for the reasons I have set out. In the meantime, the twin threats of drought and flooding were more or less everpresent. Every year large parts of the country would suffer devastating periods of flooding in the rainy season, when travel was virtually impossible unless river access was available.

The threat of renewed conflict was also never far away. The north was always tempted to interfere, to stir up trouble and keep the southern administration off balance; and the southern government itself had no incentive to demobilize their over-large army and start to devote resources to development – defence spending still amounted to over 40 per cent of the total. It was often said, and rightly, that the ruling SPLM/A continued to behave like a liberation movement rather than a government. It had some reasons for doing so, but the transition to a broader and more responsible outlook was simply too slow.

The unsettled political and security situation was aggravated by tribal rivalries endemic in many parts of the country. Long-standing disputes, often over land and grazing rights between nomadic pastoralists and settled farmers, had become much more deadly as the power of the weaponry involved had moved from spears to Kalashnikovs. Habits had also changed in dangerous ways: where once women and children had been left out of disputes, they were now increasingly seen as valuable hostages and a particularly potent means of revenge.

The overall result was that south Sudan's requirements for humanitarian aid stubbornly refused to come down as had been hoped. The continuing need for a significant humanitarian presence was brought home to me not only by the regular impassioned pleas from successive humanitarian coordinators in Juba, but also by my own visits to remote areas. In 2009, for example, I went by helicopter to Jonglei state, where intertribal fighting, unchecked by the SPLA, had killed thousands and displaced tens of thousands more. The conditions in the town of Akobo, where most of those displaced had taken refuge, were truly awful, with only one small and inadequate hospital to deal with both the casualties and the sick. Food supplies and stocks of basic non-food items such as cooking pots were extremely limited because of the virtually impossible logistics, with river barge the only means of transporting supplies. The women I met were desperately struggling to keep their children nourished and their families together.

These were areas where life was very hard at the best of times, with most people living on the edge of disaster. Any new setback could tip whole communities over the edge. We could just about cope with this kind of humanitarian emergency. But the underlying issues needed to be tackled through efforts at tribal reconciliation and disarmament. Neither the government in Juba nor the state authorities seemed to be putting anything like enough effort into this. To be fair, the physical obstacles were huge – the governor complained bitterly to me when I called on him in the state capital that he had no chance of getting round his state without a helicopter. He was right. The UN could and did help him get around from time to time, but this was not enough for the kind of sustained engagement with the warring factions that was urgently needed.

Meanwhile, there were also constant problems in the highly sensitive, oil-rich territory of Abyei. Its status, close to the undemarcated border between north and south, was and is disputed. There was a major new humanitarian emergency there in 2008, following a crisis in relations between the two largest local tribes, the Ngok Dinkas and Misseriya. The Dinkas are a dominant group in much of south Sudan, known for their great height – visits to the area usually led to a ricked neck because of the need to look up at Dinka interlocutors. They are mostly settled farmers. The Misseriya are nomads based north of the border who every year move their cattle herds south through and into Ngok Dinka areas in search of fresh grazing. Every year this causes fighting and deaths. The UN peacekeeping force, UNMIS, regularly brought the leaders together in advance to try to regulate the process and prevent violence, and patrolled the area at the most sensitive times. However, it could never entirely succeed in controlling hostility between the two groups – not surprisingly perhaps, since water and grass were matters of life and death to both.

On this occasion, in May 2008, the town of Abyei had been attacked by the Misseriya and largely burned, with the active participation of northern government forces. Most of the Dinka population had fled 30 kilometres south to the town of Agok. UNMIS had been accused, with some justification in my view, of standing by and letting this happen, despite having a significant base in the area. Unfortunately, the local command had just changed hands and the new leaders were not well plugged in to the local dynamics. In any case, the displaced were strung out along the road and in the centre of Agok. Emergency aid was much easier here than in Akobo, because it was relatively accessible, but conditions were still poor.

The question was also how long the people who had been forced to flee Abyei were going to be there. Joint mechanisms designed to run the town until its final status could be established were not working. The Dinka who had left were bitter in the extreme against their attackers and swore they would never return until the Misseriya had been expelled from Abyei for good. It was depressing to meet families expressing such hatred and venom, while in the depth of suffering themselves.

All we could do from the humanitarian point of view was to ensure that those who had fled had the basics and, at the same time, urge all sides to resolve their differences as quickly as possible. This was unsatisfactory and frustrating, but that is so often the case for humanitarians on the ground: trying to clear up the mess, and able to see better than others looking in from the outside where the areas for compromise might lie, but unable to intervene effectively themselves without becoming unacceptably drawn into the politics, thereby compromising their principles.

Sadly, the situation around Abyei remains largely unresolved as I write, with reconstruction very limited, and many displaced still in and around Agok. Northern forces occupied Abyei shortly after the declaration of independence by the south following the referendum in 2011. A UN-mandated peacekeeping force of Ethiopian troops was sent in the summer of 2011 to try to maintain peace. However, there is little sign of progress. The promised popular consultation on Abyei's future seems a long way off, with disputes continuing over the demarcation of the borders of the special administrative area and who should be allowed to vote. The prospects for the inhabitants of the area remain cloudy at best.

This is part of a wider problem. While the south has achieved its independence, many of those who fought against the north with the south, and share their desperate desire to get away from Khartoum, are trapped in areas north of the new international border. There is little or no chance of the promised popular consultations leading to a change of status for the states where they live, mainly those of South Kordofan and Blue Nile. Fighting between Khartoum government forces and militias in these areas started again immediately after independence. The international community has once again struggled to gain humanitarian access to those affected by the fighting. The prospects for the peoples of these areas are not good in the face of unrelenting pressure from the Khartoum government, which the international community is not well placed to do much about. Many are already fleeing south to get away from this northern hostility. Many more may follow, which can only increase the problems in the south in the short term.

Accepting the inevitable

All in all, there was no doubt by 2009 that we needed to reverse our plans to reduce humanitarian assistance, and re-establish a presence in some of the more remote areas to ensure that we could cope with the regular crises which could not be dealt with effectively from Juba. This meant reconnecting with the main Western country donors to south Sudan to explain to them that large-scale funding for humanitarian aid was still needed because of a combination of recurring natural disasters, tension and fighting in many areas, as well as the LRA presence, against the background of political uncertainty between north and south. There was also a renewed requirement to make sure aid supplies had already physically reached the places where they would be needed and been stockpiled there, in advance of each year's rainy season. Once the rains started, it was almost impossible to move bulk goods other than by air, which was for most purposes, other than the most urgent life-saving crises, prohibitively expensive. The UN humanitarian coordinator, Lise Grande, performed heroic work in making this system work effectively.

The donors responded reasonably well then, and indeed continue to do so. But they had and continue to have legitimate wider doubts: how long are they going to be expected to put large sums of taxpayers' money into the south, for both humanitarian and development needs? How sure can they be that the government in the south are going to use these resources well, given their track record to date of incompetence, corruption and internal division? The answer so far has been that, despite the risks, the people of the south need and deserve consistent international aid to survive and develop over an extended period if independent South Sudan is not to be the immediately failed state so many feared. If the new state is not a success, the consequences for stability in the wider region, as well as for the people of South Sudan, will be dire. I still see no alternative to that answer.

But there can be no blank cheques here, as elsewhere. The southern government must get their act together – for example, by promoting effective basic services and development and doing something meaningful about corruption – and begin to produce results which their own people can see. The international community has to show tough love and insist on better performance in return for continued support. The international community will also have to find better ways to engage the north in order to persuade them to make good their promises to respect southern independence. There is a great temptation in Khartoum to continue to play games to weaken the south, perhaps even with the ultimate aim of taking over once more after the new regime there has shown its inability to cope. But simply criticizing the north is not going to help. They have to be brought into the solution.

What is all this likely to mean for the humanitarian presence in the south in the future? The international humanitarian community has to recognize that we are in South Sudan for the long haul, with all the risks that brings with it. The authorities in the south have usually been far more cooperative with the international humanitarian community than the Khartoum government have been, but the experience has nevertheless had its frustrations, and these have been increasing. Attacks on humanitarians have risen, with little sign of action from the government, as have incidents of obstruction or even harassment from the official armed forces, the SPLA, in some states. Long-term patience and readiness for dialogue will be needed on both sides.

A better future

Overall, what are the chances that this vast land, with its relatively tiny population, can break the cycle of dependency, poverty, deprivation and violence, and begin to fulfil the hopes of a people who, at least as much as any other in the world, deserve a decent and peaceful future?

It is hard to be optimistic in the face of all the problems I have outlined. The new state will have to avoid new conflict. It will need a lot of help from the international community as a whole. It will require support particularly from its neighbours, some of whom had reservations about the precedent set by the division of an African state. In other words, a lot of things will need to come right together for independent South Sudan to emerge as the peaceful, democratic, and prosperous entity it could be. But the region and the world cannot afford anything else.

Change in Khartoum could make a decisive difference to the prospects for the south. If the Arab spring were to come to Sudan, and lead to the establishment of a new democratic government, genuinely interested in the welfare of all the people, and properly accountable to them, such a government might be ready to take a new, constructive attitude to their southern neighbour. They would certainly have enough problems on their plate already, and would not have to deal with the accusation of having 'lost' the south, as the current government do.

Reducing the constant pressure from the north could help create the time and space for the new authorities in the south to get to grips with their worst problems and finally begin to fulfil the promises they have made to their people. This is no more than a pipe dream as I write, but pressures for change in the north are undoubtedly there beneath the surface, as much as anywhere else. The military-based Khartoum regime has not only alienated the peripheral parts of the country, but also much of the old educated elite and middle class. Opportunities for the young are limited at best, and the population is constantly subject, through simplistic propaganda, to the kind of contempt and humiliation from the regime that has led peoples elsewhere in the region to demand that they be treated with dignity, not like idiots or children.

However, the government in the south cannot afford to wait on such a development. They must show themselves by their own actions to be worthy of the trust put in them by their people and the international community. Unfortunately, too often the opposite seems to be happening. For example, the South Sudan government, frustrated at the failure to resolve key issues with Khartoum, and in particular by the absence of any agreement on division of oil revenues and fees for southern oil going through the north to Port Sudan, decided in January 2012 to close down the oilfields under their control and shut the pipeline. Their argument was that they could survive the wait for agreement better than the north, since they at least were used to doing without, and that they could build another pipeline south through Kenya. Both these arguments seemed unconvincing. The southern government depend on the oil for 98 per cent of their revenues and cannot survive long without it. The alternative route out for South Sudanese oil through Kenya looks implausible and at best a very long-term bet. The donors are not prepared to fill the government's massive revenue gap with more aid money and are already reorienting their programmes away from longer-term development and back towards emergency relief, from fear of a further major humanitarian crisis which could be just around the corner.

As I write in mid-2012, the two countries may have found a way forward on this oil issue which will avert the worst. But it is far from sure that any agreement will be implemented or respected, given the huge lack of trust between them. Meanwhile, the tension over the oil and surrounding developments have once again brought the two countries close to war. Both have good reason to want to avoid this, but the chances of miscalculation are high on both sides. A new north–south war would be an unimaginable catastrophe. Even if the international community can mediate effectively in the immediate disputes and help find reasonable compromises, therefore, the prospects of genuine reconciliation and cooperation look very poor. South Sudan overall is a long way from getting out of its troubles. I fear a major humanitarian presence and funding will be needed for years to come, unless the government can somehow begin to run the country much more professionally and the surrounding political climate improves. In any case, how over-optimistic and wrong we were in 2007!

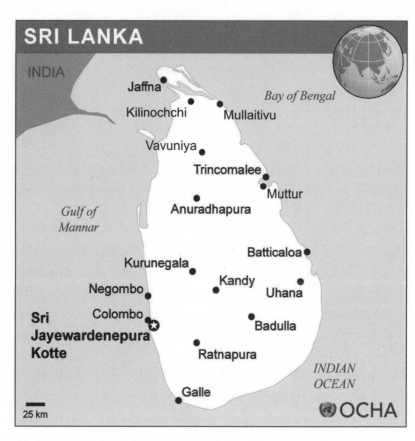

Map Sources: Gov't of Sri Lanka, UNCS. Map created in Nov 2011.

CHAPTER FOUR

Sri Lanka: the end of the LTTE

Sri Lanka was probably my most testing challenge as ERC. It dramatically illustrated the difficulties of providing humanitarian aid in a highly politicized setting, dealing with a strong, determined, and largely hostile government. The dilemma of whether to stay, despite often unacceptable conditions, or to withdraw, despite the risks to the people we were trying to help, hung over everything we did. The final stages of the war between the government and the Liberation Tigers of Tamil Eelam (LTTE) were a bloody period from which few if any came out well, including the vacillating international community. They were also an early live test of the doctrine of the 'Responsibility to Protect', and a sad demonstration of the weaknesses of international accountability for abuses of humanitarian and human rights law.

The terrorist from the UN

I first visited Sri Lanka in August 2007. The major issue was the humanitarian consequences of the long-standing political struggle between the Tamils and the majority Sinhalese population, which had become a violent conflict after 1983. Of the Sri Lankan population of about 20 million, more than 70 per cent are Sinhalese, largely Buddhist, while around 12 per cent are Tamils, historically concentrated in the north and east of the country, and mostly Hindus. Under British rule, the Tamils tended to be better educated and formed the backbone of the civil service. After independence, the majority community increasingly asserted their authority, and squeezed out the Tamils. This, in turn, led to increasing Tamil discontent, and ever louder demands for autonomy and even independence. The Liberation Tigers of the LTTE led this struggle, openly fighting for an independent Tamil state after violent ethnic disturbances in 1983. While there were many ups and downs in this struggle, by the turn of the century the LTTE controlled significant chunks of territory in the north and east. Led by Villupai Prabakharan, apparently quiet and uncharismatic, but at the same time authoritarian and brutal, the LTTE systematically rooted out and intimidated all other Tamil groups, killing their leaders where necessary, and established a repressive state within a state. They ruled with a rod of iron, and also used terrorist tactics with considerable success, both against the government, and against the Indians when the latter intervened in the 1990s; these included the assassination of the Indian prime minister, Rajiv Gandhi, by a female suicide bomber in 1991.

There were many attempts at mediation between the two communities, nationally and internationally, but all were unsuccessful, despite occasional ceasefires and apparent outbreaks of mutual goodwill. The LTTE managed to attract a lot of support and money from the Tamil diaspora around the world, and were well armed and determined. But their terrorist tactics and unwillingness to negotiate seriously alienated most of the international community over time, to the point that they were officially listed as a terrorist movement by many governments and international organizations, despite lingering sympathy for the plight and aspirations of the Tamils as a whole, and worries about the government's own often brutal response.

By 2007, and the time of my own involvement, the LTTE had just been driven out of their territory in the east by determined and effective government military action, aided by the defection of an important LTTE military leader to the government side. The humanitarians were worried about how the government were treating the newly liberated Tamil population in the east, particularly the continuing intimidation of civilians by armed men, as well as about the future fate of Tamils in the still LTTE-occupied north. In addition, I needed to raise with the government the increasing obstacles they were putting in the way of humanitarian operations.

My visit was also aimed to coincide with the anniversary of one of the worst-ever massacres of humanitarian workers. On 6 August 2006, seventeen local staff of the French-based NGO Action Contre la Faim were lined up and shot in the eastern town of Muttur. This came to be known as the ACF massacre. It was not clear who did it or why, though suspicion inevitably fell on government forces, official or unofficial, since the victims were nearly all Tamils. An official Sri Lankan enquiry was wound up in 2010 without result.

International humanitarian organizations had been in the country since the LTTE began their military campaign. Hundreds of thousands of people, mainly Tamils, but also Muslims and Sinhalese, had been driven from their homes at different times by the fighting. In theory, government administration continued in LTTE-controlled areas, with officials still supervising basic services like health and education. In practice, there was a major squeeze on the local economy, and the LTTE grip on the population was increasingly tight and brutal. International and local NGOs tried to meet the resulting humanitarian needs.

Unfortunately, these humanitarian efforts had come to be seen by some in government in Colombo as helping the LTTE enemy, or at least being complicit with them. Humanitarian contacts with the LTTE were regarded as evidence of sympathy for separatism, and aid supplies seen as likely to aid the military struggle. Such interpretations were unjustified. Most local humanitarian staff in these areas had to be Tamil to work there safely. They were certainly vulnerable to intimidation by the LTTE, either directly or through their families. But I am aware of no evidence to justify accusations against NGOs or other humanitarian organizations of broad support for the LTTE, still less actual collaboration with them – for example, smuggling of weapons, which the government and press often raised.

OCHA itself had been in Sri Lanka since the Indian Ocean tsunami of December 2004, which ravaged both government- and LTTE-controlled areas. Hopes that this tragedy would bring the communities together proved sadly short-lived, but the need to coordinate the complex relief efforts made an OCHA presence necessary. This was welcomed at the time by the authorities. However, that welcome had since soured as OCHA officials became progressively more engaged with the conflict-affected populations as well, and began to speak out about abuses of humanitarian principles and international humanitarian law by both sides.

By the time of my visit in 2007, the government were questioning more and more why OCHA needed to be there, and putting pressure on us to leave, without actually asking us to do so. Visas for replacement staff were being held up, and bureaucratic obstruction was conveying a similar message. They were also squeezing the wider humanitarian community: by all means provide the necessary relief, but keep quiet otherwise.

There were divisions within the government about this. The

technical ministries which dealt with us were sympathetic. But the military were suspicious, if not downright hostile, and those close to President Rajapaksa were certainly not prepared to let mere humanitarians get in the way of their political and military plans.

My trip was a struggle from the start. The government tried to insist beforehand that I should neither speak to the international press during the visit, nor go to the north to the Tamil areas. I told them that I could not credibly go to Sri Lanka without talking to the press and seeing the displaced Tamils. If they effectively banned me, it would not do much for their already tarnished international image. The uneasy compromise was that I would give a press conference only at the end of the visit, and that I could visit Jaffna, the historic Tamil city in the north held by the government since its recapture from the LTTE in 1995, but not the LTTE-held areas.

I was, in the end, reasonably well received, not only by humanitarian interlocutors, but also by the key players in the government, including President Mahinda Rajapaksa. They listened politely to my concerns, promised responses to specific demands about visas and conditions for humanitarian workers, and made positive if vague noises about investigating abuses, including the ACF massacre.

I was alert to the soft-soap tactics and under no illusions about the likelihood of any major change of policy. But my view was that a frank private dialogue was better than a furious public row. I could go out in a blaze of temporary glory of denunciation of the government – but I might well take the humanitarian operation with me. The real losers from that would be the very people we were trying to help. Meanwhile, we had a good chance of making short-term gains out of a visit, and registering important longer-term arguments. The bottom line here, as elsewhere, was that it was their country: if we wanted to go on working there, and standing up for the defenceless behind the scenes, we had to find some kind of accommodation with the government.

However, the government briefing to the local media about our initial discussions was disgraceful: a polite introductory remark quoted completely out of context here; a subtle distortion of what I had said to give it a completely different meaning there. There was nothing original about this black art – indeed I had already learned all about it from visiting Sudan – but the Sri Lankans were particularly shameless practitioners, briefing and stirring up their largely tame and nationalist media behind the scenes whenever it suited them.

The field trips were also instructive. The official version was that the east was now completely pacified and that the Tamil population were not only happy to be rid of the LTTE, but delighted by all the government were doing for them. The reality was that we flew into the area in an army helicopter at rooftop height, with doors open on either side to allow soldiers to lean out with their machine guns cocked. I was happy that the authorities were taking my security so seriously, but not convinced that the LTTE had disappeared as completely as the government said.

In the villages, I did not need much persuading that most people were indeed glad to see the back of the LTTE. The latter had been keeping the population effectively captive, recruiting their children, and bringing only insecurity and a lack of development. At the same time, a lot of what I heard officially about government help was clearly what people had been told to say, as they managed to convey in quiet moments when my official minders' backs were turned.

In Jaffna, there was the same contrast between the official discourse of stable peace and the security reality. A meeting with local Tamil representatives had also clearly been 'pre-prepared', in other words fixed – I was told later that the military had made clear that there were to be no statements about issues like human rights, only about economic problems caused by the LTTE blockade. This kind of attempted manipulation was both ineffective and typical of government tactics.

Both sides had behaved abominably at times in the conflict – I constantly wondered how such charming people could have such a brutal streak. The LTTE had long ago forfeited any sympathy among most of the international community, except the hundreds of thousands of Tamils living abroad. Nevertheless, I was not about to fall for government propaganda either. And I would have liked to talk to the LTTE about their humanitarian responsibilities to the people living in the territories still under their control. Talking to all parties, even those who have been labelled as terrorists, is a basic humanitarian requirement, as we will see in other contexts too.

When Reuters and the BBC pressed me for interviews before the final press conference, I therefore agreed – the government had not respected their side of the bargain. I was balanced in what I said to them about the overall situation. But I did stress that Sri Lanka was then the most dangerous place in the world for humanitarian aid workers. There had been other incidents besides the ACF massacre, involving, for example, local Red Cross staff who had been 'disappeared', to use the awful local jargon – thirty humanitarians in all had been killed in 2006. I was only stating facts, not accusing the government of responsibility, and at that moment it did not seem to cause a stir. The visit even ended on a note of cautious optimism about the bureaucratic obstructions I had been raising.

However, when my comments were published, all hell broke loose. President Rajapaksa was apparently enraged by my remarks, or a distorted version of them he had been fed by a close aide. UN humanitarian coordinator Neil Buhne was summoned to listen to strong official complaints about me, since I had left the country by then. Ministers furiously condemned me in public. The prime minister made an official statement in parliament – Sri Lanka was well known, he claimed, for the lengths to which it went to protect humanitarian aid workers. The pro-government press went to town about typical UN interference and arrogance. One minister, albeit a relatively junior one, even went as far as to describe me as a terrorist, without his statement being officially disowned by the government to which he belonged.

Ban ki-Moon, supportive as always, responded strongly to the absurdity of calling a senior UN official a terrorist. In the Sri Lankan capital, Colombo, Neil Buhne did an excellent job of defending me while calming things down. The government seemed to recognize after a while, even if only implicitly, that they might have overreacted, and we were able to resume a working relationship. But it was a nasty reminder of the prevailing atmosphere – and the terrorist label then applied to me often came up subsequently, not always in jest.

2008: the northern offensive

As 2007 ended, it became ever clearer, official statements about continuing peace efforts notwithstanding, that the government had taken the decision to go for a military solution in the north, to follow their success in the east. They had been steadily building up their forces and buying weapons. The conventional wisdom had long been that final military victory was impossible against a movement as strong and as well financed and dug in as the Tamil Tigers – they had plenty of money from the Tamil diaspora and had spent freely on weapons over the years. They even had small aircraft and submarines, as well as lots of artillery. They also had well-trained, indeed fanatical, cadres. It was therefore thought that the best the government could hope for was to put the LTTE under greater military pressure and then resume peace negotiations on more favourable terms. After all, previous negotiations had appeared close to success at times.

President Rajapaksa had other ideas. He believed, not without reason, that the LTTE leader, the vicious and secretive Velupillai Prabakharan, would never accept a negotiated compromise. Rajapaksa, at the tougher end of the political spectrum of Sinhalese nationalism, had narrowly won the presidential elections of 2005, ironically in part due to an LTTE-inspired boycott by Tamil voters. His brother Gothabaya, in charge of defence, had been a senior officer in the Sri Lankan armed forces. Bizarrely, he was also an American citizen, having worked in California in the 1990s. Another brother, Basil, was the president's chief adviser, including on the economic development of Tamil areas. He was apparently more open and conciliatory than his brothers.

Gothabaya was the driving force behind the campaign against the LTTE, together with the tough chief of the defence staff, General Sarath Fonseka. Given to bad-tempered rants, but also capable of charm, Gothabaya was ruthless in his pursuit of military success. He was particularly determined that the press, domestic or international, should not get in the way or undermine morale at home, and that the international community should keep out. He treated both accordingly, and acquired a particularly feared reputation among the Sri Lankan media.

By the autumn, it was clear that something new and dramatic was happening. The LTTE were losing battle after battle. They were gradually forced out of the Jaffna peninsula, then out of the Mannar area south-west of there, and finally confined to the Vanni, a heavily forested area further to the east, ideal for guerrilla warfare, where they had held key towns like Kilinochchi and Mullaitivu for many years.

Many of us could contemplate with equanimity the defeat of the LTTE, even if the Tamil desire for greater political autonomy could not simply be reduced to the war-on-terror rhetoric used by the government. But we were genuinely alarmed about the consequences for civilians. As the LTTE retreated, the Tamil civilian population from the area they had controlled were going with them, which obviously exposed them to huge risks. How voluntary was this? It was hard to say for certain. Many would probably have liked to get out of the LTTE zone by this time. They had already lost faith in the LTTE, after so many years of fruitless struggle and violent suppression of any dissent within the Tamil community. They had good reason to fear forced recruitment into the LTTE army, particularly for their children.

But they had little reason to trust the government either. And among them were, of course, the immediate families of the LTTE leaders and fighters, who naturally wanted to accompany their men. In any case, whatever the breakdown of views within this population, it quickly became clear that the LTTE had no intention of letting them go, preferring to use them instead as a human shield and ultimate bargaining card.

As the LTTE were beaten back further, humanitarian organizations worked with the remaining local officials and doctors to ensure that the civilians with them at least had access to food, clean water, medical care, and shelter materials. But this became increasingly problematic. The government were prepared to allow in occasional supplies but were also anxious to ensure that this did not amount to resupplying the LTTE themselves. Each supply movement had to be painstakingly negotiated with both sides, and the government position got tougher and tougher.

Even more worryingly, there was a fundamental disagreement

between the humanitarians and the government about the size of the trapped civilian population. The government claimed that there were no more than 70,000 and did not want provision made for any more. We said, on the basis of our knowledge and information from local Tamil officials, that there could be as many as 300,000 and certainly no fewer than 200,000 people moving with the LTTE and living however they could as they moved. This argument raged until the final denouement of the crisis, when the higher estimates proved to be correct. Were the government deliberately concealing the reality or did they believe their own figures? Probably the former – the truth had long been a casualty of this particular war.

Meanwhile, the position of humanitarian staff inside the ever-shrinking LTTE-controlled zone was becoming more and more precarious. Government shells and bombs damaged humanitarian offices in Kilinochchi, even though the Sri Lankan forces had the coordinates. The government denied responsibility but made very clear that they were not in a position to guarantee the safety of any humanitarian staff inside the zone. At the same time, the LTTE, while outwardly cooperative, obviously had priorities other than our security. In late September, we therefore took the difficult decision to pull the remaining international UN staff out of the zone, together with any local staff who wanted to leave. The international NGOs still present felt they had no choice but to follow suit, though the International Committee of the Red Cross (ICRC) hung on. Some local humanitarian staff also stayed, mostly because they had little option if they wanted to remain with their families – the latter were not allowed to leave by the LTTE and had to follow the civilian group as they desperately tried to survive in the smaller and smaller space available to them.

The decision to pull out was criticized at the time and subsequently, among others by the International Crisis Group in a 2010 report on the end of the war, on the grounds that we were abandoning the civilian population and helping give the government the international witness-free zone they wanted in order to finish off the conflict. As one of those accountable for this decision at the New York end, I did not believe at the time that we had any real choice, given the duty of care we owed to our staff. We also had a reasonable hope at that stage that we could run convoys into the area using international staff where possible, with a core of local staff to help on the spot. Moreover, even if we had stayed then, we would have had to leave relatively soon after, as the fighting became even more intense and the zone even smaller and more dangerous.

We did manage to run eleven convoys into the zone over subsequent weeks, but negotiating safe passage became ever more complicated. Finally, in mid-January, a convoy became trapped inside the zone by shelling all around it. Initial frantic efforts to negotiate its release proved fruitless. The bulk of the vehicles and staff managed to escape through a pause in the shelling after five frightening days, but a number of local staff stayed, with two volunteer international staff, to help establish a relief area in the government's newly declared No-Fire Zone, where the civilians had been invited to take shelter. Despite this, they were again repeatedly shelled in what became a terrifying and traumatizing experience. A group of civilians sheltering a few yards away were blown to pieces by direct hits. One of the UN international staff happened to be an artillery expert and was convinced that because of the direction and angle at which the shells had fallen they must have been fired by government forces. Repeated attempts by the UN in Colombo to get the army to stop the shelling took a long time to succeed. The government strongly denied responsibility and argued, in what was to become a familiar pattern, that the shells must have been fired by the LTTE in an attempt to incriminate the government.

As with so many other aspects of this vicious conflict, it is hard to be sure of the full truth. Both sides were fighting the propaganda war as hard as the real one. Were the government deliberately targeting these areas in order to force the civilians to flee the LTTE? Were the LTTE just as guilty of indifference to civilian casualties, firing their own artillery from areas where civilians were sheltering, in the hope that the government would not dare fire back? Or was it all more cock-up than conspiracy, as so often? Arguments continue to rage about this, as they do about other appalling incidents later in the war – for example, makeshift hospitals were shelled, allegedly fired on deliberately by the government, who knew exactly what and where they were, not least from drones which were constantly overflying the combat area. Resulting casualties were extremely high.

In any case, the stark fact was that after the last convoy finally got out, the UN had little further possibility of significant direct intervention in the LTTE-held zone. But we still wanted to follow the situation, and had some means of doing so: satellite photographs could reveal where the bulk of the population was – for example, through counting of temporary shelters – and we could also count the number of shell and bomb craters. There was also one more direct source of information: the local humanitarian staff stuck in the zone and forced to retreat with the LTTE into the ever-shrinking pocket. They still had mobile phones and were somehow able to stay in occasional contact until the very end. What they could tell us was anecdotal and, it could be argued, not necessarily objective. But what we did hear was clear and horrific enough to confirm that a major human tragedy was unfolding.

The one remaining source of help for the people on the spot was the International Committee of the Red Cross (ICRC). They managed not only to maintain a presence of dedicated local staff in the zone, but also to take a ship on to a beach in the LTTE-controlled Vanni area every few days, bringing in medical supplies and small quantities of food, and evacuating the wounded. This was an extraordinarily brave operation, working with a few heroic Tamil doctors who stayed throughout. It says something about the approach of the government that after the war, in apparent acts of revenge, the ICRC were effectively prevented from continuing their work in the north of Sri Lanka, while the doctors themselves were arrested and forced into saying publicly that they had lied about the casualties and conditions on the beach on LTTE orders – statements they later retracted again as soon as they were released.

2009: bloody endgame

In the first weeks of 2009, international alarm mounted rapidly. The number of civilian casualties was rising dramatically. The UN tried to keep track privately of the numbers of dead and wounded, using a mixture of the reports from the doctors and local UN staff, and other information about incidents which we could cross-check in some way. The system was far from perfect, but we hoped it gave us a reasonable way of estimating casualties. We judged that around 7000 civilians had been killed in 2009 by early April. We did not release these figures to the media ourselves because we did not have sufficient evidence to prove their accuracy, but they were leaked anyway. We subsequently confirmed that this was indeed our best estimate.

The reaction from the government was predictably furious, given their line that they were refraining from the use of heavy weapons in order to prevent civilian casualties, and indeed that the whole aim of their operation was humanitarian – to rescue the population (whom they had taken to describing as hostages). They accused us of falling prey to LTTE propaganda, or worse, taking the LTTE side.

We had already by that stage begun to be concerned that our casualty figures were growing steadily less reliable – both because the situation had become so confused and because of our inability to be on the ground ourselves. After much agonizing, Neil Buhne and I therefore decided that we should not give any more figures publicly, since we could not stand behind them with sufficient confidence. This led to fierce accusations at the time and subsequently that we had bowed to government pressure, and that we knew the real casualty figures, but were deliberately concealing them. Some people inside the UN strongly disagreed with our decision, and made this clear privately to some journalists. This reinforced the story that we were hiding the truth. It was alleged, for example, that we knew that up to a thousand civilians a day were being killed in the last weeks of the war, or that 20,000 civilians or more had been killed in 2009 by the time the war ended, but that we deliberately chose not to say so to protect the humanitarian operation.

The position I spelled out to the press then and later was sincere: the fierce government pressure was not the reason we had stopped giving our own casualty estimates; we simply could not say with accuracy any more what the figures were, not even the order of magnitude. In any case, the exact figures were not really the point – we continued to say, and everyone knew, that the civilian casualties were clearly very high and rising and were, equally clearly, unacceptable. Whether civilians were dying in their dozens or hundreds a day was important, but it made no fundamental difference to our attitude. It would not and did not, for example, change our criticism of the government for continuing to use heavy weapons where there were civilians in the area, nor of the LTTE for their cynical refusal to release the civilian population. Nor, in our view, would releasing figures have changed significantly the attitude of the wider international community. They knew exactly what was going on already.

Should we nevertheless have gone on giving figures for casualties, even if we could not back them up properly, in order to draw greater attention to the full horror of what was happening? Would it have made any substantial difference to the outrage of world opinion and what the international community were prepared to do about the carnage? The UN high commissioner for human rights did, in fact, go on citing high figures publicly, to little apparent effect. But I accept that there is a legitimate different view.

In any case, it was clear by this stage that I needed to visit the country again, to find out personally as much as I could about what was going on in the north, and to talk to the government face to face about casualties, lack of access and of official preparation for the humanitarian crisis we would inevitably face once the LTTE were finally defeated and the civilians released. The government were once again not keen. But a visit was finally agreed in late February. I was again able to see President Rajapaksa and his brothers. I also talked to opposition politicians, including the leader of the main official Tamil party, the Tamil National Association (TNA), which was politically linked to the LTTE and tended to reflect their views. I was not allowed to go into the LTTE zone, but did travel north, to the Tamil town of Vavuniya. A new camp had been set up there, at a place called Menik Farm, to house Tamils who had already managed to escape from the LTTE grip and the fighting, and those likely to escape in the future.

We were helping the government provide the basics to these 36,000 Tamils who had already managed to flee. But the conditions in which they were accommodated were controversial, to say the least. Menik Farm and other temporary holding centres, mainly schools, were surrounded by soldiers and barbed wire. Moreover, the government seemed to be creating semi-permanent structures in Menik Farm. This fed a story that the government were determined not to allow the Tamil population to return to their places of origin after the war, and wanted instead to recolonize the area with Sinhalese from the south.

My visit, as usual carefully controlled by the government as far as they could manage it, did not confirm these fears, but did not exactly dispel them either. It was clear enough from the conversations I managed to have with the escapees who crowded around me, and from the briefing given by UN and NGO colleagues on the spot, without official minders present, that the Tamil civilians were desperately relieved to be out of the LTTE zone alive and grateful for the help they were receiving. But they were also extremely anxious about friends and family still trapped, distrustful of the government, and fearful about their own future inside a closed camp.

Meanwhile, the most immediate humanitarian concerns we wanted the government to address were the need to reduce overcrowding in Menik Farm and the holding centres (which risked disease); to get the military out of the camps, and ensure their civilian character, as required under internationally agreed principles for treatment of civilians who had fled violence and were in need of humanitarian aid; to restore freedom of movement as soon as possible, through proper registration of those in the camps; to ensure that any screening process for LTTE cadres among the IDPs was properly and fairly conducted, with no 'disappearances' of the kind that had been prevalent earlier in the conflict; and to speed up radically the preparations for the exodus of the rest of the Tamil civilians. On the latter point, the government had not cleared enough land for the holding camps, were building shelters much too slowly, and were taking no notice of concerns expressed by the humanitarian community about water supply and drainage at the site chosen, with the future monsoon season in mind, nor about the unmanageability of one big camp.

More seriously still, I urged the government again, with all the passion at my command, to prevent civilian casualties and, in particular, to stop altogether using heavy weapons such as mortars, artillery, and air strikes in the areas where civilians were known to be. I appealed to them to help speed up deliveries of medical supplies and food to the zone, for example by allowing bigger ships; to agree to more 'humanitarian ceasefires' to let the wounded out and humanitarian teams and supplies in; to spell out publicly that they had no intention of creating semi-permanent internment camps for the northern Tamils; and to make clear their aim to respond to legitimate Tamil political demands as soon as the war was over, in order to reassure Tamils that the end of the LTTE would not spell guaranteed long-term oppression at the hands of the majority.

As usual, the government made promises about issues like freedom of movement, screening and eventual returns, and were generally reassuring about the broader political points. They were reluctant to agree to new humanitarian pauses because they said the LTTE had exploited previous ones to regroup and resupply. But the gap between their fine words and the realities yawned ever wider. For example, they continued to use heavy weapons, as indeed they did until the end of the war, with appalling consequences for the trapped civilians.

Meanwhile, I took every opportunity to remind the LTTE publicly of their obligations too: to let go of the civilians they were using as human shields, to stop forced recruitment, particularly of children, and to do all they could to avoid civilian casualties. I also used every chance I could to speak out about the risk of a much worse human and humanitarian catastrophe if there was a final deadly battle on the beaches to which the LTTE had now retreated, in the middle of the trapped civilian population.

But the awful truth was that the government were by now hell-bent on final victory, and were determined that the international community were not going to 'steal' it from them. The LTTE were equally determined not to surrender, and in the meantime to use every card they had: the wretched civilians were just about the only one they had left, and we knew from a variety of sources on the ground that they were by now shooting to kill at any who tried to flee, in order to deter any mass attempts at escape.

On returning to New York, I was able to brief the Security Council for the first time, but not in formal session. However absurd it may seem when so many innocent people were dying in such misery, Sri Lanka was not on the Council agenda. The Russians, Chinese, and others, no doubt with an eye to their freedom to attack their home-grown terrorists, were not prepared to agree that the situation went beyond an internal dispute (and therefore presented risks for international peace and security). Council members finally gathered several times in a basement room under a scarcely used, unofficial procedure called 'informal interactive dialogue'. Many Council members were anxious to make clear that they saw no political or moral equivalence between a government defending itself against terrorism and the terrorist movement involved, and were therefore not prepared to condemn what the government were doing, let alone authorize any action against them. Nevertheless, the press guidance after the meetings did at least express great concern about civilian casualties, as well as calling for restraint from all sides and asking the government to refrain from using heavy weapons – a useful reminder to the government that even the non-Western parts of the international community most sympathetic to them were watching closely.

As the situation of the trapped civilians grew ever more appalling, the large Tamil diaspora – for the most part uncritical supporters of the LTTE and only too willing to amplify its messages – cried louder than ever about government war crimes, and demanded international intervention. They bombarded public figures, including me, with well-organized text message and email campaigns, calling us lackeys of the government, and connivers in genocide. Sadly, they put no similar pressure on the LTTE to let their fellow Tamils go. Those Western countries where the diaspora was most numerous and well organized – the UK, US, Canada, Australia, and France, for example – had to take account of this Tamil lobbying. However, as these governments were not willing to take any significant action themselves, they were only too happy to deflect this political pressure on to the UN and demand publicly that we do more to stop the fighting and help the civilians. This became a rather cynical pattern, as ministers from such countries queued up to press such thoughts over the phone to me in New York.

One line of thought and potential action was the applicability of the Responsibility to Protect (R2P) doctrine, endorsed in principle by the UN World Summit in 2005. This said, among other things, that if governments were unable to protect their own populations or were themselves responsible for war crimes against them, the international community had an obligation to intervene to provide the necessary protection. Despite its unanimous adoption, many countries still took the view that R2P represented a potentially dangerous infringement of national sovereignty. I will come back to this later in the book, in Chapter Thirteen. Suffice it to say for now that some saw Sri Lanka as a test case. There were suggestions that influential members of the international community, led by the US, might intervene in some way; for example, by mounting an amphibious military operation to rescue the Tamil population from the beaches.

As far as I know, there was never much to this. A US naval operation with the agreement of both sides was indeed briefly looked at, before being quickly turned down by the LTTE, but that was all. It was clear to me from my political experience that, in the post-Iraq atmosphere of the time, no country was going to put their forces in harm's way for an uncertain cause of this kind, and that no country had strong enough interests at stake, whatever their sympathy for the trapped Tamil civilians, to oblige them to do so. Rescuing the LTTE themselves was certainly not on anyone's agenda, whatever the LTTE or the Tamil diaspora might have hoped. There was no real enthusiasm for pressing the government to go back to the negotiating table with the LTTE, given the latter's track record, or even, in truth, much support for a full ceasefire which would have suspended the action, because that would have let the LTTE off the hook. What Western governments really wanted, though they could not and did not say so, was a quick government victory and minimal civilian casualties in the process. They were, no doubt, very uncomfortable about the level of civilian deaths, and the brutality of the government approach, but were not prepared to do anything serious about either. In the meantime, the UN was a convenient whipping boy.

By late March, the so-called No-Fire Zone within the LTTE-controlled area, which had been declared by the government in January as a safe haven to protect civilians, and the boundaries of which had been constantly redrawn as the LTTE-controlled zone shrank, had effectively become a killing zone, with constant bombing and shelling as the noose tightened. We estimated that around 200,000 civilians were now squeezed into an area of around 14 square kilometres. Risks from malnutrition and disease were growing rapidly. Many civilians were being killed every day, and many more wounded. Shipments of food into the zone had improved a little, thanks to the efforts of the ICRC and World Food Programme, but these were still far short of what was needed. Four thousand people – the seriously wounded, infirm and members of their families – had been evacuated by the ICRC, but the demand and need were much greater than that. Escapes were increasing, but so were the LTTE's brutal efforts to intimidate and recruit into their ranks those who remained, as we heard from the escapees themselves. Was there any possible way out?

Talking to the LTTE

Various vain attempts had already been made (for example, by the Norwegian government, who had had good contacts with the LTTE for many years as part of international mediation efforts) to convince the LTTE leadership that their time was finally up: that they now owed it to the Tamil population – whom they claimed to represent and whose fate they controlled – to surrender in order to avoid more bloodshed; or at the very least, if they were determined to go down fighting themselves so as to keep their 'myth' alive, to let the civilians go first. As this still looked like the only hope, I decided, with Norwegian encouragement, to try my own hand with the LTTE. The idea was that a UN humanitarian figure might somehow still be seen by the Tigers' leadership as apolitical (despite Tamil criticism of the UN for failing to stop the government military assault), and worth listening to. Some contacts in the Sri Lankan foreign ministry in Colombo also encouraged me to try, though others in the government system were vehemently opposed.

It was impossible by then to communicate directly with the LTTE leadership on the ground. They did not dare to use mobile phones for fear of being tracked and targeted, and contact was only possible indirectly through intermediaries. I therefore approached a figure with close contacts to the leadership who lived outside Sri Lanka, in Malaysia: Selvarasa Pathmanathan, usually known as KP. He had, over time, built up a vital overseas network for the LTTE, using the Tamil diaspora to amass and invest money and buying arms with the proceeds.

In a series of discreet telephone conversations with KP in late March, I made clear that, based on my concern for the humanitarian consequences of the fighting, I could no longer see any possible positive outcome for the LTTE, and that the UN were willing to play a role in trying to bring the fighting to an end honourably, getting the civilian population out safely, if the LTTE wanted us to. While the conditions in the camps were far from perfect, those arriving there were being decently treated on the whole. I appealed to KP to persuade the leadership on the ground to let the people go to avoid unnecessary bloodshed and, as a first step, to stop forced recruitment. That way they could go down in history as saviours of their people, not the opposite.

He listened politely, expressed appreciation for the approach and what the UN had been trying to do, and said he would talk to his colleagues. Meanwhile, he wanted to explain why the Tamil population with the LTTE felt obliged to stay: they could never trust the government after all the broken promises and brutality to which they had been subjected over the years. Whole families were there. So even if the leadership asked them to go, he did not think they would. He argued instead for a proper ceasefire under international supervision and fresh negotiations. A political solution was needed, not a military one.

I tried to make clear to him that I did not find his account of the views of the civilian population convincing, and frankly, that I saw no chance at this stage of the kind of ceasefire and political negotiation he was talking about – the government would never agree now and the international community could not and would not force them to do so. If the leadership gave up in an agreed way, there might be a possibility of some kind of discussion about the political future of the Tamils further down the line, though I was obviously not in a position to promise even this. For now, we needed to find a way forward other than a bloody final battle.

Sadly, this initiative proved a blind alley in the end. KP seemed at one stage to be persuaded himself, and hopeful of selling something to his colleagues on the ground. But it gradually became clear that, if he had tried, he had failed. The message back from the last LTTE stronghold on the north-east beaches by the end of March was stark: there was no possibility of giving up the struggle for freedom, even with assurances about fair treatment, nor of the civilian population leaving – they did not want to go and, in any case, could not be abandoned to the brutal Sri Lankan government. Political negotiations were the only way forward and this was in the hands of the international community. KP and I agreed to stay in touch if there was anything more to say – but in truth, there was not. I was bitterly disappointed, if not totally surprised. The risk of a final death toll in the tens of thousands looked ever more likely.

The last battles

In mid-April, Ban ki-Moon decided to send his chief of staff, Vijay Nambiar, to Colombo. The hope was that the government might listen more to a fellow Asian, especially one from a sympathetic nation: India. But he too made little headway, and also fell foul of the Tamil propagandists in the process. They accused him of being a closet sympathizer with the government on the spurious grounds that his brother, a former Indian general and distinguished UN peacekeeper, had at one time been involved with training Sri Lankan special forces.

One of Vijay's specific aims had been to convince the government to agree to a longer humanitarian pause of at least a week, and allow access to a humanitarian team, which he offered to accompany himself. Such a team would try to organize better arrangements for desperately needed supplies, including with the LTTE leadership on the ground, but also in the process see whether there was any chance of a more fundamental shift in the situation. The government gave initial signs of agreeing to such a mission, at least the humanitarian part of it. However, it gradually became clear that they had no intention of allowing it to happen. Their fear that the LTTE would find a way of slipping off the hook, even at this late stage, was simply too great. They might have had legitimate grounds for concern about the security of any team going in, but security was also a convenient excuse for continuing to keep prying international eyes away from the horrors of the front line, especially, as they saw it, when those eyes belonged to dangerously naive international do-gooders.

On 20 April, government forces broke through one of the defensive earthworks the LTTE had built to protect their remaining tiny enclave of a few square kilometres, and more than 100,000 civilians escaped, with the LTTE unable to stop them. The government's reception facilities and the camp at Menik Farm almost buckled under the huge strain as the new arrivals poured in. Then, as later, there were stories of individual acts of kindness by Sri Lankan soldiers to those emerging from the nightmare – they were, after all, their fellow citizens – but also allegations of summary killings and even rapes. Evidence of either was, however, lacking. The pictures of the Tamils wading across the lagoons in long lines to get out were in any case dramatic and moving. The government were naturally eager to make the most of this with the international media, in contrast to their usual strict censorship, and provided images from their own drones overflying the LTTE-held area. Gothabaya Rajapaksa was, incidentally, able to watch these drone images live in his office and often proudly showed them to international visitors.

The people who had escaped were in dreadful shape and (not least because of the government's original denial of the numbers concerned) the arrangements to receive them were nothing like as good as we would have wanted. There was a particular problem in getting tents up quickly, since cleared land was inadequate. Rudimentary supplies of food and medical aid were provided, with a lot of help from international agencies, but were far from enough in the first days after this massive influx. I feared a still worse humanitarian crisis as the numbers increased further, as we knew they would – there were still some 70–100,000 Tamil civilians left with the LTTE in the last remaining square kilometres.

In the meantime, the government were, extraordinarily and unforgivably, still inclined to make life difficult for humanitarian organizations trying to help the Tamils who had got out. The unrestricted access to the camp we needed was a constant problem, especially for the international NGOs among these organizations, as was free discussion with those in the camp. The appointment of an army general to take over the camp operation was perhaps good news from an efficiency point of view, but hardly the right signal when our overriding concern was precisely the size and dominance of the military presence.

The lack of progress following Vijay Nambiar's mission prompted the secretary-general to ask me to go back to Sri Lanka again myself. The aim was still a UN humanitarian mission into the conflict area, courtesy of a new humanitarian pause. I was frankly reluctant. I saw little chance of achieving anything, and thought another visit risked undermining the UN's credibility further. However, Ban ki-Moon insisted – the stakes were so high that he felt we had little to lose.

The late April visit was the by now standard mixture of talks with the president and key ministers, meetings with the humanitarian community, and a trip to Menik Farm. On humanitarian conditions I made a little progress: agreements to allow more food and medical supplies into the LTTE-held zone, to give greater freedom for international NGOs to work in the north, and to grant permission for foreign medical teams to access Menik Farm. Renewed and more plausible promises about future freedom of movement for the IDPs were also made. But about a humanitarian ceasefire and a mission to the deadly beach, the answer remained the same: yes in principle, no in practice. The government again contested strongly, both privately and publicly, my accusations about civilian casualties from their use of heavy weapons, while continuing to bomb and shell as they saw fit. Determination to finish off the LTTE once and for all still trumped everything else.

Looking further forward, I also pressed the argument that after the war the government would be in a very strong position to be magnanimous. They needed to take this unique and historic opportunity to bring the two communities together and transform Sri Lanka – for example, by moving quickly to amend the constitution to allow genuine autonomy for the Tamil areas. Otherwise, the risk of the LTTE reconstituting itself would always be there, increasing as time went on.

Sri Lankan officials I was in touch with mostly agreed. But on the political level it was different. The president, a truculent character used to being obeyed, naturally did not like being 'lectured' by an outsider, still less a British one. He showed irritation at the implication that he would ever want to do anything other than what I was suggesting: the Tamils were full Sri Lankan citizens and would, after all, be his future voters. Of course he would want to bring them into the mainstream, and of course the government recognized the need to stop Tamil separatism rising again. But, he added, naturally the government would need to be careful – many Sinhalese soldiers were being killed in the war (the official toll was eventually some 6000) and majority Sinhalese sentiment could not be ignored. My impression was that while he and other politicians could understand the intellectual arguments, they were more concerned about shoring up the government's own political base in the south, and they would move only slowly, if at all.

This is, unfortunately, precisely how it turned out after the war, which finally came to its inevitable conclusion in mid-May. As the last LTTE earthworks crumbled, those who could flee did so. Almost 70,000 poured out on 16 May. To great relief, there was no final pitched battle around the civilians. My worst fears of a concluding dreadful act of a Masada-style mass suicide were not realized. The army announced that victory was theirs. But the real end did not come until 19 May, when Prabakharan and his fellow LTTE leaders were killed.

The circumstances of these deaths were – and are – heavily contested. Were they surrounded and killed as they resisted to the end, or were some shot in cold blood? Some leaders had been in touch by mobile phone as the end approached and had been passed messages by outside parties – journalists and diplomats – to carry white flags, in accordance with government responses to questions about how surviving leaders could safely give themselves up. For example, the LTTE political commissar, Balasingham

Nadesan, the leader best known to previous outside mediators, had certainly told several ambassadors in Colombo, as well as the late *Sunday Times* journalist Marie Colvin, that he was going to be coming out with a white flag. He was killed before he reached safety. Was this a result of crossfire, or a deliberate attack by the Sri Lankan forces? Or could he even have been shot by his own side for disobeying orders not to surrender?

We may never know for sure, given the fog of war. On a later visit, while proudly showing me Prabakharan's LTTE ID card (issue no. 1) which he had taken from his body, the Sri Lankan general who had been on the spot shortly after the body was discovered swore that Prabakharan and those with him at the time had been killed in the last of the fighting. Other accounts have suggested that informal instructions were given from senior levels in the government to take no prisoners from among the leaders in order to prevent trials and martyrs later. General Fonseka, the overall commander of the Sri Lankan forces at the time, gave some credence to these stories in the early days of his presidential bid the following year, hinting strongly that he had received some such orders, though he later partially withdrew the accusations under pressure from the government.

These issues were far from the government's mind in those first days of victory. There were parades and great rejoicing among the Sinhalese population, after so many years of insecurity, terrorist attacks and sacrifice. The president was hailed as a hero. He said the right things about reaching out to the Tamil population, and even spoke some words in Tamil to show his respect for their language and culture. But these were not easy days for the Tamils, however little most of them had in the end loved the LTTE. They feared the worst. Triumphalism from the government and the military did nothing to calm their fears.

Internationally, the end of the fighting was greeted with relief, but no celebration. No tears were shed for Prabakharan and his colleagues, except by parts of the shocked Tamil diaspora, who had supported and believed in him until the end. But the relief was strongly coloured by concern about how the victory had been achieved, and the appalling loss of civilian lives. Voices were immediately and rightly raised to insist on a full and independent investigation into what had happened.

Ban ki-Moon flies in

Even before the end of the war, the secretary-general had been pressing the Sri Lankan government to allow him to visit the country himself. Now, finally, the government were ready to welcome the secretary-general. I was not in favour of him visiting so soon. It could too easily be interpreted by the ill-intentioned as tacit support for the government in their celebration of their victory. I thought it would be better to wait until the febrile atmosphere had calmed a little, and the president might be more inclined to listen to unpalatable political messages about the future. But Ban took the view that being seen to visit was a sign of action in itself, was good for the UN, and could do no harm. He liked being the first international leader on the scene after dramatic events.

He therefore set off on a lightning trip on 22 May. I accompanied him, along with Lynn Pascoe, the USG for political affairs, and a good chunk of the UN press corps. The majority of the twenty-four hours in Sri Lanka was spent travelling – to the camp at Menik Farm, on a rather ghoulish overflight of the newly liberated final-conflict zone, to see the president in his private residence in Kandy, and finally to Colombo for a press conference.

The camp visit was chaotic, but that at least helped to counter the government's usual attempts at control and manipulation, because everything was so rushed and confused. Overcrowding was acute, with 280,000 Tamils now crammed together on the site. Several families were often crushed into the same small tent. The condition of those who had come out in the final wave was particularly serious – malnourished, many suffering from skin and respiratory infections, weak, and traumatized. There were also many wounded. Supplies were still insufficient, though we were catching up fast, and there were particular complaints about poor sanitation.

I was able to slip away from Ban's entourage and talk to as many IDPs as I could. They were in shock, but still articulate. Their main worries were not aid, but lack of information about missing members of their families, and acute anxiety about what might happen to them next. They feared the worst from the government. And they had some reasons for this – despite all the government's promises, the registration and issuing of new ID cards to previous waves of IDPs was still moving extremely slowly. This was the vital first step before they could be allowed out of the camps. The prospects for rapid release and freedom of movement did not, therefore, look at all good.

There were particular worries about what the government might do to those who had been separated from the main body of the IDPs and identified as LTTE members. Rumours had spread about renewed 'disappearances' and extra-judicial killings, long a feature of the war. There was little hard evidence of this that we could see, but the methods of so-called screening were certainly worrying. There was an assumption on the outside that the government must have a good database of LTTE members. In reality, below the top leadership, the government had surprisingly poor information, as they themselves admitted.

The screening process was therefore mostly carried out via self-identification – those coming out of the conflict zone were asked whether they had worked for the LTTE or not, and threatened with worse treatment than they would receive otherwise if they did not own up straight away. A surprisingly large number did so, though not necessarily the worst offenders. The other method was by using informers. They were often seen in the camp, faces covered, identifying to the military the former LTTE cadres who were hiding among the IDPs. This may have been effective in some cases, but it was certainly unacceptable in judicial or human rights terms. The government practice of paying informers by results was hardly likely to be an objective process. It also lent itself to every kind of individual score-settling imaginable.

Lack of knowledge about LTTE membership may also at least partly explain the military's continuing reluctance to allow the IDPs to move around more freely. They would not even allow our own local staff out of the camp for some weeks, which caused me particular outrage. Their great worry was that LTTE sleepers might somehow find a way to restart the war, using weapons caches prepared for just this eventuality. We tried hard, but mostly in vain, to persuade the military that while such fears were not necessarily fanciful, they were exaggerated. Meanwhile, they were taking greater risks by not allowing freedom of movement, because they were alienating the Tamils they had rescued from the LTTE all over again, and creating a new generation of grievances. Some politicians and officials understood this, but not apparently those giving the orders.

The helicopter overflight of the area of the LTTE's last stand was horrifying. The beach where the final act had been played out – an area fearfully small for accommodating so many people – was by now empty of civilians, and largely of soldiers too. No bodies were visible. But the detritus of war and flight was all around – abandoned rudimentary shelters, some burned and still smouldering, amateur trenches, shell holes, bicycles in piles, clothes and rags everywhere, some flapping from poles, possessions of all kinds, scattered and lost in the final desperate flight. It was only too easy, and awful, to imagine the plight of the tens of thousands of civilians caught between the men with guns, crouching in shallow foxholes, clutching on to their children and aged parents: wondering how they would find food and water for another day, how to secure some kind of medical treatment, just trying to survive the hell somehow. How many had died there? How many bodies and horrors had already been cleared away in the few days before we swept low over the pathetic remnants still visible?

The contrast with the relaxed and confident President Rajapaksa in Kandy was extreme. Ban-Ki Moon carefully avoided congratulating him and instead concentrated on the next steps. He went through the humanitarian concerns, and the importance of reaching out to the Tamils quickly. But he also emphasized the need to investigate the many allegations about the conduct of the war. This would be a vital part of re-establishing confidence between the communities for the future. He proposed including language to this effect in a joint communiqué. Rajapaksa was extremely doubtful, to say the least. But since his line was that the Sri Lankan forces had conducted the most humane military campaign in history – he occasionally claimed that there had been no civilian casualties at all, which even his close colleagues found embarrassing – it was difficult for him to oppose it openly.

In the end, after a difficult tête-à-tête with the secretary-general, he agreed to a version of the language we sought: 'The secretary-general underlined the importance of an accountability process for addressing violations of international humanitarian and human rights law. The government will take measures to address those grievances.' We had no illusions about the likelihood of the government being ready for an independent enquiry any time soon, but this was at least a valuable peg for the future.

In the end, I thought the visit had just been worthwhile: for the frank points Ban ki-Moon had been able to make in person to the president, and for this language on accountability. But some of the press, as well as the Tamil diaspora, still took it as a tacit UN endorsement of what the government had done on the battlefield. That was certainly not what we had had in our minds. But it was not easy to get this message across to those who did not wish to hear it.

Post-war recovery

The end of the war was far from the end of our problems. Indeed, in many ways arguments with the government intensified. Many outside and inside the country still believed that Menik Farm was intended to be an internment camp – some even called it a concentration camp – and that it might be years before the Tamils got out. Allegations of government plans to fill the north with Sinhalese were still being made by some outside journalists and the Tamil diaspora. I was personally convinced by my own intense discussions with the government that, whatever they might have thought when they started building the camp, they now realized that they would not be able to keep the IDPs in there for years, politically or otherwise. External pressure had been an important part of getting them to that conclusion. But they now needed to show their intentions through actions as well as words.

Moreover, the fate of the former LTTE cadres was still far from resolved. Four hundred or so were expected to be tried. But another 11,000 'surrendees' were in so-called rehabilitation centres, which were prison camps by another name, at least initially. No rehabilitation was happening, and it was not clear when the surrendees might be released – the government talked vaguely of a year or sometimes two. Meanwhile, the legality of their detention was dubious, even under Sri Lankan law. Accusations by the Tamil diaspora that the surrendees were being tortured or even quietly got rid of did not appear to be true on a large scale – after a while relatives knew where they were and could communicate with them – but there was no independent access to them and no way of verifying such stories. The obvious candidates for this verification task, the ICRC, had not been allowed to resume work in the north. The government wanted international donors to help organize and pay for the rehabilitation of these LTTE detainees, but the donors were rightly unwilling to do so in such circumstances.

The donors were in any case increasingly unhappy that their resources were being used to support a humanitarian operation in which those to be helped were being dealt with by the government in ways that were not in accordance with internationally agreed norms for the treatment of IDPs. Some Western donors threatened to withdraw their funding. The government bridled at any suggestion that Western aid would have conditions attached and said they would throw out the international agencies before they accepted any such conditions (even though they needed the help since they had spent all their own money on the war). I strongly agreed about the desperate requirement to see conditions improve, but thought we needed to stay in there if we could. Withdrawal might make our consciences easier because we would not be complicit with government behaviour, but it would do nothing for the Tamils. They needed not only our practical help, but also the constant pressure we put on the government to improve conditions and respect the promises about return which had been made.

I also thought that the government could be moved in the right direction, at least on the humanitarian issues, if not on the broader issue of how to deal with the Tamil problem politically in the long term. They were certainly frustrating to deal with, and obstructive at every stage. During the war they had countenanced many unacceptable practices by those working for them and those sympathetic to them, and no doubt still did. They remained paranoid about further attacks from some LTTE remnant somewhere. Nevertheless, there were decent officials and ministers, and a still persistent democratic tradition, despite everything. And even the hardliners did not want in the end to be complete international pariahs.

Slowly and painfully, therefore, there was movement. Those in the camp were gradually given new ID cards and allowed to leave – at first for a few days only, and later for good. In September the government promised that 80 per cent of the IDPs would be back home by the end of the year. A package of aid for those returning was put together – not enough, certainly, and conditions in the areas of return were extremely difficult. But at least the process of returns was starting to accelerate. Indeed, as summer turned to autumn, the complaints gradually began to be about the authorities pushing people back too soon, when operations to remove the tens of thousands of mines laid by the LTTE had not been satisfactorily completed. The irony of this was not lost on the government. I always made a point of emphasizing our welcome for the commitment we had long sought: for the early return of the IDPs to their homes.

But the concerns about the process were also genuine: thousands of IDPs would be herded on to buses early one morning, with virtually no advance warning, either to them or the aid agencies, taken back to near their homes and left there with little support or help. We pressed for a better system, with greater preparation and consultation. The worry about the de-mining was also real. When a zone was declared open for returns, that did not mean all mines had been removed, but simply that the roads and some of the open areas had been cleared. The rest was taped off rather amateurishly, and left for later. Some areas were riddled with mines, planted over many years, with no maps. The risks for the returning civilians, particularly for children, were only too obvious.

To spell out what we needed as a humanitarian community, we drew up detailed criteria about increased openness of camps and transit areas, as well as about de-mining and returns; these would have to be met if our aid was going to continue beyond the end of 2009. We set the bar high, but at a level which the government could meet if their intentions were as they said they were. The government disliked the process intensely. There were more expulsion threats and mutterings about unacceptable conditionality. But in the end they did just about enough in meeting our demands and making the necessary moves and improvements to prevent any break in the aid pipeline.

Nevertheless, there was still enough controversy within the humanitarian community and between the international aid community and the government for me to make a fourth 2009 visit in November. This was also part of a deliberate UN strategy of a series of high-level visits to ensure that the government knew we were watching every move. Lynn Pascoe, the political USG, had visited in September, and the SG's adviser on the human rights of IDPs, an excellent Swiss expert called Walter Kaelin, in October. Attempts to persuade the government to allow in the UN high commissioner for human rights, Louise Arbour, were, however, unsuccessful. This was disappointing, but not surprising. A senior official openly boasted to me at one point during the war that the best decision they had ever taken was to refuse to allow the opening of a Colombo office by the high commissioner.

During my visit, I was assured by everyone from the president downwards that full freedom of movement for the IDPs would be restored as from 1 December – as it more or less was in the end, though there was still argument over the meaning of 'full'. The camp population had already been reduced by well over half to 140,000. It was agreed to step up de-mining efforts still further. Measures such as the reopening of the main north–south A9 road, closed for years because of the war, were beginning to be taken. This was a key demand of the northern Tamils, to allow them to move freely around the country. The extent of high-security zones in the north, which had left a lot of houses and farmland abandoned, was being looked at. Normalization after the war was beginning, however timidly, for the first time.

However, on the increasingly controversial issue of accountability the government said only that they were thinking about it. The same was true of political change. I went through – yet again – the arguments about the dangers of the government missing the great chance they had to transform the country and reach out to the Tamils. Their answer was that the president had decided to present himself for re-election in the spring, followed by parliamentary elections. Until then, serious action was postponed. I was sure this was a fundamental mistake.

As I write, in mid-2012, the most controversial humanitarian issues have been largely resolved. The camps are virtually empty. The only IDPs left are from one particularly contaminated area yet to be de-mined. Nearly all the 'surrendees' have been released and are being reintegrated into society. A semblance of normality is returning to the north, as people gradually rebuild their homes and their lives. The worst fears about government policy and Sinhalese colonization have not been realized, though there are still issues about the size of the military presence and high-security zones.

Yet sadly, and predictably, there has not been much progress on political reconciliation. President Rajapaksa was comfortably re-elected in April 2010, though only after an extraordinary episode involving a rival candidacy from his former armed forces head, General Fonseka, who had resigned in a huff in early 2010 because he thought that his role in the successful military campaign had been inadequately recognized by the government. During the campaign the general decided to speak out publicly, if vaguely, about orders to take no LTTE prisoners at the end of the war. After the campaign he was arrested and charged with treasonable activity. None of this reflected at all well on Sri Lankan democracy. Meanwhile, government pressure continues and has even intensified on the press and human rights defenders to refrain from criticizing official policies or talking about the more unsavoury episodes of the conflict.

The LTTE has disappeared from Sri Lanka, but separatist sentiment continues, at least among the diaspora. If the government does not change the political dynamics between the two communities, the chances of a successor to the LTTE emerging remain significant in the long run. KP, with whom I had tried to negotiate, took over the LTTE leadership briefly after the end of the war, and declared he was turning it into a peaceful political movement, and a government in exile. But he was then himself arrested in Malaysia and returned to Sri Lanka. In another bizarre twist, he has since been released and has called for Tamil cooperation with the government.

Reflections

What conclusions can be drawn from this tragic and still incomplete story?

The biggest single issue for me was the balance to be struck between speaking out to denounce abuses, whether by the host government or the LTTE, and the need to work with both to address genuine humanitarian needs. Should we have pulled out altogether at some stage in the face of unacceptable conditions imposed on our work? Was there more we could have done through tougher advocacy to influence both sides and save civilian lives? Reflecting on it now, I am not sure we could have achieved more in the absence of real determination by the international community to change the course of events.

Despite the intimidation and pressure, we did not just keep quiet and get on with practical humanitarian aid. Our constant private and public criticism, and pressure on the government over humanitarian conditions, bore fruit over time, however frustratingly slowly. Importantly, in my view, we were tougher in private than in public – importantly because nothing is so counterproductive as a foreign interlocutor who has a friendly conversation in private, but then goes out to a press conference and blasts the government he has been talking to, claiming to have been very tough all the time. More confrontation might have earned plaudits from the media, Western governments, and even some humanitarians. But it would have set up a counter-reaction and helped no one very much in practice.

The underlying question is where the humanitarian community should draw its red lines in dealings with governments and non-state actors. If we always allow the humanitarian imperative and practical considerations about keeping aid flowing to overcome worries about observance of our principles, are we not doing a wider disservice to humanitarianism? If we give the impression that we will accept almost any humiliation in order to stay and help, will not governments and rebel movements elsewhere notice and behave accordingly? I recognize the risk and agree with the argument in general. I do not think personally this red line was ever quite crossed in the case of Sri Lanka. But this is a matter of judgment.

Why were the Sri Lankan government able to ignore the weight of international opinion, and maintain their ruthless military campaign despite the casualties and the criticism? I have already suggested two important parts of the answer: virtually no one had any sympathy left for the LTTE; and Sri Lanka had important backers in Russia, China, and India, who did not believe in intervention, wanted to preserve their own free internal hand to deal with terrorists, and had business interests in the country too. The Sri Lankan government also had a lot of developing-country sympathy. This, with the changing balance of power in the world, meant that the West (and the UN) could be ignored with relative impunity, including from an economic point of view.

This was graphically illustrated immediately after the end of the war, when not only was a Western-backed resolution in the UN Human Rights Council calling for an enquiry into the events of the last stages of the war thrown out by a big majority, but a resolution was passed which praised Sri Lanka's conduct. This really was too much. But the Sri Lankan government used to great effect the argument that not only had they just been defeating domestic terrorism, as any self-respecting government was bound to do, but that they were also, as a small developing country, the victims of classic Western double standards. Where, they asked, was the equivalent resolution about American crimes against civilians in Iraq or Afghanistan?

Of great concern at the time and since has been the fear that the Sri Lankans were setting an extremely dangerous precedent in showing how ruthlessly opposition could be crushed in the absence of the usual witnesses provided by international journalists and humanitarians. It remains to be seen how far others will follow this example. There may not in practice be too many occasions when it will be as easy to keep out foreigners as it was in north-east Sri Lanka, due to a mixture of geographical isolation, real danger from intense fighting, and the lack of any significant international sympathy for the opposition group. Moreover, we have since seen in Libya and Syria how mobile phones with cameras can now be used to reveal to the world what is happening, however much the regime in place tries to conceal it. We are now in a completely different news age. Nevertheless, it is important that the international community maintain the pressure against invisibility and impunity for governments acting in similar fashion. We will come back to this issue in the case of Gaza, where Israel's Operation Cast Lead just preceded the last stages of the LTTE war.

Hence the importance of accountability, the issue which continues to have most resonance for the future, not only of Sri Lanka, but also of wider respect for international law. The International Criminal Court has no competence here, because Sri Lanka has not ratified its statute. The ICC issue will only arise in practice in this context if the Security Council refers the Sri Lankan case to it, which looks highly unlikely given the balance of views there. Human rights groups and others such as the UN have nevertheless kept up the pressure for an independent investigation. Several weighty accounts have already appeared: the US Congress produced a report in late 2009, setting out the evidence, without attempting to draw any conclusions. The International Crisis Group produced a powerful and detailed report in late 2010.

President Rajapaksa did eventually create a domestic Lessons Learnt and Reconciliation Commission, which included some respectable local figures with a reputation for independence. This heard powerful evidence from a number of Tamil witnesses. It concluded that there had been abuses on an individual level, and that there had, for example, been shellings of hospitals. But it took the view that the government had not targeted civilians deliberately and pulled most of its punches otherwise. In any case, no one outside Sri Lanka believes this has been or could be a full and properly independent exercise. Frankly, the government is not going to countenance any process which could lead to some of its own members being prosecuted for war crimes.

Ban ki-Moon kept up his own pressure on the Sri Lankan government to respect the agreement on addressing grievances they had signed up to immediately after the end of the war. But in the predictable absence of real progress inside the country, he finally decided in June 2010 to appoint an international Panel of Experts to look into possible domestic and international accountability mechanisms in Sri Lanka. The government tried every diplomatic trick in the book to prevent the creation of this panel. The secretary-general had what he told me was the most unpleasant conversation he had ever had with any world leader when he telephoned President Rajapaksa to inform him of his intentions.

The panel was nevertheless established. Led by a distinguished Indonesian lawyer, Marzuki Darusman, it consulted widely, though it was unable to visit Sri Lanka. It finally reported in April 2011 that it had found credible reports of possible war crimes by both sides, including government killings of civilians by shelling and denial of humanitarian assistance, and LTTE use of civilians as human shields and killings of civilians trying to flee. It recommended that the Sri Lankan government mount a proper investigation of these allegations, but that otherwise a full and independent international investigation be held. The government violently denounced the panel's conclusions. And nothing has yet come of its calls for a further independent enquiry, although the UN Human Rights Council did finally pass a resolution to this effect in March 2012 (with China and Russia voting against). Meanwhile, there have been continuing media investigations with deeply worrying allegations and (contested) video footage of apparent atrocities, particularly from the UK's Channel Four.

The awkward reality here is that any full and meaningful enquiry requires official Sri Lankan cooperation. This is not going to happen until the present Sri Lankan government have left office and greater democratic transparency becomes possible. A future government, particularly one from the opposition, may well want to see the truth established as part of a fuller reconciliation exercise between the two communities. Whether they will contemplate any domestic or international prosecutions for a military victory which was popular with most of the voters may be a different story.

It is crucial meanwhile to ensure that the testimony of those prepared to give it is not lost, and that events are recorded and documents preserved as far as they can be. We must also be careful not to focus exclusively on what the government did, simply because the LTTE leaders are no longer there to answer for their actions. Many LTTE actions need proper international investigation. Both sides must be under equal scrutiny. But above all, the international community must not lose interest, because of the important principles at stake and the need for a lasting accommodation between Tamils and Sinhalese. Sri Lanka has returned to being a pleasant tourist destination, with charming and welcoming people, and is enjoying some economic success. This is good news for everyone. But the nasty realities must not be swept under the carpet.

Map Sources: ESRI, Europa Technologies, UNCS. Map created in Dec 2012.

CHAPTER FIVE

The Democratic Republic of Congo: not losing hope

Of all the crisis zones I visited, the DRC was the one which I was almost guaranteed to leave more depressed than when I arrived. This is not because it is naturally poverty-stricken, or short of able people. On the contrary – it has natural resources aplenty, water and fertile land almost everywhere. But its people have been plagued by incompetent and corrupt governments, fattening themselves on the country's natural riches, while doing nothing for the population; and they have been further deprived of what is rightfully theirs by foreign companies and governments exploiting the situation for what they can. The lack of basic infrastructure in most of the country – which is the size of Europe but has a population five times smaller at around 80 million – is staggering.

DRC is a test of the staying power of humanitarian agencies. The needs are immense, and we can only hope to tackle the most urgent and accessible. Working with a weak government creates a different set of problems from those we saw in Darfur and Sri Lanka. In addition, the problems of a large international humanitarian community coexisting with an overstretched UN peacekeeping force are there in even more acute form than in Darfur, exacerbated by the fact that the state's own armed forces are at least as much a part of the problem as of the solution. Sexual violence by armed groups is the scourge of the east, as we will see. Meanwhile, the appalling destruction caused by those elements of the Ugandan Lord's Resistance Army who finished up in the north-east of the country raises serious questions about the international community's will to tackle such atrocities, and, again, about the role of the International Criminal Court, as we will see.

DRC is an extraordinary place to visit. While conditions in Kinshasa are in many ways better than elsewhere in the country, much of the city – especially in the rainy season – still resembles a scene from the scary futuristic movie *Blade Runner*. The roads are dreadful, even the town-centre boulevards. People swarm in every direction. It is not a place to lighten the spirits, despite its vibrancy. But many areas of the country are stunningly beautiful. On my last visit in 2010, I was summoned to meet President Kabila at his farm 30 miles outside Kinshasa. The countryside looked more like rural France than central Africa. It was hard to believe you were in the same country.

In the east, the lakes are tranquil and magnificent, even if the water is full of bilharzia, not to be drunk or swum in by unwary foreigners. One of the run-down lake hotels we used had once been one of King Leopold's hunting lodges. The hills and forests are equally striking. I particularly remember one helicopter journey to the eastern town of Walikale, looking at the wonderful rolling country we were flying over, dotted with peaceful-seeming villages of huts with elaborately woven roofs of straw. The tourist potential if the country ever gets its act together is huge.

Unavoidable history

The last 120 years of Congolese history are a sad tale, starting from the brutalities of the country's origins in the Congo Free State, the private property of King Leopold, then fifty-plus undistinguished years as an official Belgian colony. Independence in 1960 promised a fresh start. But hopes of progress and development quickly disappeared in a maelstrom of political and personal struggles, heavily influenced by US and Belgian fears of supposed communist influence, and secessionist movements, notably from the copper-rich state of Katanga. A 1965 army coup led by the US-backed Colonel Mobutu brought apparent stability, but only at the heavy price of government incompetence, repression, corruption, and an oppressive cult of personality. In the 1970s and 1980s, as the Mobutu kleptocracy creamed off mineral profits from what they had by now rechristened Zaire, any infrastructure left by the colonial administration rotted away.

The 1990s and the end of the Cold War saw Western support for Mobutu finally evaporate. Instability in the east also spiralled upwards as the consequences of the 1994 genocide and civil war between the Hutus and Tutsis in neighbouring Rwanda spilled over into the DRC. The defeated genocidal Hutu militia, known as the Interahamwe, fled into Congo, vowing to continue their struggle from there. Hundreds of thousands of refugees also crossed the border, leading to an acute humanitarian crisis. Cynically, the Congolese armed forces began to work with the Interahamwe against local Tutsis who were disillusioned with the central government. In 1996, the Rwandan and Ugandan armies, both concerned about instability on their borders, invaded to stop this and enabled a coalition of rebels led by Laurent-Desire Kabila to march on Kinshasa. Mobutu finally fled in May 1997, and Kabila took over, rechristening the country the DRC. But when Kabila asked his foreign backers to leave, they were unwilling to do so, and attacked his army. The latter were supported, in turn, for a variety of personal and political reasons, by forces from Angola, Zimbabwe and Namibia, in a kind of African version of World War One.

Kabila was assassinated by unknown hands in 2001, and was succeeded by his son, Joseph. This change of personality at the top assisted in the conclusion of a peace deal involving a power-sharing government and the withdrawal of all foreign forces, with the help of a new UN peacekeeping mission, MONUC (Mission de l'Organisation des Nations Unies en République Démocratique du Congo). Multi-party elections in 2006, supervised by MONUC, were controversial, but Kabila was eventually declared elected. This democratic election was a considerable success in the circumstances. Unfortunately, as we have discovered to our cost in Iraq and Afghanistan, even successful elections do not make a real democracy in the absence of a strong civil society and democratic culture. Kabila's victory did little to solve the underlying problems of the country.

Troubles in the east

Eastern DRC in particular remained plagued by an alphabet soup of illegal militias. One of the biggest threats was the self-styled General Nkunda, leading the largely Tutsi CNDP (Congrès National pour la Défense du Peuple), with close links to the Rwandan Army. His claim to be defending the local population against the Interahamwe gave him a degree of popularity. However, his CNDP forces were themselves responsible for many abuses, not least in 2004 when they captured briefly the capital of South Kivu, Bukavu. Nkunda finally overreached himself in late 2008, when his forces threatened Goma, the capital of North Kivu. His Rwandan allies, who had by then repaired relations with the DRC government, made him back off, to relief all round, and put him under effective house arrest in Rwanda not long afterwards.

The disappearance of Nkunda allowed the UN and the government's army, the FARDC (Forces Armées du République

Démocratique du Congo), aided for a time by the Rwandan Army, to focus their efforts on the Interahamwe, now known as the FDLR (Forces Démocratiques pour la Libération du Rwanda), who had proved themselves the most brutal and licentious of all the militias. Some progress was made in 2009 and 2010, but not enough to get rid of them, and the effort has since more or less fizzled out. The FDLR continue to prey on the local villagers in their areas of control, particularly the women, with an appalling brand of sexual slavery and violence. Meanwhile, other local militias such as the Mayi-Mayi, supposedly a village self-defence organization, have also continued to spread violence and terrorize local civilians. The result is a lawless and largely ungoverned region.

The tragic importance of minerals

If this brief history is vital to understanding DRC's travails today, the same is true of its geography. Virtually landlocked at the heart of Africa, it has nine neighbours: the Central African Republic and South Sudan to the north; Uganda, Rwanda, Burundi, and Tanzania to the east; Zambia and Angola to the south; and the Republic of Congo (often known as Congo-Brazzaville) to the west. Many of them cast covetous eyes on its mineral wealth, much of it in the east: gold, copper, silver, manganese, bauxite, diamonds, and above all coltan, vital for the construction of mobile phones, and cassiterite, a tin ore also used in modern circuitry.

Grasping Congo's problems is impossible without appreciating how far those involved are driven by the desire to get their hands on these resources. All militias and political forces have their own mines, and all have ways of smuggling the products out of the country. Very little of the revenue goes to the government, which does not control or own the mines, and even less is used for the benefit of the population. Alliances between different armed factions, including the DRC's own forces, constantly shift under the pressure of political events and military fortunes. But the mineral extraction business always goes on.

The result is a chronically weak government, with few resources. Its writ only just runs in the capital, and hardly at all elsewhere in the country. Local government has little or no financial muscle or authority, and is widely ignored. The official armed forces are badly equipped, badly trained, badly paid, badly housed, badly disciplined and, as an inevitable result, bad in all senses of the word. They often prey on the population as much as any of the illegal militias. Meanwhile, the police scarcely exist as a disciplined force either, particularly in the east. The judicial system is more or less non-functional there too, with virtually no courts, no secure prisons, and no money to feed prisoners even if there were any who could not bribe their way out.

Humanitarian needs and problems

Combine all this with severe underdevelopment, the prevalence of debilitating and fatal diseases, and recurring natural calamities, and it is scarcely surprising that there are desperate – and unmet – humanitarian needs virtually all over the country. There have been relief operations of different kinds for many years. But it is the long-running crisis in the east which has turned humanitarian efforts in Congo into the second-biggest operation in the world, after Darfur, costing not far short of $1 billion per year. A 2007 mortality survey by a US-based humanitarian NGO, the International Rescue Committee, estimated that 5.4 million deaths had been caused by conflict and deprivation in DRC since 1998, mainly in the east. The vast majority of these were not due to violent killings, but were early deaths brought on by neglect, malnutrition, stress, displacement, and disease. The figure of 5.4 million is a staggering one: the exact methodology by which it was estimated can no doubt be questioned, but it has not been seriously disputed by those who know the region well.

Millions have also been forced to leave their homes by various bouts of fighting. There are still almost 2 million displaced in the east at the time of writing. While most displacements are relatively brief, their frequency has had a disastrous cumulative effect. People have lost any possessions or resilience they might have had, leaving them ever more vulnerable and traumatized. Those I saw on my visits to camps or villages in the worst-affected areas were more deprived and hopeless than any I came across elsewhere in the world – filthy and malnourished, with nothing to their names except the rags they wore. Their stories of the constant disruption of their lives and unending abuses by armed groups about whom they knew little or nothing were truly heartbreaking, with no end to their troubles in sight.

While the humanitarian problems could rise and fall in intensity, in parallel with the recurrent security crises, the main agencies and actors, UN and non-UN, were still almost constantly at full stretch, geographically, financially, and psychologically. They needed regular support, and intervention with the government and the political/peacekeeping side of the UN, to allow them to operate successfully. Discussions in New York were often fraught. But support on the spot was also crucial. During visits in 2007, 2009, and 2010, I spent most time in the east, and in the area of LRA activities further north. However, I also talked at length to the government in Kinshasa, including meetings on each occasion with President Kabila.

The issues were multiple: ensuring coordination of the international humanitarian effort over a vast area; trying to guarantee the safety of staff in a dangerous and volatile environment where just flying round the country was extremely risky (two staff members of OCHA were tragically killed in an air accident in appalling weather in 2009); raising enough funds from an international donor community never quite sure it was really interested in Congo; liaising and mediating between the humanitarian and politico-military international efforts in Congo, especially with the MONUC leadership and local contingents; urging the government to control the dreadful Congolese armed forces, responsible for far too many of the atrocities; and pressing for much greater action, political and military, by the government and the international community to protect the local population, particularly from the appalling scourge of sexual violence.

There were no easy solutions in DRC. But the commitment of the humanitarians at all levels was truly inspiring. Many I met were burned out by the stress under which they worked, but carried on because the needs were simply so great. DRC was also, astonishingly in some ways, the site of much innovative work in implementing the humanitarian reforms which had been agreed in 2006, particularly the idea of local pooled humanitarian funds, the allocation of which was decided on the spot, rather than in donor capitals.

The humanitarian community faced overwhelming challenges just trying to do its basic job. The transport infrastructure was awful at the best of times, and more or less impossible at the height of the rains. Even communities near the so-called main roads could be reached only intermittently. Remote villages were often inaccessible for long periods. The armed groups were usually uncooperative and at times hostile. Even where they had nothing against the humanitarians as such, they usually had an interest in stealing what they could, from vehicles to supplies. The same applied to the official armed forces. The population themselves were mostly welcoming to humanitarians – I always found them friendly, despite their desperation – but powerless to influence attitudes around them.

International failures and MONUC

The problems of the humanitarian community could not be seen in isolation from the constantly debated issue of the role of the wider international community. Was it doing enough, and was it doing the right things? While the UN was at the heart of these questions, it was also legitimate to wonder whether the governments of the world with the clout to change the course of events in Congo were really committed to doing so. The situation was an international running sore, and was often on the Security Council agenda. I briefed the Council frequently. Ban ki-Moon's chief advisers spent endless hours debating the right way forward. But it was not clear that those in charge in Washington, Moscow, Beijing, Paris or London were prepared to put in the tough diplomatic miles to turn the situation around. World leaders rarely, if ever, visited the DRC, and even phone calls to the key actors were few and far between.

DRC was, in fact, something of a diplomatic orphan. The French took a natural interest in a francophone country and were prepared to champion them up to a point. But they were not the former colonial power, and felt less of a responsibility than they did towards, for example, Côte d'Ivoire. Belgium continued to take a close interest, but did not have the influence, or the local credibility, to make much of a difference. The UK was for much of the time too obsessed with its close relationship with Rwanda to play a role in Kinshasa, at least while relations between the two neighbours were at their nadir. The Americans were interested, but only up to a point.

It may seem offensive to some in Africa to say that having an influential former colonial power engaged can help. But the reality is that having a powerful friend at court in the counsels of the international community, and a country ready to intervene and take risks at the right moment, can make a big difference. Perhaps the most obvious recent example was the British intervention in Sierra Leone in 2000, which stopped the rebellion in its tracks, and led to a gradual turnaround of the situation. Former colonial powers can certainly also make things worse if they get it wrong, by inflaming local feelings. But where a country is incapable of resolving its problems by itself, a motivated outside mentor can be a positive force.

However, the biggest controversy in DRC has been about the UN and particularly the peacekeeping force MONUC. Was it doing enough to stop conflict, restore stability, and protect civilians? MONUC was first established in 2000, to protect the military monitors of the ceasefire which ended the so-called African world war. It progressively increased its presence in the DRC, particularly in the east, to help tackle the security problems there. But its 2003 strength of 10,000 troops was still manifestly inadequate for the task: an EU-led force had to come in to re-establish order in the eastern province of Ituri. And when the rebel forces of General Nkunda took Bukavu from the government in 2004, MONUC was again able to do little to stop them. This led to major demonstrations in the rest of the country, particularly Kinshasa, which threatened the whole UN presence.

MONUC nonetheless survived and its numbers were gradually increased to 16,000. Its role in protecting the elections in 2006 was particularly vital. But numbers had to be further increased by the Security Council to 22,000 in 2007, as violence worsened again. In 2008, when General Nkunda attacked the capital of North Kivu, Goma, the biggest city in eastern DRC, MONUC was ordered to be robust in its military response, with fears of renewed demonstrations and attacks in Kinshasa if Goma fell. This was a welcome sign of firmness for all concerned, including the humanitarian community in the area. But in the end it was not MONUC which saved the city, but Nkunda's backers in Rwanda telling him to stop his advance.

The Security Council subsequently authorized a yet further increase in MONUC's numbers in 2009, up to 26,000. But sadly, an old challenge had come back to haunt the country by then – fresh attacks by the Lord's Resistance Army, led by Joseph Kony. Expelled from northern Uganda in 2005, after spreading chaos there for many years, they had taken refuge in the forests of north-east DRC, with occasional forays into southern Sudan and the Central African Republic too. A previous attempt to get rid of the LRA in 2006 had ended disastrously when MONUC special forces, lacking sophisticated communications equipment and detailed knowledge of the bush, had apparently attacked each other while Kony and his men slipped away from the trap. I will come back to the LRA. But meanwhile, the inability of MONUC to deal decisively with Kony or protect civilians from him was added to the already heavy charge sheet against them.

How fair is it to blame MONUC for failing to stop the continuing instability, help the government establish its authority, and end the chronic vulnerability of the civilian population?

The basic problem of MONUC is that it has an impossible mandate from the Security Council. Like UNAMID in Darfur, they are a classic case of peacekeepers with no real peace to keep, sent there because the international community could not think what else to do with an intractable conflict in an area where none of the major powers really wanted to get its own hands dirty. They are supposed to support the government, but the government writ does not run in most of the country. They are asked to work with the official armed forces, but these are out of control themselves.

MONUC's basic mission has increasingly, and rightly, been defined as protecting civilians. They have worked hard to implement this. But protecting all civilians against all threats is clearly well beyond them, even just in the east of the country. While they are the biggest single UN peacekeeping force in the world, made up of several national contingents, mainly from South Asia, they are still very small indeed compared to the size of the country. After the conflict with Serbia in 1999, 50,000 well-armed and well-equipped, mainly NATO troops policed Kosovo, a relatively modern territory of some 4200 square miles, about the size of Wales or Connecticut, and struggled at times. Twenty-six thousand UN soldiers have been trying to police Congo, a territory of 905,000 square miles, with no infrastructure to speak of. Even the east is many times the size of Kosovo. MONUC can never be behind every bush and in every village to prevent attacks. The reality can never live up to the expectations which the mandate creates.

However, there are also more fundamental factors in the set-up and operating methods of UN peacekeeping forces which make them incapable of carrying out the complex multiple tasks they are now given:

- They are made up largely of national military contingents with little or no experience of, and relatively rudimentary training in, the tasks of a UN force, which are very different from those of a classic national army. In particular, their knowledge of what protection of civilians should mean is wholly inadequate.
- The contingents rarely speak the language of the country where they are operating. Interpreters can help, but are

never sufficient in numbers or availability to make up the difference. In the case of Congo, most contingents were English-speakers from the subcontinent, while the international language around them was French. Their chances of understanding the dreadfully complicated political and military scene around them were always limited.

- The contingents, and their commanders, rotate too frequently: usually every six months. This means that they tend to disappear just as they are acquiring the experience and knowledge of the local conditions to do a better job (this is not, of course, exclusive to UN forces).

- The contingents are only partly under the control of the UN commander, since they are also answerable in reality to the national governments to whom they belong. These governments usually have views of their own about policy in the area of operations, and certainly have no interest in seeing robust action which would result in body bags turning up at the local airport.

- Many of the tasks really require police contingents or civilians, rather than soldiers. These are much harder to find and to persuade to participate in a UN force operating in remote and dangerous environments.

- The intelligence capability of the force is usually poor.

Against this background, it is worth taking a closer look at the official mandate to see just how much a force like MONUC is actually supposed to be doing, namely:

- protecting civilians (a broad and complex task which goes well beyond just physical protection)
- protecting all UN personnel and installations themselves

- fighting sexual violence and human rights abuses
- promoting law and order and reform of the security and judicial sectors
- stopping the use of child soldiers
- helping refugees return
- supporting the Congolese armed forces in operations to defeat rebels
- trying to bring fighting to an end overall
- supporting disarmament, demobilization, and rehabilitation of former rebel soldiers
- trying to stop LRA atrocities
- supporting elections
- preventing illicit trade in minerals
- de-mining
- facilitating humanitarian aid
- encouraging and facilitating stabilization and economic development.

These are all reasonable and necessary objectives in themselves, but achieving them all would need an army of miracle workers. How far are they realistically attainable by an inadequately trained force which often struggles simply to maintain and protect itself, and has nothing like the number of professional civilian staff needed?

Peacekeepers and humanitarians

Relations between MONUC and the humanitarian community were often difficult. Like many in the Western media, the humanitarians were highly critical of the peacekeepers, particularly over protection of civilians. They pointed to the fact that massacres and other atrocities often took place close to

MONUC bases without any apparent attempt to stop them. They repeatedly called attention to MONUC's close cooperation with the official armed forces, and accused them of turning a blind eye to their abuses for political reasons. They seized on the apparent involvement of some MONUC troops in sexual abuse of local women, or illegal trafficking, to cast doubt on the integrity of the force as a whole. Some called for MONUC's withdrawal, believing that they had become part of the problem, not the solution.

I shared such concerns, and voiced them frequently to the UN peacekeeping authorities in New York and Kinshasa. From a humanitarian point of view, MONUC's performance did indeed leave a huge amount to be desired. It was important, for example, to make sure that MONUC did not become complicit in criminal activity by the Congolese armed forces, and that they knew how to deal sensitively with situations where the civilian population gathered round their bases for safety, as frequently happened.

But I was also conscious of the underlying structural weaknesses within the peacekeepers, and the difficulty of addressing them in the short term. The individual contingents I met were clearly sincere in their desire to do a decent job. I also had to keep in mind the bigger picture. We had to work with MONUC. Its bosses were aware of the problems and doing their best to improve the force's performance. I certainly did not believe it was sensible to fuel demands for MONUC to leave, and often warned NGO colleagues to be careful what they wished for. Whatever MONUC's shortcomings, the situation would have been much worse without them. They offered some protection in some places, their presence was a deterrent, and they were at least a check on the worst aspects of the behaviour of the Congolese armed forces.

MONUC also pioneered some effective new techniques for protection of civilians, including small forward-operating bases in known trouble spots and joint civilian/military protection units. The forward-operating bases were very good at stopping trouble in local hot spots, and acted as a genuine deterrent as long as they were there. The problem was that they could not stay remotely deployed for too long without major logistical problems. There were also always far more demands on them than they could cope with. The Joint Protection Teams could offer a more sophisticated analysis of the threats and provide a more subtle response than the military units alone. These innovations were picked up and replicated elsewhere.

The acid test of all this came when the Congolese government themselves started to ask for MONUC's departure in early 2010, in the run-up to the celebrations of the fiftieth anniversary of independence. The request was partly out of national pride, but mostly because the generals found the force's presence unduly constraining on their money-making activities through their ability to observe exactly what was going on in terms of illegal mining and corruption.

It was clear to all in the international community at that point that the situation in the east had in no way reached a stage where MONUC could leave. There was an almost universal outcry in the international community, including from the fiercest critics among the NGOs, that MONUC had to stay longer. I and other senior UN officials intervened at the highest level we could with the government to make this argument. My discussions with President Kabila on my last visit in 2010 were all about this.

Luckily, the president – an intelligent man if no great leader – did seem to understand the reality of the situation. He therefore managed it in the end in such a way that national honour was satisfied but MONUC stayed: the force was renamed

MONUSCO, the 'S' added to its title standing for 'stabilization' to show that it was now working towards the end of its mandate. There was also agreement on a largely token withdrawal of some 3000 troops.

This was a sensible outcome, but the 2010 demands highlighted a fundamental dilemma. MONUSCO cannot stay for ever. They will never be able by themselves to fix the problems of a country with such deep-seated difficulties as Congo. And their very presence may well also contribute to a kind of involuntary dependency which militates against the development of the kind of genuinely home-grown solutions which alone are capable of resolving DRC's political and security problems, however great the need for outside assistance at the same time. They are also expensive at $1.5 billion per year. Critics argue that this money would be much better spent on development. However, this point ignores two realities: if the force left, the money would be saved by the contributing governments, rather than redeployed to development aid; and development without security is an illusion. But cash is nevertheless a factor in the minds of those who have to pay the bill – the UK and France, for example.

In any case, the question of when MONUSCO should withdraw will have to be faced again before long. The classic answer has been that it should leave when certain benchmarks are met, not in response to some arbitrary timetable. This is no doubt true and the ideal. But if the benchmarks are set where the main players in the international community would like them to be set – in other words, representing the return of lasting stability – the chances of them being met satisfactorily in any reasonable timescale are very low. Meanwhile, how long will troop contributors be willing to stay, how long will those who pay for peacekeeping be ready to go on stumping up, and how can dependency on the peacekeepers be minimized?

Working alongside a peacekeeping force like MONUC/ MONUSCO also poses another set of questions for humanitarian organizations. How close should the relationship be, given the humanitarian need to maintain their independence, impartiality, and neutrality? I will explore this broad question in greater detail elsewhere in the book, in relation, for example, to Somalia and Afghanistan, but suffice it to say for now that the degree of integration of the humanitarian coordinator into the peacekeeping operation was a major bone of contention for many NGOs. The doubts were not about the individual (Ross Mountain, a tough and effective New Zealander with a lifetime of humanitarian experience behind him), but about his simultaneous position as deputy special representative of the secretary-general, i.e. he was the deputy to the head of MONUC/MONUSCO. Did not such a position mean that he was inevitably too close to the political and security aims and operations of the force, thereby risking compromise of the independence of the whole humanitarian operation?

These were legitimate questions in principle. However, in my experience, the system worked reasonably well in practice, since OCHA itself remained physically and administratively separate from MONUC. This one foot in, one foot out compromise was the default option for humanitarian coordination and leadership in conflict contexts. It ensured coherence, while preserving sufficient freedom of action and independence. But it was still a problem in the minds of many humanitarians in DRC.

'The rape capital of the world'

The greatest single human rights and humanitarian preoccupation in the DRC, once again most pressingly in the east, is sexual violence. It is more or less routine for militias attacking a village to rape women they encounter, often in the most casual and brutal way imaginable, and to kidnap others to serve as sex slaves for as long as it suits them, or until the women either die or somehow manage to escape. While the figures for reported rapes are bad enough – tens of thousands every year – in practice there are no reliable statistics: the incentives to report to the authorities are limited at best. In the absence of a functioning law-and-order and judicial system, the chances of those responsible being caught or otherwise held accountable are minimal.

Moreover, rape carries with it a dreadful social stigma, as if the woman could somehow be held responsible for what has been done to her. Husbands regularly reject their wives if they have been sexually attacked, and village life often becomes intolerable for the victims. Unable to continue their normal lives and with little or no means of support, too many have drifted away to terrible fates or have taken their own lives. It is hardly surprising that many women stay silent about what has happened to them if they can.

All this would be bad enough, but it is not all. Frequently, rape is accompanied by the most dreadful violence, for example, the use of gun barrels, bayonets, sticks, and other objects to destroy women's internal organs. Tens of thousands of women have been disfigured and maimed for life. Many have been left with a condition called fistula, where the separation between reproductive organs and the urethra and anus has been torn or destroyed. Chronic incontinence is one of the results, as is high vulnerability to infections. Women with this condition, which also occurs naturally in some cases, are often shunned by their fellow villagers in the most soul-destroying way.

The worst of the armed gangs behind these rapes are believed by most observers to be the FDLR (previously known as the Interahamwe). It is perhaps not surprising that those responsible for the Rwandan genocide, so steeped in horror that all conscience must have long ago been stilled, do not shrink from such bestial treatment of women. But there are young cadres as well, too young to have been part of the genocide, who are every bit as bad as their elders. How have things come to such a pass?

What happens in the east goes far beyond any notion of rape as an inevitable accompaniment of war through the ages. Extreme sexual violence has become a weapon of choice, deliberately used to terrorize and subjugate the population of the villages around which the armed groups operate, to prevent resistance and allow them to live off what the villagers are forced to provide. Men and boys too have sometimes been targeted, because the humiliation and shame associated with male rape can be an even more effective means of preventing resistance.

There is almost total impunity for those responsible. Even more chilling has been a gradual acceptance that this behaviour is the cultural norm. In a telling sequence in Lisa Jackson's excellent film, *The Greatest Silence: Rape in the Congo*, young rebels are interviewed about why they do these things. Most shrug and mumble about the lack of women in the bush. Asked how they would feel if someone raped their mother or sister, they are clear that they would shoot anyone who tried. When the interviewer points out that the women they are raping are themselves someone's sisters and mothers, the thought seems to strike them for the first time.

As time goes on, the culture of impunity and amoral acceptance of rape as normal is beginning to affect civilian behaviour too. This is one of the reasons why the international community has been so determined to tackle this horror. Let me be clear about this, since those trying to raise awareness about sexual violence in the DRC are sometimes accused of a kind of racism, by appearing to suggest that these things only happen in Africa. Rape and sexual violence have been used by others too as weapons of war, most recently, for example, in the Balkans in Europe. No group of people can point fingers at any other as uniquely capable of these crimes. But the long internal conflict in this part of Congo, the absence of the rule of law, and the influence of those fleeing from their guilt in the Rwandan genocide have combined to bring about a uniquely ghastly and widespread plague of sexual abuse. No one can or should ignore this.

Horror can also produce heroes. I was hugely privileged to meet on one of my visits Dr Denis Mukwege, founder and medical director of the Panzi Hospital just outside Bukavu. He set up the hospital in 1999 to treat the victims of sexual violence, and to repair their broken bodies wherever possible. His surgical interventions to put back together those suffering from fistula or other internal damage have given countless women a new chance to live a normal life. I met some of those women before their surgery, and could only marvel at their courage and dignity in the face of pain, humiliation and savagery. They were shy, but still determined to tell their shattering stories.

I was also able to meet some of the women who had been through this hell, been repaired, and somehow come out on the other side. Dr Mukwege recognized that many of the women needed psychological as much as physical repair, and could continue to face rejection by families and communities. He therefore set up a rehabilitation area in the hospital, where those whose immediate wounds had healed could mix with others who had been through the same ordeal, and begin to learn basic trades of sewing and basket-weaving, to enable them to survive in the outside world. A group of them sang to me in joyous fashion. This demonstration of the ability of the human spirit to triumph over barbarism was even more gut-wrenchingly moving than the medical miracles.

Yet mending the physical and mental wounds of the women, however admirable and crucial, is not enough. Nor would it be enough, however desirable, to establish meaningful police and courts to hold accountable those responsible for these abominations, however vital. This sexual violence has to be stopped, not just treated. Efforts to raise international awareness have attracted the attention of millions all over the world. Personalities like Eve Ensler, of *Vagina Monologues* fame, have spoken out in dramatic fashion, and enlisted the help of Congolese women too, including President Kabila's wife. Films and TV programmes have been made, and countless articles written. Money has been raised to treat the victims. New Congolese legislation has been passed to outlaw sexual violence, as strong as any in the world, in theory. Politicians have adopted the cause, and made moving speeches. UN agencies, NGOs and the Red Cross have poured resources and people into the struggle. A joint comprehensive strategy was agreed in 2009. The UN appointed in 2010 a new special representative of the secretary-general, Margot Wallstrom, with the sole task of fighting sexual violence, and Congo as a top priority. One DRC perpetrator has even been convicted by the International Criminal Court.

This is all good. However, the sad reality is that none of it has yet made much difference on the ground. The incidence of rape, sexual violence and sexual slavery remains largely unchanged. The Panzi Hospital and its analogues, such as the Heal Africa Hospital in Goma, remain overwhelmed, despite extra resources, more doctors, and new equipment. How can this be?

Part of the answer is that no one has yet succeeded in changing the culture which allows such behaviour to be seen as normal. Local institutions, such as the powerful Christian church, have not been as outspoken and active as they should. We have not been able to get to the leaders and ordinary soldiers of the armed groups. They do not read political speeches or UN resolutions. The world's condemnation means little or nothing to them.

The rest of the answer is that until the underlying conflicts are resolved, and the illegal militias disarmed and disbanded, there is little chance of stopping sexual violence. As long as armed groups are making money out of the mineral wealth which lies so abundantly beneath their feet, with the complicity of the government's own armed forces, and as long as outside buyers are not interested in where the precious metals they are buying come from or at what human cost they were acquired, the fighting and the rapes will continue. The world, if it really cares about the scandal that is sexual violence in the Congo, needs to step up dramatically its efforts to re-establish lasting peace and stability. The very least we can do is to ensure that we are not contributing to the mess by our readiness to benefit from its mineral wealth – for example, the coltan we all need for our mobile phones – without asking too many questions.

The uncomfortable reality is that the international community has paid little more than lip service to peace in DRC for far too long. MONUC/MONUSCO is just one symbol of its preference for palliatives over solutions. As I have already suggested, no major country feels a sufficient sense of responsibility to take the lead, and no major country really thinks it matters to them whether it is sorted out or not. This is an historic mistake. Congo may not be in an historically oil-producing region, and may not involve a great clash of religions. But it is a vital country at the heart of Africa with huge unexploited resources which the world needs, not least its tropical forest as a vital carbon sink. If Africa is to emerge as the last great investment frontier and take off economically, eventually lifting its 1 billion people out of poverty (as we have seen in China and India), then Congo cannot be left to fester.

Of course, the DRC should sort out its own problems. Ultimately, the government and its people will have to take responsibility for their own fate. I recognize the dangers of infantilization of a country's politics from too much international interference. The government need to be confronted with their own failures and shortcomings. The people need to expect more from their government and go on demanding it. An African spring in countries like this surely cannot be long in coming. But Congo's tragic history and the curse of mineral wealth mean it is simply not able to solve its problems on its own yet.

Some ask whether Congo is not a hopeless basket case, doomed to bump along the bottom of the international indicators. I do not believe this, even if some of what I have written sounds very gloomy. The Congolese people are as capable as any other of prospering if given a chance by an even half-competent government, and freed of the presence of armed groups threatening their lives and livelihoods on a daily basis. They want to see their country take its place as a proud and thriving African nation. The vibrant artistic and musical scene shows what they are capable of. We owe it to them to do whatever it takes to help them escape their present plight.

The humanitarians will have to go on trying to mitigate the worst effects of conflict and neglect, and working with the development actors to promote economic and social progress. But without solving the security issues and taking the illegal militias out of the equation, little will change.

As I write, the situation in the east has again taken a terrible turn for the worse. A Tutsi-based group of soldiers called M23 (named after the 23 March 2009 peace agreement between General Nkunda's former forces and the government troops) has mutinied because of lack of pay and poor conditions, attacked government forces, and installed yet another reign of terror. They are apparently led by Bosco Ntaganda, indicted and wanted by the ICC for child-soldier recruitment and atrocities. He believed the government were about to hand him over to justice, as indeed they should have done. There are, once again, accusations (the truth of which is hard to judge) of Rwandan support for these rebels. Government forces are once again tempted to make common cause with Hutu FDLR militia, despite their dreadful reputation, not least for appalling sexual violence. The central government and MONUSCO once again seem powerless to restore order. Civilians are once again being displaced in large numbers. Humanitarian needs are once again rising rapidly.

All this is extraordinarily depressing for anyone who has been involved with DRC. The east of the country seems to be going backwards again. Relations between DRC and Rwanda, one of the bright spots of the last few years, are once more under threat. But the reaction of the international community cannot and must not be a shrug of the shoulders, with the implication that nothing can be done. Instead, attention and diplomacy need to be stepped up dramatically to tackle the underlying issues for once and for all. It is possible. This is not the inextricable Middle East peace process, or rocket science, and a small proportion of the international effort which has gone into the Middle East peace process could make a huge difference.

LRA nightmare

One security problem which ought, in theory, to be relatively easy to sort out is the presence of the Lord's Resistance Army. I had already seen for myself the devastating consequences of their murderous reign of terror in northern Uganda, driven by their ruthless leader Joseph Kony and his tactics of murder, rape, and forced recruitment of child soldiers. More than a million people had been terrorized and displaced by their raids in the 1990s. Nearly all of them remained in camps many years later, still too traumatized to go home, though confidence was just beginning to return when I visited in 2007. But their good fortune, the disappearance of the LRA from Uganda, signalled a new trauma for countless others in neighbouring countries.

In late 2008, after lying relatively low for a couple of years, the LRA attacked towns and villages in the north-east DRC region of Haut Uele, including the capital, Dungu, killing around 1000 people in the so-called Christmas massacres. As a result, Ugandan forces were finally allowed by the Congolese authorities to enter the country and mount a new offensive against Kony and his followers. This did not have the results that were hoped for. The initial supposedly surprise air attack failed to kill the leadership as planned, and Kony and his men scattered again. While a continuing Ugandan-led offensive did have some success in tracking and killing LRA elements over the following months, most evaded capture and began to cause even worse mayhem among remote village communities in the north-east, displacing hundreds of thousands, killing and maiming hundreds of others, and continuing their usual dreadful practice of kidnapping women to be sex slaves and children to become new fighters.

In response, MONUC deployed all the way up to Dungu, and beyond, where they could, to try to afford some protection to the worst-affected areas. But it quickly became clear that this was an impossible task, even by DRC standards. The area where the LRA were operating was huge and virtually without roads. In the places that MONUC could actually reach, using helicopters or even building roads themselves to enable access to one particularly badly hit area, they were able to deter the LRA up to a point and to reassure terrified villagers. But this was only a drop in the ocean, as other threatened regions remained completely out of reach.

Humanitarian coordinator Ross Mountain, and the steely head of the OCHA office, Gloria Fernandez, worked hard to build up the humanitarian presence in the area too, to offer at least some help to the victims. But this was also a major undertaking, for both security and logistical reasons. And in this case, whatever our position of principle about keeping our activities separate, we were more or less totally dependent on MONUC – their helicopters and their security presence – to reach affected villages. The alternative of inaction would have been unacceptable.

I visited the area twice, in 2009 and 2010, to push MONUC to do more, and to keep the issue on the international map. Each time, I had the unenviable task of explaining to local communities that while the UN was doing its best, we simply could not guarantee to protect them against the LRA. They were outraged. How could a group from Uganda, which had absolutely nothing to do with them or their lives, create such devastation? And how could I seriously tell them that the mighty Security Council could do nothing about this?

They were unable to work their fields, and lived in constant fear of LRA raids. The raiding parties were tiny – a handful of individuals in most cases – but they had AK47s, and also used their machetes without compunction, not least to save precious ammunition. I met one girl in hospital who had had her ear and lips sliced off. An LRA group had surprised her in her fields, and mutilated her without explanation, perhaps to spread terror further and decrease the chances of resistance, or perhaps through random evil. It was enough to make one despair of humanity.

My predecessor Jan Egeland had been so incensed by the lack of progress in dealing with the LRA by the world and his UN political colleagues that he had taken the initiative to meet Kony himself in the jungle in November 2006, to urge him to sign a peace deal. This had at least helped give fresh life to negotiations started earlier that year. These talks continued through 2007, supported by the UN, including special envoy Joaquim Chissano, former president of Mozambique.

A peace agreement was finally agreed, including detailed provisions on how to deal with issues such as demobilization and disarmament, without granting any kind of blanket amnesty for past crimes. But, despite repeated promises that he was going to come out of the bush to sign, Kony never turned up. The stumbling block seemed to be the indictments against him and four fellow LRA leaders issued by the International Criminal Court in 2005. The indictments had been instigated by the Ugandan government, sickened by Kony's atrocities and despairing of any peace deal at that stage. But by 2007, they were prepared to see the indictments withdrawn, and replaced either by the use of traditional reconciliation justice practices from northern Uganda, or trials in Uganda itself, in order to enable a lasting peace and the end of the LRA threat. The people of northern Uganda themselves seemed prepared to forgive, if not to forget, despite all they had suffered. A group of escaped LRA child soldiers I met confirmed to me that this was their view too, notwithstanding the horrors they had been forced to be a part of.

However, the Ugandan government discovered that they did not have the power to withdraw the indictments. Only the ICC itself or the Security Council could do this, and neither was prepared to do so, given the gravity of the crimes of which Kony and his henchmen were accused. This meant that the chances of a peace agreement and the LRA deciding to come out of the bush were hugely reduced. Although the agreement was left open for signature in case Kony changed his mind, in practice peace hopes had disappeared by 2008.

Would Kony really have signed the peace agreement in 2007/8 if a way could have been found to withdraw the ICC indictments or otherwise give some kind of assurance about his future? He may never have been serious about peace, simply using the ceasefires which accompanied the talks to regroup and resupply (the UN were, at one stage, feeding his fighters who had assembled in southern Sudan). But the opposite is also possible, which would have spared many, many lives. This poses some real questions about the relationship between peace and justice to which I will return in Chapter Thirteen.

Why has Kony not been taken out before now? None of the major powers has enough at stake. Meanwhile, the local governments concerned, Ugandan and Congolese, have been reluctant to accept the infringement of their sovereignty and slur on their reputation involved in handing over the task to someone else. They have frequently been guilty of exaggerating their military success and minimizing the threat. There was much talk in 2009 and 2010 of the defeat of the LRA, with only final mopping up needed, even while the LRA were continuing to wreak havoc. No one knows for sure how many men Kony has, scattered as they are. But the truth is that he needs very few to terrorize and kill defenceless and petrified villagers.

LRA atrocities and attacks continue as I write. The US offered 100 military advisers in late 2011 to help in the search to track them down. I had long urged some such step on my political UN colleagues and the major powers who had the capacity (if not the will) to do something about the LRA, but obviously had to have full support from the DRC and Ugandan governments, who were themselves reluctant to admit they were largely powerless. For example, a Security Council resolution could have authorized anyone with the capacity to do so to take out Kony and his band of villains, with the cooperation of the local governments concerned. This was not exactly a standard position for a humanitarian, but I was as outraged as the DRC villagers that the international community appeared unwilling to prevent such appalling consequences from such a small group of desperadoes. The LRA are experienced jungle fighters, able to melt away when threatened. Killing or capturing Kony would be no easy task. But it is not impossible. We have the capacity, and we have intervened elsewhere in the world about far less. The LRA have killed and terrorized far more than Al Qaeda – it's just that their victims weren't Western citizens.

SOMALIA

Gulf of Aden

DJIBOUTI

SOMALILAND

Boosaaso

Baki

Ceerigaabo

Hargeysa

Burco

Laascaanood

Garoowe

ETHIOPIA

PUNTLAND

Gaalkacyo

Dhuusamarreeb

Beledweyne

Garbahaarey

Xuddur

Jawhar

INDIAN
OCEAN

Baidoa

Afgooye

Mogadishu

KENYA

Bu'aale

Marka

Kismayo

100 km

OCHA

Map Sources: ESRI, UNCS, UNDP, UNHCR. Map created in Apr 2012.

CHAPTER SIX

Somalia: endless night

Somalia was a daunting challenge throughout my time at OCHA. The two self-governing but internationally unrecognized areas in the north of the country, Somaliland and Puntland, had many problems but were not in need of major humanitarian relief. The same was sadly not true of south-central Somalia, including Mogadishu and other major towns, such as Baidoa and Kismayo. Drought, floods, and disease were regular features for people who were in any case living on the edge of food insecurity. But the absence of government and the addition of conflict over such a long period gave a new dimension to their needs.

The main issue for the humanitarian community was simply to cling on, despite the threats and insecurity, because of the depth of these needs. We were not helped by the political games going on around us, including the tendency of some Western governments to look at the situation mostly through a war-on-terror lens, more concerned about what might be the impact on Western streets of infiltration by Al Qaeda into Somalia than about the underlying political and economic mess which was allowing this to happen. Resisting attempts to integrate humanitarian aid into (dubious) political strategies, by both the government and UN colleagues, was therefore a constant preoccupation. Trying to work in militia-controlled areas proved a gradually worsening nightmare. Continuing to deliver aid against this background – while also facing accusations that we were allowing it to be stolen, and even of helping the Islamic rebels – became increasingly impossible. This was not helped by inflexible US anti-terrorist legislation, which was driven particularly by worries about the Al Shabaab militia group and its links with extremist Islamic groups elsewhere, notably Al Qaeda. The problems we faced changed and evolved over time, but tended to become worse, rather than better.

Outsiders beware

The history of south-central Somalia is too complex to go through in detail. The key point is that after the 1991 collapse of the Siad Barre regime, no group or movement has been able to establish secure control of the territory for long. Warring clans have been supported at different times by outside powers, but have never really been controlled by them. The international community has made several attempts to intervene to sort out Somalia and bring stability, but so far always unsuccessfully. The most notorious was the entry in 1992 of a UN force, UNOSOM (the United Nations Operation in Somalia), to try to restore order and prevent the famine from getting worse. When it was unable to make progress in its early days, it was strongly reinforced by US troops. But the Somali clans continued to resist fiercely, led by Mohamed Aidid, a well-known tribal leader and fierce opponent of the West. After the humiliation of US soldiers in the 'Black Hawk Down' incident, when a US helicopter was brought down and the bodies of its crew dragged through the streets, the US lost interest and gradually withdrew its forces. The UN force stayed until 1995, but never managed to establish its authority.

This familiar pattern from Somali history, of invaders rapidly regretting their presumption and finishing up by withdrawing, continues. In 2007, the Ethiopians sent in their troops to eject the Islamic Courts Union (ICU), a group of local Islamic leaders which had taken control the year before. The main Ethiopian motive was to prevent attacks on their own ethnic Somali territory of the Ogaden, which the ICU had been unwise enough to threaten to take over. But they withdrew again in 2008, after suffering significant casualties in and around Mogadishu.

The African Union has had its own force, AMISOM (African Union Mission to Somalia), in Mogadishu since 2008, to help establish the authority of the Transitional Federal Government (TFG), which had been set up as the legitimate and internationally recognized government in 2004, with the support of the UN and the AU. But for long periods they could scarcely move out of the airport. In each case, whatever their internal differences, the Somali clans have tended to unite against the invading foreigner, and the intervening force has quickly become part of the problem, not the solution.

An explosive visit

I learned the hard realities early, on a visit in May 2007. I went to see the humanitarian consequences of a particularly intense burst of fighting in Mogadishu. Some 400,000 people had fled the city. It was the first UN visit to Somalia at USG level since the mid-1990s, for security reasons, and it turned out to be as potentially perilous as it was fascinating.

The security briefing from a tough South African UN security official in Nairobi beforehand was stark. A plane had been shelled on the runway at Mogadishu airport a few weeks before. It was still there, pushed out of the way, but very visible. His overall message was that we stood a strong chance of being attacked on the roads inside the city, but only if we managed to survive our landing and arrival …

I took this with a pinch of salt. I knew that the situation was unstable and risky, but also that the security authorities would not let me go at all if they really expected serious danger. However, my South African briefer was close to the mark. We landed safely enough, trying to ignore the sight of the shattered plane. But as we reached the UN base just outside the airport, a large bomb went off at a road junction a couple of miles away, killing three TFG officials. As we tried to absorb this, since we were due to be heading to the same junction a few minutes later, reports reached us of bomb explosions in other parts of Mogadishu that were on our itinerary. Our Somali-based UN security officials were immediately on the phone to their local contacts to find out whether I was a target. The message back suggested that I was not, at least not directly. The aim was rather to make clear in the context of my visit that the conflict was not over and the city was not safe.

We quickly decided to cancel the planned programme – we had intended to visit different parts of the city, stay the night, and move on to an area seriously affected by flash floods. But I was not prepared to go back to Nairobi with my tail between my legs, having seen nothing and no one. We therefore opted to take a different route into the city, riding in an AMISOM armoured personnel carrier, with a serious military escort from the Ugandan contingent. That way I could at least visit Villa Somalia, the beleaguered headquarters of the TFG, and meet the then President Yusuf – who was, incidentally, both a British citizen and also at that time the world's longest-surviving liver-transplant patient.

I arrived at Villa Somalia hotter than I had ever been in my life. Several tense miles stuck in the APC, with the outside temperature around 45°C, and a heavy flak jacket on top of my going-to-see-the-president suit, meant I more or less melted on the way. However, I did at least get there in one piece, despite the conspicuousness of our convoy. I was also able to see on the way how depressingly little remained of the handsome, Italianate port city that Mogadishu had once been.

Unfortunately, my discussion with the president and his prime minister left me wondering whether the effort had really been worthwhile. I urged them to stop using force indiscriminately inside the city (both government and rebels were shelling more or less at random), to facilitate desperately needed humanitarian aid, and to abandon plans to move long-standing displaced people (IDPs) out of public buildings, given that they clearly had nowhere else to go. The president and prime minister were unresponsive, and in denial about the seriousness of the situation. They claimed, for example, that only 30,000 people had left Mogadishu. They also complained that relief organizations were in effect helping the rebels in some places by working with them.

The meeting did not, therefore, go well. As I made my frustration clear, the president turned to me at one stage and asked threateningly whether I really thought I cared more about his people than he did. It was on the tip of my tongue to say, 'Yes, obviously!' However, years of diplomatic training kicked in and I moved the conversation on. The basic problem was, of course, that the TFG had virtually no control of most of Mogadishu, let alone the rest of south-central Somalia, and we both knew it. But my point was that the least this ineffective government could do was to facilitate the help their people so desperately needed, rather than posturing and getting in the way.

As we took the coast road back to the airport, I insisted that we stop to visit some of the long-standing IDPs camped all round the city. Our convoy pulled up at random outside a large compound facing the sea, inhabited by around 150 families. Many of them had been there for almost twenty years, pastoralists from the south who had lost their herds in the early years of the conflict and headed for the capital in search of work. Their living conditions were appalling – makeshift tents of rags and sticks – with no work and no prospects. I could only guess at the miserable futures of the many children running round. But I was also astonished to be told that the compound was the site of the former British Embassy, which had been abandoned in 1991. The outline of the chancery building could still be seen, together with a large depression in the middle of the courtyard, obviously where the swimming pool had once been. I do not believe in the significance of coincidences, but this was certainly an odd one.

While in Mogadishu I also met representatives of civil society, whose struggles to survive and be heard were little short of heroic, and a group of locals working for UN agencies and international NGOs – few if any expatriates were able to stay in south-central Somalia for more than a day or two at that stage. Talking to them brought home the dangers they faced. Most of their families had themselves left Mogadishu as IDPs. They themselves had stayed out of a sense of duty and to try to safeguard their houses. But they were extraordinarily vulnerable, not only to the fighting around them, but also to clan pressures. Working for an international organization was a highly suspicious activity in clan eyes. The risks of blackmail and intimidation, and diversion of aid, were correspondingly high. I was hugely impressed by their dedication in the face of these pressures, but also realistic about how far they could resist them.

Getting aid through

The amount of aid which could be delivered in such circumstances was obviously limited. Yet the World Food Programme,
UNICEF, the World Health Organization, Concern, Care, the
Danish Refugee Council, the Norwegian Refugee Council, and
others were continuing to operate, and indeed trying to increase
their programmes, relying mostly on national staff. But the needs
were much greater than they could possibly cope with, while
security was steadily deteriorating. At that stage, in 2007, the
fundamentalist Islamic militia group, Al Shabaab (The Youth),
were still relatively small and disorganized. They had not yet
established the kind of grip over towns and rural areas which later
encouraged them to try to veto aid from international
organizations. But roadblocks with armed men demanding 'taxes'
to pass were already a constant feature.

I went back to south-central Somalia in December, this time
to see the plight of those who had fled Mogadishu, by then
numbering some 600,000 – around half the normal population
of the capital. There were no bombs on this occasion: intensive
discussions by UN security officials with the local warlords had
paid off. We flew into a rural airfield some 50 kilometres west of
Mogadishu, known for that reason as K50. There was nothing
there but a couple of huts, but as we drove out we were surprised
to see a large gaggle of women outside the gate. They were
waiting for the arrival of the daily flight bringing in supplies of
khat, the mildly narcotic leaves which are an essential daily
chewing requirement for most Somali men – a reminder that
some things worked in Somalia, even in the middle of mayhem,
drought and conflict. The other obvious thing which worked,
for reasons not unconnected to the khat trade, as well as to piracy
and other criminal activity, was the mobile-phone system.

BlackBerry smartphones worked more reliably, even in deepest rural Somalia, than in London or New York! Some businessmen, if that is the right word, have continued to make a lot of money in Somalia through all the troubles.

The idea behind arriving at K50 was easy access to the so-called 'Afgooye Corridor', which housed most of those who had fled Mogadishu, in some seventy disorganized camps strung out along 15 kilometres of road. The IDPs I met told harrowing stories of the fighting which had made even hardened veterans of trouble in the capital flee – shelling of residential areas and sniping which spared no one. Most had left with only the clothes on their backs. Conditions were poor in terms of shelter, but other aspects of the relief operation were more encouraging. Clean water was being trucked in, and vaccination campaigns were under way. All this was still being done almost exclusively through local NGOs or local staff of international agencies and NGOs, because of security concerns. Visits like mine were only just beginning to become possible – and the window for foreigners to get in with any degree of safety closed soon afterwards.

In Afgooye I met another true humanitarian hero, Hawa Abdi Dhiblawe – a Somali doctor who had been running a clinic there for the previous sixteen years, including a therapeutic feeding centre run by Médecins Sans Frontières, with sixty beds full of severely malnourished children. She had steadfastly refused to be intimidated by the warlords and clan leaders of the area – fortunately, since her clinic was more sorely needed than ever. She and her colleagues were doing extraordinary work in the most difficult and dangerous circumstances imaginable.

Three years later, when things had deteriorated even further, even Dr Abdi was pushed out of her hospital by an armed gang from the Hizbul-Islam extremist militia group, who smashed it up and insisted at gunpoint that she give up her work. However, she was still not intimidated: from Mogadishu she used her media and other contacts to relay the news of this outrage to the outside world. In the weeks that followed, she not only forced the gunmen to back down, but even made them apologize publicly before she would agree to go back and reopen the hospital. That's courage and commitment.

From Afgooye I went to Baidoa, then home of the country's 'parliament', to meet the new TFG prime minister, Nur Hassan Hussein. As a former president of the Somali Red Crescent Society, he was far more responsive than his predecessor and made clear that the humanitarian crisis was one of his top priorities. But the problem of TFG incapacity and impotence remained, and the prospects for progress were still bleak. As always, while the aid community could work away to minimize the humanitarian consequences of the conflict, the real need was for political progress and reconciliation to create peace and stability. There was also a desperate need for all sides to the conflict to recognize that the overwhelming majority of the victims of the fighting were the helpless civilians. But such appeals fell on deaf ears in Somalia.

It was no easy task in these circumstances to persuade the international donor community that they should be putting more money into relief in the country. They had been giving aid for so long that they had little faith that the task would ever end. They were also increasingly hard to convince that the aid was reaching its destination, rather than being diverted by one or more of the armed militias – and it was true that none of these had any compunction whatsoever in stealing supplies if they could. We nevertheless successfully used the UN appeal system to raise more cash, as needs went from around $300 million in 2007 to almost $900 million in 2009. Successive UN humanitarian coordinators for Somalia, Eric Laroche and Mark Bowden, were dedicated advocates. But I suspect the donors also felt, despite their doubts, that relief aid was the one positive thing they could provide while progress otherwise seemed so remote. Attracting funds became much harder subsequently, until the 2011 famine unleashed a renewed flow of donor money.

The further deterioration of the security situation after 2007 meant I was unable to visit again myself, but south-central Somalia remained an intense preoccupation, and not just from a humanitarian point of view, where we were constantly battling to keep the aid flowing. Policy towards Somalia was the subject of constant and difficult debate within the UN Secretariat throughout my time there. Ban ki-Moon wisely observed on more than one occasion that Somalia was the issue on which he felt most at a loss. There were equally intractable problems, not least Israel–Palestine, but at least you knew what you were trying to achieve there, however remote success might seem. In Somalia, the mess was so long-standing, so deep, and so impenetrable from the outside that it was almost impossible to know where to start.

I shared this frustration. Like Ban ki-Moon, I found it hard to say what exactly the international community should be doing to help change the situation. At the same time, I had strong views about what it should *not* be doing. Because some of the Western powers, particularly the US, looked at policy towards Somalia almost exclusively in the context of the international struggle against terrorism (a nonsensical notion in my view, in any case, since terrorism is a tactic, not a movement or an ideology), they came to see the TFG as a vital bulwark against extreme Islamicist influence in the area, including Al Qaeda. Arguably, the TFG could have played such a role, if it had had real influence and a meaningful political creed, but in practice it had neither. This reliance on the TFG led to two mistaken judgments: first, a belief that any internal political deal involving rebel Islamic forces was bound to be bad news for the West and good news for terrorists, when the only chance of removing the causes of the terrorism and engaging those who supported it was to involve these groups politically and bring them into the political picture; and second, that the TFG not only needed support, but was actually getting stronger and doing an increasingly good job, ignoring all the evidence from the ground that this was a misreading of the realities. This was based on wishful thinking and the same unwillingness to deliver bad news to Western capitals we have seen in Iraq and Afghanistan too. The truth was that while they certainly had to face many difficult problems, the TFG were corrupt and incompetent on a grand scale.

As a consequence of this policy of reliance on the TFG, considerable efforts were made by various outside parties, including parts of the UN who bought into this vision of events, to recruit and train TFG army and police forces. A lot of international money was spent on this. Sadly, most of the recruits melted away after the training, if they even stuck around that long. Many of them later joined the very Islamic militias they had been trained to fight, whether from conviction or because the militias actually paid them, unlike the government. Despite these multiple failures, the TFG were effectively given a blank cheque to go on with the same policies. The same attitude lay behind US encouragement to Ethiopia to intervene militarily. The ICU were duly thrown out, but nothing effective was put in their place, and the Ethiopians' later withdrawal was humiliating for all concerned.

There were also severe doubts in the humanitarian community about the African Union force, AMISOM, which, in practice, relied on Western financial and political support, as well as UN help. AMISOM was certainly vital to the continued existence of the TFG, since they were all that stood between them and complete collapse between 2008 and 2010. But for most of that time, the force controlled little more than a small area of territory around Mogadishu airport and the area round the TFG HQ in Villa Somalia at the other end of town. And while the AMISOM contingents were courageous, hanging on and taking significant casualties from opportunistic shelling and attacks by the militias, and living in very difficult conditions, they were also responsible for many civilian deaths themselves: their habitual response to attacks was indiscriminate shelling of areas of Mogadishu where they supposed their attackers were based. Their international backers preferred to turn a blind eye to this.

Inside the UN, the policies of basing everything on backing for the TFG found support in the Department of Political Affairs (DPA) and from the secretary-general's quirky but experienced special representative, Ahmed Ould Abdullah. The latter had a habit of criticizing the humanitarians for not supporting the TFG more. He also constantly suggested, on the basis of no visible evidence that I could ever see, that a breakthrough in terms of political reconciliation was just around the corner, brokered by the Western powers and the Saudis.

The DPA meanwhile wanted the UN to deploy its own peacekeeping force, to take over from AMISOM. The Department of Peacekeeping Operations (DPKO) themselves, who were separate from the DPA, but supposed to work very closely with them, had absolutely no desire to do this. They had more than enough on their plate already, in Sudan, Congo and a dozen other places, and saw no reason to suppose that the experience in Somalia would be any more successful than it had been in the 1990s. They pointed out forcefully that there was absolutely no peace to keep, and that they would be putting troops into a highly dangerous vacuum, to support a government whose writ did not run beyond the gates of its highly fortified compound, with no visible exit strategy.

I supported these DPKO arguments, not because as humanitarians we were opposed to a UN peacekeeping force as such, but because we knew what was happening on the ground, through our own constant exposure in humanitarian operations, better than the theoretical analysts in New York or in Western capitals. UN political reports on Somalia constantly painted an over-rosy picture of the situation. It was clear to us that the conditions were simply not there for a successful UN military intervention, which would only end up becoming part of the problem and a common enemy for all the Somali factions. These policy debates were often fractious and bitter.

The battle over 'integration'

This friction also helped explain why the DPA was constantly pressing for full 'integration' of the UN presence, in other words subordination of the development and humanitarian sides to political objectives and instructions. This issue, already brought up in the DRC context, was fought on many fronts inside the UN, and deserves further explanation. In one sense, it was obvious that the UN should be unifying its efforts and making sure that its various arms and agencies were pushing in the same direction. This was what lay behind the 'One UN' initiative in countries where many UN agencies were represented, each with their own offices, budgets and programmes, and little apparent coordination between them. I strongly supported these efforts from a development point of view, and the parallel need to strengthen the hand of the UN resident coordinator, in order to bring together the agency programmes. Where there was no conflict, it made sense to have the UN working together as closely as possible. I also supported better general cooperation between humanitarians and other parts of the UN.

However, I quickly came to understand why, where the country concerned is still in a conflict or an immediately post-conflict situation, structural integration with the rest of the system can prove a real problem for the humanitarians. The point is that humanitarian aid is a moral imperative, not part of a political strategy. It has to be given purely on the basis of need, objectively assessed, if it is going to be effective and acceptable to the warring parties and the populations in need, and if those delivering it are going to be able to work safely and usefully. In other words the consent of those engaged in fighting and the communities on the ground is needed, if at all possible. This can never be forthcoming if the aid is being used – or is perceived as being used – as a political or security tool for one side or another.

Where the UN is actively engaged politically in a country with an internal conflict, as it almost always is when there is a peacekeeping force (Sudan, DRC, etc.) or a large political mission (Afghanistan, Somalia), it is of course trying to act impartially. But the UN as an institution cannot be *neutral* between the warring parties if its mandate is essentially to support the legitimate government, as it usually is. This means that if the humanitarian parts of the UN are fully subsumed into the overall UN set-up, physically and administratively, they too will automatically no longer be seen as neutral, with all the risks entailed by this perception.

As we will see, this has been a huge problem in Afghanistan. But it was a major issue in Somalia too. The UN's political side was trying to strengthen the TFG, and working closely with Western powers trying to defeat and exclude fundamental Islamic forces. Our mission was certainly not to do anything which might undermine those objectives, but at the same time we had a serious problem if we were seen to be part of that effort. We wanted to be able to operate in areas not controlled by the TFG, i.e. most of the country in this case, and to be able to talk to all the forces on the ground in the country, including Al Shabaab and others denounced as terrorists, about humanitarian issues. We could not do this if we were looked upon as part of, or too-close to, a hostile political strategy.

Unfortunately, selling this view to others was a constant uphill struggle. For traditional political actors and diplomats, from whose ranks I had come, the desire for separation simply looked like special pleading from a typically humanitarian ivory tower point of view. In the Somalia case, some in the DPA and the TFG did not, or would not, understand the point, and believed some humanitarians were playing their own political games.

Part of the 'political' argument against the humanitarian position of principle was that we were kidding ourselves if we thought that the average terrorist could or would distinguish between political and humanitarian parts of the UN. So our desire to keep our distance was theoretical and naive. I strongly rejected this counsel of despair. It was true that in many contexts we struggled to establish our difference. No doubt we could never have persuaded Al Qaeda themselves of our neutrality. But there was plenty of evidence, from Afghanistan and elsewhere, that many armed groups *were* capable of drawing sophisticated distinctions between different organizations on the ground, on the basis of what they did and how they positioned themselves, and that they reacted accordingly, leaving alone those they believed were genuinely humanitarian groups and targeting the activities of others.

In any case, the difficulty of tackling perceptions was, to my mind, not an argument for not trying to explain why humanitarians were different, but on the contrary a reason for increasing our efforts, given the importance of being able to operate all over a country affected by conflict. Moreover, the need to be perceived as being separate from the UN's political and peacekeeping sides was absolutely paramount for the humanitarian NGOs. These independent organizations made clear in many places that they would refuse to be coordinated by OCHA and the UN humanitarian coordinator on the ground, or even to visit our offices, if we were structurally and physically part of a UN political/security set-up. They feared the 'contamination' would make it impossible for them to operate. This NGO threat to withdraw their cooperation, with all its potential consequences for effective coordination and efficient aid delivery, remains a problem in several crises around the world.

For all these reasons, we resisted strongly the proposal that our efforts in Somalia should be integrated with those of the special representative of the secretary-general (SRSG), whose role was primarily in the political and security field, and put together in one office with his staff. We did succeed, but it was a constant struggle. And, as we shall see, it was hugely complicated by separate concerns in parts of the international community and the press about the effectiveness of aid delivery in Somalia. There were even accusations from some that the UN World Food Programme had been involved in diversion of aid, going as far as collusion with extremist opposition groups.

Working where the 'terrorists' are

Through 2008 and 2009, the situation for the population in south-central Somalia steadily worsened, as the effects of conflict reduced agricultural production, drought tightened its grip, and Al Shabaab and allied Islamicist militias took more and more territory. Links between Al Shabaab and Al Qaeda strengthened, and the area came to be seen as one of the international battlegrounds against terrorism, drone strikes and all. Meanwhile, our attempts at a humanitarian dialogue with Al Shabaab only got so far. There was no consistent policy between their leaders in different areas. Some would not talk to humanitarians at all on principle, since we were foreign infidels. Others talked, and could see the need for us to keep the population fed. But they also issued a constant stream of threats to close humanitarian offices and operations, unless the organizations concerned complied with their demands: to register officially with the Al Shabaab authorities, to pay fees for permission to work, to hand over part of the aid to them to distribute, or to agree to conditions, such as employing no women.

We dealt with these unacceptable demands as best we could, never complying but trying to avoid outright confrontation. But this became progressively more difficult as time went on. We had in the past been protected in many places by pressure on the militia leaders from local elders, who knew the importance for their people of the aid provided by the humanitarians. But intimidation gradually silenced most of these voices. By 2009, even large and resourceful NGOs were recognizing that it had become simply too difficult to maintain meaningful operations to the required standards, and were beginning to think about pulling out.

Against this background we had to face a new and even more difficult set of challenges, which led to the abandonment of humanitarian operations in much of south-central Somalia in 2010. This had two separate but linked origins, both driven by increasing Al Shabaab military success and presence. The first was a growing drumbeat of accusations that aid was not reaching those for whom it was intended and was indeed being used to fuel the insurgency. These accusations came from a variety of sources: people inside the TFG who had always suspected the World Food Programme of too close a relationship with the rebels; SRSG

Ould Abdallah and some of his colleagues, who sympathized with that point of view and wanted to control the humanitarians more; and some observers sitting in Nairobi whose scepticism about WFP's operations in Somalia was encouraged by an unnecessarily secretive approach from local WFP representatives.

These accusations came to a head in a report in early 2010 by the Monitoring Group on Somalia, an investigation unit set up by the Security Council a couple of years before. The report claimed inter alia that WFP had deliberately used only a very small group of Somali trucking companies with close links to the rebels; had ignored the dodgy connections of companies it was working with locally; had turned a blind eye to, or even actively connived at, large-scale diversion of food aid; and had otherwise fallen short of the required standards and principles in its operations. WFP strongly denied all these accusations, and issued a detailed rebuttal. But some of the mud stuck, not least because previous similar accusations from British TV station Channel 4 had never been convincingly refuted. Under pressure from me and others, they therefore agreed to an independent enquiry into the allegations.

The second prong of the attack came in the shape of new US legislation in 2009 which prohibited any US aid going to agencies which could not demonstrate to the administration's satisfaction that none of their money or goods could reach terrorist groups, including Al Shabaab. Aid organizations were required to sign binding certificates to this effect, and risked prosecution if such assurances turned out to be unfounded. This threatened to undermine most humanitarian operations in south-central Somalia, of which the US were by some way the biggest funders, because the agencies and NGOs operating there could not sign in good faith the certificates demanded. The main problem was that all aid in the areas in question, whether specifically under Al

Shabaab control or not, had to pass through roadblocks where 'taxes' were routinely demanded by the armed men manning them. Those concerned did not wear uniforms or openly declare their allegiance. Much of it was simple criminality. But it was impossible to say with certainty that none of these funds was reaching those classified by the US government as terrorists.

A long argument ensued. The aid agencies argued that the sums involved in such fees were tiny in the great scheme of things – the hundreds of dollars potentially involved were not going to make the difference between successful terrorist operations or their absence, given other lucrative sources of support for Al Shabaab; and that the Americans were using a sledgehammer to crack a nut, with the likely effect of increasing the risk of death or serious malnutrition for many hundreds of thousands of innocent civilians through the withdrawal of crucial humanitarian aid. I strongly supported these misgivings about the US administration's policy. The aid side of the administration was sympathetic, but others in Washington were not, and in any case did not feel inclined to go back to Congress to argue the case for an exception for aid agencies in Somalia.

Withdrawal

WFP were at the forefront of all these worries since their operations were by far the biggest in the areas concerned. The arguments were also particularly sensitive for them since they relied to a large extent on US funding and had close links with the administration. In late 2009, WFP decided to suspend their operations in a significant part of south-central Somalia, in particular those parts most clearly controlled by Al Shabaab and affiliates. They said that they were doing so because of new threats to their staff which had made continued activities in these areas too dangerous. They made clear that they would continue to operate in other areas, including Mogadishu and the Afgooye Corridor, and would return to the abandoned areas as soon as conditions allowed. Nevertheless, their withdrawal meant hundreds of thousands of people relying on their emergency food efforts would now have to manage without them.

This WFP decision was much criticized in private by other agencies, from the UN as well as NGOs, who found it hard to believe that security conditions had suddenly deteriorated so much in these areas that a pull-out was justified. Others who were working there did not see the same immediate need to pull out themselves, though all were obviously under increasing security pressure. Some were inclined to think that WFP had become too uncomfortable about operations in the area concerned because of the accusations and the pressure from Washington and the media, and therefore preferred to get out from under, in order to preserve their funding and credibility with the administration and Congress. WFP strongly denied such claims and stuck to their security story. There was no doubt that southern Somalia was a dangerous place for aid workers – dozens had been killed and many more kidnapped over the previous two or three years. WFP was always in the front line because of the size, visibility and sensitivity of its operations. Some of its offices and warehouses had certainly been attacked and ransacked.

Whatever the truth about their motivation, concerns about the effects on the population in the areas from which they had withdrawn were severe. Coming at the same time as increasingly difficult experiences in Afghanistan, Pakistan, and Yemen, what was happening in Somalia also propelled a fresh bout of introspection inside the humanitarian community about how to maintain effective operations in remote and dangerous environments. OCHA launched a new system-wide study, drawing on the views of those who had seen this problem at close quarters. For its part, WFP convened a conference on new technical solutions to the problem of remote monitoring of aid delivery – ideas such as using locals on the ground with mobile phones to report how much aid they had seen, if any; tagging aid shipments; and satellite monitoring of convoys.

There are no easy answers to these problems. In most cases of humanitarian aid, the levels of diversion and corruption are remarkably low – aid does not pass through the hands of local governments, and tracking it is reasonably straightforward. In 'normal' environments, if such a concept makes sense in the context of humanitarian aid, agencies such as WFP take huge care to follow what happens to aid being delivered by their local partners. They monitor every step in the deliveries themselves wherever possible, often using expatriate observers from outside the operation as an independent check. But if aid is to be provided in remote and dangerous locations, little of this may be possible. The reality is that more risks have to be taken and some degree of 'leakage' may have to be accepted.

Even in favourable circumstances, small amounts of WFP food will always tend to turn up in local markets, because some of the recipients will prefer to sell it for cash or exchange it for other goods. As long as this is a small percentage and the leakage is coming from the recipients themselves, this need not cause undue alarm. But if it goes above a certain level, e.g. 5 or 10 per cent, and especially if the aid is finding its way straight from the food trucks into the markets, to the profit of those supposed to be delivering it, this is no longer tolerable. Aid deliveries may have to be halted. There is always reluctance to do this because of the potential effect on those in need. To repeat, risks have to be taken and accepted in humanitarian aid delivery, and donors and the media need to be aware of them. But there have to be red lines too.

Famine

In the case of south-central Somalia, the legislation-driven reduction of US funding from late 2009 onwards, followed by other donors equally reluctant to appear to be funding 'terrorists', cut the amount of humanitarian aid dramatically. Other agencies and NGOs more or less had to follow WFP's lead in withdrawing. This did not result immediately in the kind of humanitarian catastrophe that some had feared. There had been some rain in previous months. But drought struck again in deadly earnest in 2010, and famine was officially declared – a rare event – in a number of south-central areas in July 2011, reflecting even worse conditions than elsewhere in the Horn of Africa. Some 4 million Somalis, including 3 million in the south-central region, a very high proportion of the population, were assessed to be at severe risk. The international community reacted well once the alarm bells were rung by the 'famine' word, but much later than ought to have been possible, since the facts of drought were known months before that.

The spectre of famine pushed the US terrorism legislation concerns to one side for the time being. However, Al Shabaab's reaction was cynical in the extreme. On the pretext that agencies and NGOs were collaborating with their enemies and, for example, providing targeting information for US drone strikes, an increasing number were simply prevented from operating in the regions which Al Shabaab controlled, culminating in the outright banning of sixteen agencies and NGOs in late 2011/early 2012. Compounds and aid were seized. Large numbers of Somalis meanwhile fled southwards to Kenya, swelling the already massively overcrowded and explosive camps of Daadab and Kakuma in northern Kenya. Others walked to wherever they could find some relief.

We will never know exactly how many died, or what the true toll has been in terms of retarded physical and mental growth among the young children in the affected areas in the months before the famine (though not the crisis) was declared officially over in February 2012. But we can be sure that the figures were high. We will also never know whether the situation might have been better, and the resilience of local populations higher, if politics from all sides had not already been interfering with aid delivery in the months and years preceding the famine. But we can be sure that it is not the last time that that dreaded word will be heard in an area so chronically plagued by conflict, drought, and food insecurity.

Military efforts and political solutions

In the meantime, the conflict continues. After local Kenyan officials, as well as Western aid workers and tourists, were attacked and kidnapped by Al Shabaab in the border areas, the Kenyan government decided in late 2011 that enough was enough, and sent an invasion force and bombers to 'pacify' Somali towns. The Ugandans have been helping too. The Ethiopians have also been intervening again, sending their troops over the border once more, whenever they sense an opportunity. This encouraged repeated talk of the TFG successfully extending its authority in the country, with the help of AMISOM, and of Al Shabaab being militarily 'on the run'. Al Shabaab have certainly suffered severe setbacks in some places. The international community believe, as I write in mid-2012, that they might be finally turning a corner in the struggle against Al Shabaab.

Politically, a new constitution has been agreed and elections are supposed to be held to produce a new, more representative government to take over from the TFG, whose mandate has run out. There is a bit of optimism in the area about Somalia and its political and economic future. Is this justified?

I certainly hope so. But I remain sceptical. Somalia still risks suffering from the same kind of wilfully blind happy talk in Western circles as Afghanistan. The political institutions remain weak in the extreme, and the constitution unlikely to be respected in reality. Like the Taliban, Al Shabaab can lose many battles without losing the war. Even if their oppressive behaviour has made them few friends among the local population in most areas, and their alliance with Al Qaeda looks like a fundamental mistake, a hated foreign presence is the best argument they can have for continuing their activities. The risk is, therefore, that the Kenyan incursion will go the way of so many other foreign interventions in Somalia. It is certainly far from clear that the Kenyans have the money, capacity, or will to stick to what is bound to be a difficult and lengthy task.

The reality is that in south-central Somalia, as in Afghanistan, no one would wish to start from the point that we have reached. No good solutions now seem available. There are also vested interests everywhere who do not really want a solution – including commercial interests in Somalia itself, and cynical outside powers like Eritrea, fighting a proxy war against Ethiopia through Somalia. And while the international community would genuinely like to see progress, Somalia will never be able to command the undivided attention of the world's major powers, except perhaps over piracy. And even on this issue there is a wilful desire to ignore the reality that the problem of piracy is unlikely to be solved until there is a wider political solution. This will have to be one which provides alternative livelihoods, and which removes the incentives for the militias (and even some in government in south-central Somalia and Puntland) to connive in this lucrative business by turning a blind eye to what is going on, or even quietly helping the pirates in return for a cut of the profits.

More widely, until policy-makers, especially those in the West, look the stark realities in the face, drop our distorting security lenses, and understand the importance of locally driven solutions, we are destined to go on repeating the same mistakes. I do not think that the outside world can now solve south-central Somalia's problems. The clans, militias, and Islamic forces will have to find a way forward to build peace and a state themselves, while the international community facilitates and helps where it can, but does not try to direct. Somaliland to the north has shown it can be done.

Meanwhile, the uncomfortable reality is that humanitarian aid will go on being needed in south-central Somalia for the foreseeable future. But the problems of delivering it safely and reliably are likely to remain too. On the humanitarian side, too, we therefore have to learn the lessons. Donors must recognize that a consistent attitude to the needs of the people, not one driven by political concerns, is the only viable and acceptable approach to humanitarian aid. They also need to accept that there is bound to be some leakage in aid in such desperate circumstances. The aid will certainly not itself solve the political problems, but without it thousands will die and the chances of an eventual political solution will be that much less.

For their part, agencies and NGOs need to do more to ensure that they can answer the questions about the destination and effectiveness of the aid they are delivering, without suggesting that 100 per cent guarantees will ever be available in circumstances like those of south-central Somalia. Remote working practices need to be improved and technology exploited to the full. Full transparency is the only way forward, not an attempt to hide the realities.

Map Sources: UNCS, Europa Technologies, ESRI. Map created in Oct 2011.

CHAPTER SEVEN

Myanmar: cyclone strike and government obstruction

On 2 May 2008, Cyclone Nargis struck the Irrawaddy peninsula, dealing a glancing blow to the country's main city and former capital, Yangon (Rangoon), as it passed. It was one of the deadliest cyclones in recent history. One of Myanmar's most fertile areas, the peninsula is densely populated with small farmers. Unlike neighbouring Bangladesh, Myanmar had little recent experience of big tropical cyclones. There was no early warning system in place, and no shelters. Its weather forecasters did not see anything dramatic coming, or at least did little or nothing to raise the alarm effectively if they did. The cyclone found those in its way unprepared in every sense.

The 160-kilometres-per-hour wind did huge damage. But it was not wind which caused the major catastrophe. Nargis drove a 15-foot tidal surge which swept across a large part of the flat delta at high speed and destroyed virtually everything and everyone in its path. Only those strong enough to cling to trees, or lucky enough to be swept out of harm's way, survived. The final death toll was over 140,000, many of them women and children, though 80,000 bodies were never found. Houses and livelihoods were destroyed along with lives, as the salt water polluted everything it touched. Two million people were badly affected.

Nargis had not only hit a country and people physically unprepared. It had struck a regime isolated and in the grip of advanced paranoia about the outside world. They were in the last stages of preparations for a referendum on the future political path of the country. The result of the referendum was hardly in doubt, but sensitivities were even higher than normal. This was the worst possible backdrop for a rapid and effective aid operation. Even with good cooperation, the logistical problems of reaching many parts of the delta would have been horrendous: there were few if any roads, in many areas water transport was the only means of moving about and getting in goods, and most of the boats and landing stages had been destroyed. In the absence of a decent working relationship with the government, such problems looked almost insurmountable.

The crisis was to monopolize my attention and that of Ban ki-Moon for the next two months, and to remain the focus of international governments and media for almost as long. It raised many questions about how to deal with a government bent on excluding meddling foreigners; about the applicability of the Responsibility to Protect (R2P) doctrine; and about the interaction between the UN and a regional organization like the Association of South East Asian Nations (ASEAN).

Isolation and paranoia

A look at the troubled politics of Myanmar, a country with plenty of natural resources, as well as a population of almost 60 million, can help to explain how a natural disaster nearly led to armed conflict, and why those affected had to flirt with death and disease for much longer than necessary.

The military had held Myanmar in a tight grip since a coup in 1962. When the relatively free election of 1990 was convincingly won by the National League for Democracy (NLD), the party of Aung San Suu Kyi (ASSK), the regime refused to accept the result, and effectively banned the party. ASSK herself had already been put under house arrest in 1989. She remained in some sort of detention for fifteen of the next twenty-one years.

The almost fifty years of military rule were marked by sporadic and brutally suppressed democracy protests. Myanmar fell behind the rest of the world – and in particular the rest of Asia – politically, economically, and in almost every other way. Human rights abuses, internal repression, unresolved conflicts with ethnic groups in the north, lack of investment, and underdevelopment were the hallmarks of the regime. They led to Western sanctions, absence of meaningful dialogue, and a sense of persecution, for which support from other countries less concerned about the internal issues, such as China and India, could only partly compensate. Myanmar was part of the regional grouping of countries trying to promote cooperation and integration in key areas, the Association of South East Asian Nations (ASEAN), but it was always on the margins, as a slightly embarrassing member of the club.

The 2008 referendum was claimed by the government to be part of the process of putting Myanmar on the path towards genuine democracy, but no one took it seriously in this sense at the time. It was widely assumed, both inside and outside the country, to be a fig leaf to cover continued military rule, with the generals putting on civilian clothes but behaving in the same old repressive way. In any case, when the disaster struck in 2008, the regime was in no mood to trust outside powers, particularly from the West; and the outside world was certainly not ready to give credit of any kind to the regime. Previous attempts to start an exchange of views about reform had come to nothing. The only diplomatic game in town was a sporadic discussion between the government and Ban ki-Moon's special representative,

Ibrahim Gambari, a Nigerian who had previously been head of the UN Department of Political Affairs in New York. Even this dialogue was constantly on the point of being abandoned, on the grounds that it was giving diplomatic cover to the regime for nothing in return.

The excellent UN resident and humanitarian coordinator, Charles Petrie, had been thrown out of the country the previous year for a statement about the need to address human rights abuses which could hardly be seen as provocative in the circumstances. Ironically, he was the one person who had struggled for years to keep channels of communication between the outside world and the regime open, and to convince the regime to accept humanitarian help in some of the conflict zones in the north, working to persuade them that such help carried no political significance or risks from their point of view.

Reacting to catastrophe

News of the scale of the Nargis disaster filtered out gradually from such a closed country. But within a day or two even the generals could not hide from the world the fact that the delta had suffered a major catastrophe. Their initial reactions were slow in the extreme. It was several more days before they announced any real measures to help the population, and the initial sum pledged – $5 million – was hopelessly inadequate. Gradually, they began to use military resources like helicopters to reach the affected areas, and to work with the Myanmar Red Cross. But it took even more days for the government to say, under pressure from the world's media, and with every apparent reluctance, that they would accept cash help and goods from the outside world.

In practice, they were doing all they could to *prevent* the UN agencies and NGOs already in the country from getting to the affected area, and stopping anyone new from getting in. Even the regular UN Disaster Coordination and Assessment (UNDAC) emergency team, immediately despatched by OCHA to a disaster-stricken country on such occasions, had been delayed, and two of its four members turned away on nationality grounds. The government made increasingly clear that no new visas would be granted to international relief workers, and no permission to work given to international NGOs not already in the country.

This was highly unpromising, to say the least. Nevertheless, given the severity of the emergency, I decided that we should do what we normally did, and launch a 'flash appeal' in New York – in other words, our best assessment of needs, and the resources required to address them. In a presentation on 9 May to all UN member states, I made clear that I had been tempted to cancel the event, given the authorities' uncooperative attitude, but that the suffering of those affected had to take precedence. The appeal asked for an initial $187 million, to cover the needs of 1.5 million people for three months. This embraced, above all, emergency food aid, clean water, health, shelter, and the transport logistics needed to reach the remote parts of the delta.

Donor countries made clear that they wanted to help, but that their readiness to do so on a large scale would depend on how far the government was prepared to cooperate with the international relief community. Frustration with the regime was in fact already mounting quickly on all sides. Their decision to press ahead with the political referendum despite the catastrophe they had just suffered, except in the areas worst affected by the cyclone, seemed to symbolize their indifference to the suffering of their own people. Ban ki-Moon and I had no hesitation in letting our frustration show. But we also took the view that we had to go on working with the regime to persuade them to change their attitude, rather than just lapsing into full public denunciation mode, which might have been temporarily satisfying, but would have achieved nothing, particularly for the hundreds of thousands of people desperately looking for help.

Part of the frustration was the sheer difficulty of communicating meaningfully with the regime. Ever since the disaster, Ban ki-Moon had been trying to speak on the phone to the head of state, Senior General Tan Shwe, while I tried the same with the relevant ministers. There was no response whatsoever. We were told that the senior members of the regime did not take phone calls from overseas because there was no tradition of responding off the cuff to policy questions. We therefore had to rely on the Myanmar ambassador to the UN, who was well-meaning, but had no real clout, and on painfully slow exchanges of letters. Ban ki-Moon addressed increasingly urgent appeals to Tan Shwe to issue visas to UN and NGO personnel, and to allow free movement to humanitarian staff already there. The only response was a bland letter thanking the SG for his concern, assuring him that the government was tackling the problems, and repeating that donations of money and emergency goods from abroad would be welcome, while failing to address the critical issue of letting in experienced aid workers.

Although it did not, of course, say so openly, the regime was clearly terrified that if it allowed in foreigners at this time of weakness and political sensitivity, the country would be swamped by a wave of intelligence agents looking for secrets and stirring up sedition. For the same reasons it was even tougher about allowing in journalists. We had to convince the regime that such fears were unfounded: those needing visas were bona fide relief workers, not the CIA in disguise, and no one would blame the authorities just for the fact that they needed outside help, faced with such a huge catastrophe. Unfortunately, our efforts to do so were not helped by the growing and outspoken criticisms of the regime from key Western capitals, and by a rapidly rising drumbeat of suggestions that if the Myanmar government would not willingly allow in aid workers, international help should somehow be forced on them.

French foreign minister of the time, Bernard Kouchner, led this charge, saying that the doctrine of R2P meant that the international community had an obligation to intervene in Myanmar to ensure that aid reached the victims of the disaster. Chapter Thirteen looks at the wider advantages and drawbacks of R2P from a humanitarian point of view. But there were at least three reasons why it was neither applicable nor likely to be helpful in this case:

- The texts on R2P made clear that its application was restricted to conflict situations, not natural disasters, and to prevention of specific and defined war crimes such as genocide or ethnic cleansing.
- There was no chance of any R2P action being approved by the Security Council, as in principle it should be. Russia and China, among others, had no intention of allowing Nargis even to be discussed in the Security Council, let alone of voting for any kind of intervention. They had not long before jointly vetoed a draft Council resolution calling on the Myanmar government to stop political repression and human rights abuses.
- Even if the applicability and authorization hurdles could be got over, it was clear, as in the Sri Lanka case discussed in Chapter Four, that no country was actually willing to put its troops in harm's way.

The glib talk of forcing in aid also ignored the reality that this would have meant effectively declaring war on Myanmar. The regime would have resisted strongly any landings of aid by military forces, or attempts to create so-called safe havens or humanitarian corridors. Meanwhile, all talk of the use of force, far from convincing the regime that they should cooperate, simply tended to confirm their suspicion that the international community's insistence on getting in aid workers was a cover for intervention aimed at regime change, Iraqi-style. This suspicion was reinforced by the fact that the US and the French happened to have naval ships in the area, and were calling on the regime to allow them to dock in Myanmar ports in order to deliver aid. These were genuine and sincere offers, and could have helped a good deal. But it was all too easy for a paranoid and ignorant regime to add two and two and make seven.

None of this is to cast doubt on the sincerity of those whose frustration with Myanmar obstruction was boiling over, or to condone in any way the actions of the regime. But the reality was that there was not going to be any international military intervention, that it would have been catastrophic if there had been, not least for those we were most concerned to help, and that talking about it was not helping the essential task of convincing the regime to back down from their absurd insistence on no international aid workers. Our UN argument to the regime was that humanitarian aid had nothing to do with politics, and that they had nothing to fear from it. That argument could only be undermined by outside governments making highly political statements, however well meant.

One obvious issue was what ASSK herself thought. And since she was cut off from contact with the outside world there was, unfortunately, no way of finding out reliably. However, indirect indications suggested that she was *not* in favour of exploiting a natural disaster for political reasons, nor of using military resources to force in aid, and agreed with our diplomatic effort to persuade the regime to change course. She certainly did not allow her name to be attached to those pushing for more radical courses of action.

There were real fears at the time that unless we could get aid in quickly, we would face a secondary disaster potentially as devastating as the initial cyclone, in the shape of a major outbreak of water-borne diseases hitting a weakened population lacking food, clean water, and shelter. Large areas of the delta were flooded. Malaria was already endemic in the area. Malnutrition rates were high. And measles, cholera, and dysentery outbreaks were a strong possibility if health care could not be provided quickly, including vaccination campaigns for the most vulnerable, particularly children.

I was conscious in all this of the risk of exaggeration of the dangers. This is a besetting sin of humanitarian organizations, albeit one committed with the best of intentions. Those concerned want to ring the alarm bells loudly to draw the attention of a jaded media. They are desperate to alert governments and publics all too prone to donor fatigue to the real suffering out there, and convince them to respond with appropriate generosity. In an emergency, the implicit argument goes, a little hyperbole is surely forgivable and even necessary, if that's what it takes to get a headline and jolt people out of their complacency?

I understood these arguments, but did not share them. My view was that every time humanitarians exaggerated for effect, and were caught doing so, they were damaging their overall credibility. Over time, this had negative effects on attempts to raise money and persuade governments and publics to take us seriously. Yes, we had to appeal to hearts as well as heads, which meant giving the drama a human face. But unnecessary alarmism, and too much shroud-waving, was ultimately counterproductive. At a slightly later stage in this crisis, one large and well-respected international NGO claimed that if they were not allowed in to the affected area in the next couple of days, 30,000 children would die the following week. There was no evidence to back this up. Indeed, it was implausible in the extreme, however worrying the situation. Making such a claim simply risked challenging our seriousness and our efforts to make an impact on the government.

Opening up

How then were we to make progress? We had some things on our side. Even an isolated and paranoid regime could be susceptible to reasonable outside arguments, properly applied. Those close to the situation on the ground were already aware that they really could not deal with a catastrophe of this magnitude without international assistance. The government gradually began to give way. Their first step was to say, nine days after the disaster, that their immediate Asian neighbours could send aid workers to help – Bangladesh, China, India, and Thailand. This first crack in the wall was quickly followed by the announcement that they were allowing ASEAN to send in an 'Emergency Rapid Assessment Team'. The idea was that while regime relations with their neighbours, particularly Thailand, were not always good – ASEAN was regarded with suspicion in Myanmar, though usually seen by the West as too soft on the regime – individuals from these countries were not likely to be the spies and provocateurs they feared. They were also much less likely to be critical of what they saw, or inclined to run to the Western media with nasty stories.

Unfortunately, while neighbours could provide useful resources such as medical teams, this half-opening was not the solution. Neither ASEAN itself nor ASEAN countries could put much real expertise in the field. Regional generosity also had its limits since the countries concerned faced regular disasters of their own. But we clearly needed to exploit this move. Luckily, we found willing partners in ASEAN, particularly Secretary-General Surin Pitsuan. He was well aware of the organization's lack of humanitarian capacity, but was keen to help open up the situation. We were quickly able to agree that ASEAN's rapid-assessment team should consist of individuals with international experience whom we knew and trusted. This early partnership was to lead to extremely effective UN–ASEAN collaboration as the crisis progressed.

Meanwhile, however, this glacial movement was not placating the regime's external critics. Fears about disease and other risks continued to grow. They were fed by wild stories about the dangers posed by the many unburied and decomposing bodies, despite guidance from the World Health Organization that while bodies could certainly be a threat in water sources, they were not otherwise a significant source of disease in themselves. The clamour for more radical action therefore continued to grow, together with accusations that the UN was being too soft and letting the regime off the hook.

Our efforts to convince the government to move faster were helped by the local credibility of the acting UN resident and humanitarian coordinator, Dan Baker. Although, as an American, he was the wrong nationality from the regime's point of view, he had nevertheless been able to establish a degree of trust as a professional who was not trying to score points or take his problems to the media, but simply to solve problems. Gradually, our combined efforts to reassure the regime that accepting humanitarian workers from the UN and NGOs could be done in an entirely non-political way, without risk to the regime's stability and security, began to bear the first signs of fruit.

Nevertheless, the aid effort was still building up very slowly. Some local Myanmar staff from UN agencies and international

NGOs had managed to get into the delta, and were working heroically. But in most cases they simply did not have the experience or expertise to make the necessary difference. They were also rapidly becoming exhausted. Ban ki-Moon and I therefore decided on a more direct and high-level diplomatic effort, with a visit by me as soon as could be arranged, and a visit from him to follow immediately, if there was any prospect of success.

Potemkin lives

The government initially pleaded unavailability of key inter-locutors, in the classic fashion of authorities trying to avoid an inconvenient visitor, but firm pressure from the UN and Myanmar's neighbours led to a change of mind. Two weeks after Nargis, the way was finally cleared for me to go to Myanmar. We had also proposed to the government an aid-pledging conference in Yangon itself, to help focus international minds – and, of course, to help press the regime to start delivering.

I arrived in Yangon on 18 May, having visited Bangkok briefly on the way to concert tactics with ASEAN, and took a tour of the affected area the following day. There had been a row about this, with the government wanting to dictate where my helicopter should land, and the UN team on the spot insisting that we should be able to choose, since we had well-founded suspicions about government manipulation. The end result was a compromise, with agreement that I would go to a government-run camp, but that I would land elsewhere too.

The fly-over was revealing and worrying. In parts of the delta, including several major towns, the flooding was very serious, even two weeks after Nargis. Much physical destruction of buildings was also visible. Nevertheless, life looked as if it would be able to continue after a fashion once a decent aid effort could be mounted. But in other areas the tidal surge had swept the landscape clean of virtually all signs of human habitation. The foundations of houses showed where villages had been, but there were no buildings or villagers to be seen – only the occasional body showing up white in the mud or stuck in the remains of a tree. Splintered debris was piled up anywhere, including large boats upside down, miles from the watercourses they had previously plied. The reasons for the huge death toll were painfully clear.

The visit to the government camp was an even worse sham than we had feared. It was small and ridiculously neat. The people in it, while no doubt genuine victims of the disaster, looked bemused at suddenly finding themselves in capacious army tents with undisturbed piles of relief goods surrounding them, while army minders took a bunch of foreigners around. Their answers to our questions, when we were able to pose any, were bland in the extreme, and we could not shake off our minders enough to get at any underlying truths. We made very clear to our accompanying foreign ministry officers that we did not take kindly to this sort of Potemkin village farce.

Talks with government ministers followed, including those responsible for planning, health and social welfare. The discussions were painfully slow and formal, with endless official presentations of how much the government were doing, and no substantive response to the insistent questions about access we were posing. Local hands explained to us that this was the unavoidable Myanmar way of doing business. We would have to work our way up the chain, getting our messages across as best we could, and hope for real answers when we eventually got to the top. Only the ruling generals, and in particular Senior General Tan Shwe, would be able to break the deadlock. But there were, meanwhile at least, warm words, and even hints of likely progress from some interlocutors when we were able to speak more informally. Some junior officials went further, making clear that they regarded their own government's policy as wholly misguided, and that they were personally right behind my efforts.

The culmination of these meetings was an encounter with Prime Minister General Thein Sein, officially number five in the regime. It was yet another stiff occasion, where my demands were listened to politely, but no answers were given. Yet I thought I could detect that beneath the protocol, messages were beginning to sink in about the sheer wrong-headedness of the government's stand on outside aid workers, and about the need for them to separate humanitarian aid from political disputes, lest the whole issue become politicized beyond repair. The mood music seemed increasingly positive, though no explicit promises had been made. I therefore strongly encouraged Ban ki-Moon to come to Myanmar himself as soon as possible, to take our demands straight to the senior general in the new capital of Nay Pi Taw, some 250 miles north of Yangon.

We had, in the meantime, been working with ASEAN to develop a so-called tripartite mechanism to coordinate national and international aid efforts, and resolve problems in relief delivery. The three legs of the stool were the government, ASEAN, and the UN. The aim was to use the political cover of ASEAN to give ourselves direct access to the decision-makers in the government, once the principles of a genuine international operation had been accepted at the highest level. ASEAN were again more than happy to work together in this way. Apart from their lack of humanitarian capacity, they were anxious to defuse the gathering international political storm over Myanmar. They were uncomfortably stuck in the middle, getting much of the blame, while having relatively little leverage.

I told Ban ki-Moon that he would have a good chance of

success if he could establish a constructive working relationship with the senior general, and set out five immediate aims:

- agreement to access for accredited international aid organizations and aid workers, including fast-track visa procedures
- agreement to improved logistics in the affected areas, including use of World Food Programme helicopters
- agreement to the tripartite mechanism, with ASEAN as the symbol of a relationship of greater trust between the international aid community and the government
- acceptance from the government that relief operations would have to continue for many months, and run in parallel with recovery efforts (the government had been repeating, absurdly, that the emergency relief phase was over, when, in fact, it had hardly started)
- agreement to do everything to make the Yangon pledging conference turn out positively, including explicit statements about improvements on the above lines.

Ban ki-Moon's visit was, in the event, a considerable success, including for him personally. He made a similar helicopter tour to mine, and had to endure the same excruciating visit to the show camp. This was despite our strong advice to the government that this would be a serious mistake, not least since the press travelling with him would see through it straight away, as they did. He also had to work his way up through the ministers to Prime Minister Thein Sein, as I had done. But he was able to strike up an informal and positive relationship with the prime minister over dinner, and to use that channel to make sure that the senior general would be in no doubt of what was expected of him the following day in the new capital.

Nay Pi Taw

The visit to Nay Pi Taw was surreal. The capital had been moved there from Yangon a couple of years before, with ministers and civil servants given only two days' notice before having to shift their operations lock, stock, and barrel. It had been under construction for years, but was still only a quarter complete. It sprawled across a huge area, literally in the middle of nowhere, in order to be nearer the geographical centre of the country.

From the new but empty airport, our party of officials and journalists was taken down a deserted eight-lane highway to a new hotel for refreshment. The hotel had no guests, despite its lavish accoutrements. The highway was deserted not for security reasons, because of our VIP delegation, but because there was hardly anyone else to use it, apart from the odd bullock cart belonging to a local farmer. It was immaculate, with workers toiling away at the side of the road to trim the grass by hand. The occasional (unnecessary) roundabouts were decorated with huge murals and other examples of dictator kitsch. We were told that there were no fewer than six golf courses in Nay Pi Taw, golf being a habit the country's military rulers had picked up from the British. But there was little sign of ordinary facilities or shops, beyond the flats for the civil servants to live in. The skyline was dominated by the outlines of grandiose, classical-style buildings being erected by a workforce mainly composed of Indians. The gargantuan Greek temple of the planned parliament building seemed particularly incongruous for a country without a functioning parliament at the time.

This was an obscene monument to dictatorial whim. It was not needed, had no heart or soul, and was costing a fortune in a country where most people were living in poverty. Nay Pi Taw would have seemed an extravagance at the best of times, but appeared ludicrously out of place when so many people were suffering so much only a couple of hundred miles south.

The sense of unreality was reinforced when we set off to see Senior General Tan Shwe. His lavish mansion at the other end of the city was approached by another huge and deserted highway, well away from all other signs of human habitation. How could someone living here have any real idea of what was going on in his own country, never mind the rest of the world? We were told he watched satellite TV, and therefore was not only subject to his own media propaganda. He had even ventured out briefly a couple of days before to see for himself some of the devastation in the delta. But he can only have had the most limited grasp of the ghastly reality, given that he had spent most of his time in the Potemkin camp we had already visited.

The meeting was long and not easy, dominated by the senior general's seemingly endless opening statement, involving detailed accounts of how much the government was doing, and lengthy complaints about the hostility of the international community. Tan Shwe was accompanied by the other high-ranking military figures of the regime, some of whom were reputed to be even harder-line than he was. They also made clear their absolute rejection of any political interference, and of the use of any Western military assets in the aid operation. Ban ki-Moon stuck doggedly to his script in response and, without lecturing, pressed hard for the agreements we needed to allow international aid workers in and to improve the logistical capability on the ground. It was uncomfortable and tense, but in the end, his persistence had its reward. After ninety sticky minutes, Tan Shwe finally gave the basic assurances we sought. We could leave with the mission apparently accomplished, a message quickly conveyed to the accompanying media circus.

This was good news indeed. But we were also well aware that

the proof of the pudding would be in the eating. How quickly would the decisions of the senior general filter down to the rest of the bureaucracy, and how clear would the instructions be? The first objective, on return from Nay Pi Taw, was therefore to persuade Prime Minister Tein Shein that he not only had to attend the pledging conference himself a couple of days later in Yangon, but also had to repeat in public the senior general's promises – and, if possible, to do so wearing civilian clothes, not military uniform. That would send the right signal to the Western and other ministers who were by then planning to attend in force.

I was left in Yangon to try to ensure this happened while the secretary-general went on a lightning visit to the site of the devastating Sichuan earthquake in China, which had struck a few days earlier. The Chinese had made clear that they would, as usual, deal with the relief operation themselves. But unlike the Myanmar regime they at least had the capacity and experience to do so.

The pledging conference was, in the end, a significant success, not so much for the new money raised, since most donors remained suspicious, but for the symbolism of the increasing openness. Fifty-one countries were represented, many at ministerial level, and were able to hear for themselves the reassurances of willingness to accept outside help, given by the prime minister in his opening address, and delivered, as requested, in his smart civilian suit. His words were not quite those we had wanted – we had fed in to his office exactly what we thought he should say to be effective – but they were close enough to convince those listening that attitudes at the top were indeed changing, and the aid operation was likely to be worth supporting.

The focus was now, therefore, on rapid implementation. Logistics were already beginning to improve. The Thais had offered a large former airbase at Don Muang as a staging post to the crowded and badly organized airport in Yangon. Relief flights had begun to arrive at the much-increased rate of ten to fifteen per day, though this was far from enough. The World Food Programme had government agreement to operate ten helicopters in the delta, which was set to transform delivery capability to the remote areas where the needs were greatest.

Local v. international

One of the continuing frustrations was the sheer difficulty of finding out what aid had already been delivered and where. Good information is always an issue in a major disaster. Often in my time in New York, harassed by a press pack in full cry, my colleagues and I would tear out our hair at the absence of reliable real-time facts. In the Myanmar case, this was compounded by the lack of access to the delta, and by the reluctance of the government to tell us exactly what they were doing themselves and where. This led to an immediate assumption on the part of the media and some Western governments that the local effort was small, useless, and misdirected.

The reality was more complex, and an interesting lesson in the complementarity of national and international assistance. There were several elements to national efforts. First, there was the official aid effort led by the army. The soldiers were efficient in classic military ways, dividing up the affected area into sectors and assigning a commander and troops to each. But they had little or no idea of what they were doing in the provision of effective relief. They tended to assume that once they had rescued those who needed to be rescued and put them somewhere safer, that was the end of the emergency phase. Reconstruction ought then to start immediately. Their rigid military background tended to show through in everything they did. For example, their idea of rebuilding a village at a later stage was to reproduce a barracks in all its impersonal structure and regularity. They were also, with good reason, not trusted by the locals, and programmed to pretend that all was fine and well organized when it was clearly not. None of this means they did not do some useful work. But it did not go very far or very deep.

Second and more effective was what the local inhabitants around the affected areas were doing themselves. As always, they were the first responders, providing basics of food, water, and shelter to neighbours, and taking in families or individual survivors themselves when there was no alternative. The local Buddhist monasteries were an important focal point, acting as collection and distribution points for supplies. In contrast to the army, they were trusted by the locals. The monks did a lot of great work.

Burmese people from outside the delta also gave generously and informally, particularly when it became clear that the regime were not responding as they should. Many simply drove to the affected areas with supplies or money and gave it out as best they could. This was disorganized, and tended not to reach those most in need, who were a long way from the road system. But it was a contribution of a kind. The Myanmar Red Cross also did sterling work, especially after they were boosted by help from outside societies like the British Red Cross.

An interesting innovation in Myanmar was the mobilization by the government of major local construction and other companies, who had been asked to help in specific areas. Many in the aid community were sceptical. They thought the companies were just in it to make money for themselves, or that it was all for show, since the companies were all stooges of the government. There may have been some truth in this, but the company I saw working in one area a few weeks after the disaster seemed to be doing a genuinely committed job: mobilizing transport, bringing in goods, and starting on reconstruction tasks such as reroofing houses.

The combination of all these local efforts was significant, even if we could not measure its impact with any degree of confidence, and its distribution was largely random. Even once the international agencies were able to operate with some degree of normality, the local efforts remained important. This is usually the case in most emergencies. Humanitarians need to avoid suggesting, as we do too often, that only international aid really counts.

Does this mean that all the fuss about getting in international aid workers was unnecessary, as some in Myanmar regularly tried to suggest? My clear answer is no. Only an agency like WFP could provide the logistic skills and assets to mobilize food for 1.5 million people for six months. Only specialized UN agencies and NGOs could organize and carry through with the necessary speed the immunization campaigns (for example against measles) without which the population would have been far more vulnerable to disease. Only the medical agencies could fill in the huge gaps of elementary care left by the destruction of most health facilities in the worst affected areas. Only international specialists could import, operate, and maintain the mobile water treatment plants which were a lifeline for hundreds of thousands of people whose wells were flooded or polluted by bodies and debris. Only international agricultural experts could analyse the effects of salt-water pollution on the fields, recommend the right solutions to avoid long-term damage, and bring in salt-resistant varieties to help farmers get going again. International agencies could also help ensure that there were no political distortions in aid, which the government were always tempted to introduce.

Making it happen

For the next few months we closely monitored the fulfilment of the senior general's promises. I reported regularly to Ban ki-Moon, to the donors, and to the media. Implementation was far from perfect, and often delayed. We had to intervene frequently to keep things like visas moving. The tripartite mechanism with ASEAN proved absolutely essential in troubleshooting. But the bottom line was that the government did, ultimately, allow what they had promised to allow. We were gradually able to operate with a decent complement of international experts on the ground in the delta. The aid operation in the end came reasonably close to what we would normally expect to provide for similar disasters. There was no secondary death toll of any significance.

If that makes it sound easy, it was not. Some in the international press seemed to want to prove that we had been wrong to negotiate in the first place, and were now being taken for a ride by an indifferent and manipulative regime. The government kept trying to say that the emergency was over, and that they needed to revert to 'normal' procedures. Some visas were refused or delayed on incomprehensible grounds. The government tried to say almost every week that WFP no longer needed to use their helicopters. There were press accusations of all kinds; for example, that the government were manipulating the exchange rates for international aid efforts and skimming off massive profits (not quite so, but we were only able to resolve the actual problem with the government after some tough discussion). The government were initially reluctant to cooperate with a full assessment of how far the relief effort had reached all the areas and people affected. And so on.

A major problem throughout was donor scepticism. Their political antipathy to the regime meant many were less generous than they might have been otherwise. By the time a revised appeal for $482 million was launched in July 2008, the initial appeal for less than $200 million was still only about two thirds funded. This was less than we would normally expect for the first stage of a major emergency of this kind and far from enough in these circumstances, and the funding pipeline had all but dried up. Many donors were insistent that their money should not be used to bolster the regime in any way. This was not so much a problem for emergency relief aid, since it went straight to UN agencies and NGOs, and thence to those in need. But reconstruction, inevitably, had to be managed in close coordination with the government. Reconstruction aid could arguably free up government resources for use elsewhere, including repression of the population. This was where the main Western donors drew the line, just as most had refused to fund development aid before Nargis.

We did not want to undermine Western policy. At the same time, unless there was a decent reconstruction effort, many of the people affected would be left without long-term shelter or livelihoods. Farming and fishing in the delta were essential both for the local people and for Myanmar's overall food security. With the tacit agreement of Western representatives in the country, we therefore fudged the always rather artificial line between relief and reconstruction aid by emphasizing the requirements of so-called early recovery in critical areas like agriculture, shelter, rural infrastructure, water/sanitation, and health. We still struggled to attract enough funding, but at least this enabled the foundations of recovery to be laid and a reasonable aid effort to continue for at least a year after the disaster.

The other focus was how to prevent a recurrence of the disaster. Myanmar had been almost completely unprepared for Nargis. Unlike in Bangladesh, there was no early warning system, no shelters and no standing instructions to the population about what to do in the event of an emergency. Natural barriers such as mangrove swamps on the coast had been removed to make way for profitable rice growing and shrimp farming. This might have been a rational calculation in the absence of previous big cyclones in Myanmar, though it was more likely the product of poor governance. In any case, such a casual approach was obviously no longer good enough, particularly as climate change was likely to mean more Nargis-style disasters in the future.

Building back better was, therefore, clearly a major priority, as well as improving Myanmar's weather forecasting and early-warning capacity. Resources needed to be allocated accordingly.

This being Myanmar, nothing was straightforward. Much effort was required to deflect the government from costly white elephants like building protective walls along the most vulnerable parts of the coast – an approach which had been rightly rejected in Bangladesh many years before. I fear that in practice little if anything else has so far been done, as is sadly too often the case for disaster risk-reduction measures. Myanmar remains highly vulnerable to another major disaster.

I returned in late July to see how the aid effort was moving forward. While the picture was mixed, overall the situation had improved significantly. Towns were beginning to buzz with activity again. Houses were being repaired. School was resuming, even if under canvas in many places. Ploughing for the next harvest was under way across much of the delta, despite fears of the effects of the salt water. Several hundred international aid workers were working in the area. Cooperation with the government, with the help of ASEAN, was at reasonable levels. My conclusion was that the agreement we had negotiated in May had, in essence, worked, however imperfectly.

Political change

In the months that followed, the situation continued to improve steadily. But the emphasis by this time was shifting back to politics and the need to try to find a better way forward for the people. One hope was that the positive humanitarian aid experience might have created a little more trust and readiness to open up on the Myanmar side. A fresh attempt at dialogue was, therefore, needed.

The early signs were not promising. Ibrahim Gambari resumed his visits, but to no apparent effect. Ban ki-Moon eventually decided to visit again himself in July 2009, despite the fact that he had not received the assurances he had sought in advance (for example, on political prisoners and the removal of ASSK from house arrest). I and others were doubtful whether he should go ahead in such circumstances. But he was determined to try and convinced he had managed to establish a working relationship of some confidence with the Myanmar senior leadership.

The visit was fruitless in the short term: he was unable to see ASSK, no political prisoners were released, and no worthwhile assurances about the future were received. He got some credit for trying, but rather more criticism from the usual quarters, in Western capitals and the international press, for naivety. However, his persistence began to be rewarded, as signs of a thaw in the regime's attitude to reform emerged. Some political prisoners were released. ASSK herself was let out in November 2010, just after the elections in which she and her party had refused to take part, won overwhelmingly by the newly created party of the former military regime. And when former prime minister Thein Sein was appointed head of the newly elected government, the pace of change began to accelerate dramatically, to almost universal surprise in the outside world – and much initial scepticism. More political prisoners were released, freedom of expression increased, economic reform started, a political dialogue between Thein Sein and ASSK began, and a real sense of openness and readiness to change could be felt. ASSK and the National League for Democracy decided in early 2012 to contest by-elections in order to be able to take part in parliamentary discussion, and won them triumphantly.

As I write, the reform process is continuing to pick up speed and even the greatest sceptics are beginning to accept that something real and different is happening. Thein Sein seems to have taken the wise view that the country could not go on as it was. Whether he has unleashed forces and processes he did not anticipate and will struggle to control, as Gorbachev did in Russia, remains to be seen. But for the moment Myanmar seems to be changing significantly for the better, which is profoundly to be welcomed. And I think there is reason to believe that the experience of Nargis played some part in this, through the genuine help the international community was able to provide without political strings, and the dialogue that Ban ki-Moon opened up at the time with the future leader, as a fellow Asian concerned to assist and to understand, rather than to lecture.

Conclusions

Why was the regime so insistent at the beginning on not allowing in international relief workers? One driving force was certainly fear of infiltration, and strong suspicion of anything foreign, especially anything with a Western label. But there were other powerful elements too: a deep instinct to retain control of everything; a top-down and bureaucratic structure, with those making the decisions likely to be the most cut off from on-the-ground realities; a heavy dose of national pride – 'We can do this ourselves' – plus a long-standing Potemkin culture; lack of knowledge and experience of disasters on the scale of Nargis, and unwillingness to accept at the beginning that it really could be as serious as we and others were suggesting; and concern that their long-planned political/referendum process would somehow be derailed.

Were we right to take the approach we did, by trying to get beyond the chorus of condemnation and calls for punishment of the regime? As always, it was a tricky judgment call. The argument that such regimes only listen to the language of threats and pressure, take dialogue as a sign of weakness, and respond accordingly, was put forward with great insistence by many pundits. But I was convinced at the time that we had to go a different way, and do everything we possibly could to persuade the government to see reason. This was both because we had no real choice if we actually wanted to help effectively – it was their country and they controlled what we could actually do on the ground – and because I believed that even the most apparently closed regimes could respond to reason in certain circumstances, if they were engaged and approached with a degree of respect. The alternative of trying to bludgeon them into submission was even less likely to work when they had the backing of big local powers like China and India, offering them political support and protection. But if these powers could also be brought to see the advantages of a different approach by the government, and apply pressure in their own subtle ways, we had a decent chance of moving forward.

The dramatic political opening from 2010 onwards also suggests that the wider logic of only external pressure and sanctions being able to bring about change is flawed or, at best, not universally applicable. Western policy too often seems to lack nuance and understanding of local dynamics. In Myanmar it had for many years failed to achieve anything significant, as even the Americans had privately begun to recognize. I was struck on my own visits by the fact that the regime, while certainly brutal, paranoid and isolated, was neither as monolithic, nor as efficient in its repression, as I had expected. The chances of progress may always have been there somewhere, behind the oppression, if the right notes could have been struck, and the right openings found at the right moments, rather than just the same old lecturing and sanctions.

What is vital now is to respond in the right way to the new opening. Genuine progress should be welcomed and rewarded, without assuming that everything is now all sweetness and light. Practical measures to liberalize and democratize should be recognized for what they are, but the implementation monitored and problems not glossed over where they occur. Western sanctions should be suspended, but not necessarily removed, until the reform process is judged effectively irreversible. ASSK should continue to be honoured for her courage and consistent commitment to democracy, but not treated as the leader of the country, which she is not, or at least not yet. Engagement with the actual government to encourage them is crucial. Fortunately, the main Western countries do seem to be going down this path. Optimism in this case really does seem to be justified for now. Long may it last.

occupied Palestinian territory

LEBANON

Lake Tiberias

ISRAEL

JORDAN

EGYPT

Mediterranean Sea

Gaza City

Gaza

Khan Yunis

ISRAEL

EGYPT

Tulkarm
Nablus

West Bank

Ramallah
Jericho

Jerusalem
Bethlehem

Hebron

Dead Sea

--- Armistice Demarcation Line
--- Boundary of former Palestine Mandate

1 5 km

2 20 km

OCHA

Map Sources: Europa Technologies, OCHA, UNCS. Map created in June 2012.

CHAPTER EIGHT

Gaza: collective punishment, conflict and controversy

There is no more politicized place in which to support humanitarian causes and deliver humanitarian aid than the occupied Palestinian territories of the West Bank and Gaza, oPt in the UN jargon. Every move is scrutinized for evidence of political partiality or intent. As elsewhere, I faced questions of balance between denouncing unacceptable behaviour and continuing to deal with those responsible for it; of how far we should deal with those regarded as terrorists by much of the Western world; of how allegations of war crimes should best be investigated; and of the degree to which humanitarian solutions could play any role in political progress. But the degree of sensitivity was always in a league of its own.

What crisis?

The issues start from the basic question of whether there is even a serious humanitarian problem to deal with. The Israelis maintain that, whatever the problems in the territories, there is no humanitarian crisis in either, at least not one comparable to crises elsewhere, in which large numbers of people risk dying of starvation or disease. Humanitarian organizations working in the territories therefore must be doing so mostly for political reasons, as part of what the Israelis see as the institutional bias of much of the international community in favour of the Palestinians. For their part, the Palestinians and their supporters claim that the Israeli occupation and policies towards the Palestinians in the territories are not only profoundly unjust but also produce dire humanitarian consequences: poverty, deprivation, and abuse of basic rights. They believe that these are consistently played down by parts of the international community.

The original establishment of Israel in 1948 certainly threw up a major humanitarian problem in the shape of the millions of Palestinian refugees who fled or were effectively expelled. They have been looked after since, in the West Bank and Gaza, as well as in Lebanon, Jordan, Syria, Egypt, and elsewhere, by the specially created UN Relief and Works Agency (UNRWA). There are many controversies about these refugees – for example, whether they have been deliberately encouraged for political reasons to stay in camps rather than resettling elsewhere, and misled about their real chances of ever returning to their homes, in order to keep their suffering in front of the international community. Whatever the truth of this, they are a continuing reality whose existence cannot be ignored and whose fate will not be settled until there is a lasting peace. But needs also exist among communities other than the refugees; for example, the Bedouins of the West Bank, effectively prevented from using much of their lands by the ever-expanding Israeli settlements, and those Palestinians who never left their homes in the occupied territories but face increasing problems from Israeli activities.

Gaza has always been the biggest humanitarian issue, and one of the worst running sores of the conflict: a narrow strip of land running down the coast to Egypt with a young and growing population of over 1.5 million, more than two thirds of whom are officially designated refugees, living in crowded and sordid camps. The withdrawal of the Israelis from Gaza in 2005 was warmly welcomed at the beginning, but the mood soon soured on all sides. The Palestinians deliberately trashed any trace of the occupation. Some took an increasingly aggressive attitude towards Israel. Israel left no troops in Gaza, but retained strict control of its borders, and even – indirectly – the frontier with Egypt.

Hamas takeover

Political ferment in Gaza came to a head in 2006, when Hamas won the Palestinian elections in both territories, taking 56 per cent of the seats. A national government was set up, led by Hamas, but with the participation of Fatah, the original Palestinian group behind the PLO. However, it was not recognized by most Western governments. They had insisted on the election, but were then, unforgivably, unwilling to accept the result. They called on Hamas to renounce violence and recognize Israel's right to exist before there could be any dealings with them. Funding for the Palestinian Authority was effectively cut off. Hamas was also not popular with most Arab governments, worried about their links with Iran and with the Muslim Brotherhood.

Relations between Fatah and Hamas, never good, deteriorated sharply. Open fighting broke out in early 2007. By June, Hamas was fully in control of Gaza. Fatah had effectively been expelled from the territory, and severely curtailed any Hamas presence in the West Bank in turn. Each side treated the other with great brutality. This was the signal for the Israelis to impose even stricter controls on Gaza.

While often described as a blockade, Israeli action rarely, in practice, amounts to a full embargo. Rather, the Israelis usually allow in the minimum of basic goods to keep the population alive and services just about running. Apart from fuel oil and diesel, supplied through a pipeline whose tap is firmly under Israeli control, all goods have to be brought in by truck, through designated crossing points. This involves the most laborious imaginable method of trans-shipment by hand from Israeli to Palestinian trucks, all under close Israeli military supervision, during limited weekday hours. While there was a range of crossing points originally, these were gradually closed, until only the ill-equipped and physically limited crossing at a place called Kerem Shalom remained open.

Increasingly, the situation became one of more or less open war between Israel and Hamas, as well as other even more extreme factions in Gaza, particularly Islamic Jihad. These groups were firing a regular stream of crude rockets from Gaza into southern Israel, while the Israelis retaliated with air strikes and occasional ground incursions. Hamas blamed Israel for the privations of the population, while Israel, more and more, regarded not only Hamas, but the whole of Gaza, as a hotbed of terrorists bent on Israel's destruction, and closely linked to the hated regime in Iran. The Israeli government declared Gaza a hostile entity in September 2007.

Living conditions in Gaza deteriorated further as the restrictions bit. Food became scarcer and more expensive, malnutrition grew, and health indicators worsened, especially for children, who made up more than half of Gaza's population. Dependency on humanitarian supplies from UNRWA, for the refugees, and the World Food Programme (WFP), for the rest of the population, increased steadily as jobs and incomes disappeared. The power was off much of the time. Lack of maintenance and electricity meant that the sewage system, poor and patched up at the best of times, collapsed further. Millions of litres of raw sewage were released into the sea every day. Most agricultural and industrial activity ground to a halt for lack of fuel, materials, and spare parts. Any possibility of exporting the results had in any case disappeared.

Repeated attempts by humanitarian organizations to clarify exactly what was and was not allowed by the Israelis got nowhere. Essentially, everything was banned except what was allowed; there was no definitive list of what that was; and the criteria used in decision-making seemed arbitrary and unpredictable. Often, there seemed to be a bias in favour of local Israeli commercial suppliers of food at the expense of others, including humanitarian agencies.

Israeli restrictions were, in fact, only partly effective because of smuggling through a maze of tunnels under the Gaza–Egypt border. New tunnels were being dug constantly, despite the dangers from collapses and regular Israeli raids and bombings. An amazing variety of goods could be brought in. Most things could therefore be bought on the Gaza black market. But this was only partly helpful for the income-starved population, since the prices were inevitably high. Moreover, the smuggling favoured criminal and extremist elements in the population, who depended on Hamas and supported them in return, and penalized legitimate business owners and moderate forces, who were natural Fatah supporters.

First visit

OCHA had had an office in Jerusalem for some years. Over time, it had become an authoritative source of information on the effect on ordinary Palestinians of Israeli policies in the occupied territories: settlements, house demolitions, obstacles to free movement, and the Barrier/Wall which the Israelis had begun to build in 2000 to seal off most of the West Bank from Israel, to prevent terrorist infiltration. A call at the OCHA office became an indispensable part of any high-level visit. Collecting and analysing this information was not a political act. The aim was rather to allow the international community to understand what was happening on a human level and to be correspondingly ready to contribute to the humanitarian efforts to mitigate these effects. But the Israeli authorities disliked what we were doing, viewed us with great suspicion, and were constantly threatening to close us down. Only the flow of senior international visitors and support from Western donors kept us in business.

I was urged from the start of my mandate to visit the oPt, but in the early days there always seemed to be more urgent demands. It was therefore February 2008 before I finally reached Gaza and the West Bank, as well as Israel. I had long followed the Israel–Palestine conflict as a diplomat, and was indeed in the early 1980s the first non-Arabist to become FCO desk officer for the Arab–Israel dispute. I was, therefore, well versed in the sensitivities and the deep-rooted clash of rights between Israelis and Palestinians. But I had not been there for some years and was shocked by what I saw on the ground.

In the West Bank, the visible reality of the steadily expanding settlements, commanding the hilltops with their bright newness virtually wherever you looked, contrasted depressingly with the dilapidated Palestinian villages beneath. Checkpoints, restrictions on movements of goods and people, blockages and closures of roads to the local Palestinians had created a two-tier system which some even compared to apartheid. The Wall or Barrier, in most places a bleak concrete wall 8 metres high, was a particularly sad sight, cutting off many Palestinians from their lands, and from services they had previously been able to access in Jerusalem. The Palestinian population in Jerusalem itself was under constant pressure from expanding settlements and other measures seemingly designed to squeeze them out over time. In Hebron, I was struck by how the presence of a group of settlers in the middle of the town, protected by Israeli soldiers, had divided the city, severely affected the lives of its citizens, and created constant tension and threat of violence.

Israel had significant and continuing security concerns. Measures to stop terrorists infiltrating had been largely successful, but they seemed to go well beyond that aim. The cumulative effect on the Palestinian population, politically, socially, and economically, was dramatic and deeply counterproductive. More fundamentally, it was hard to see how the Israelis could ever give up the physical positions they were busy creating, particularly the settlements, or how the territory of the West Bank, carved up as it was, could ever be the planned core of a viable Palestinian state.

Gaza was worse. Getting in was difficult enough. The checks seemed specially designed to humiliate even the few foreigners trying to visit, let alone the rare Palestinians allowed to cross. The first view once in was one of utter desolation: all buildings near the border had been razed to the ground for security reasons. It also became clear that the eight months of severe restrictions had already had a profound effect, coming as they did on top of years of isolation and decline. Only about 10 per cent of the goods which had been previously imported into Gaza were now getting through the crossing points. The people of Gaza were effectively prisoners. Only a few urgent medical cases were allowed out, and even these were often delayed, sometimes with fatal consequences. Palestinians from the West Bank were also not allowed in, meaning the two territories were increasingly going their separate ways.

I was unable to talk directly to senior members of Hamas myself since the UN had decided, most unwisely in my view, to continue to adhere to the 2006 ban on such contacts, agreed by the so-called Quartet of the US, EU, Russia and the UN, until

Hamas met certain political conditions. These conditions were not unreasonable in themselves, but the political reality was that Hamas were simply not going to sign up to them in the absence of wider progress. The ban should not have excluded humanitarian dialogue, but the sensitivities were considered too great even for that. I was, however, able to meet a wide range of representatives of civil society. They were universally despairing about the consequences of the restrictions, not least in terms of strengthening Hamas's grip on the territory and discouraging moderates, and strongly urged me to bring about a change in international as well as Israeli attitudes.

In Israel, I visited the southern town of Sderot, the main target of the rockets from Gaza. Over 4000 had fallen since 2004. The people there were clearly traumatized, especially the children, by random attacks which had no military objective and were bound to kill and injure civilians above all. Luckily, the home-made rockets at that stage were still so crude – not much more than flying metal pipes with rudimentary fins – that the casualties and damage were much more limited than they could have been. But their sophistication and range were increasing steadily, as new materials and supplies reached Gaza through the smuggling tunnels.

The rockets were the main reason given by the Israelis for the restrictions, and for the constant raids and air attacks. They wanted to make sure that the legal crossing points were not used for supplies which could enhance the military capability of Hamas and Islamic Jihad. Suspect items went well beyond weapons to items like metal pipes and cement which could have dual uses. But there were other motives too. An Israeli soldier, Corporal Gilad Shalit, had been captured by Hamas on a cross-border raid in 2005, and was still being held somewhere in Gaza. The Israelis wanted to force Hamas to release him or at least to start negotiating seriously about this. They also said they wanted to convince the people of Gaza that their best interests lay in rejecting Hamas, and turning to the path of moderation and dialogue.

These were plausible aims. But it was highly questionable whether the tactics were likely to work. Many Gazans might well be inclined to blame Hamas and their intransigent pursuit of rocket attacks for their plight. But they were bound to blame Israel more – and indeed Fatah too, since some in Fatah, whatever they said publicly or felt emotionally, were in certain ways complicit with the Israelis in trying to weaken Hamas. Even on the purely security side, the proliferation of smuggling tunnels, over which the Israelis had little control despite the bombing raids, meant that arms and supplies to strengthen Hamas and other arsenals could enter relatively easily, with no checks whatsoever. Moreover, while the Israelis could have tried to demonstrate, through favourable treatment of the West Bankers, that moderation and dropping Hamas would have clear material rewards, that was not what they were doing in practice – the West Bank too continued to be tightly controlled, with economic activity struggling as a result.

All in all, Israeli tactics did not seem to outside observers like myself to be well thought through or effective. They were certainly increasing alienation, bitterness, and despair in Gaza, which would do nothing to improve the prospects of longer-term peace. But I and others were convinced that they were wrong in principle too. The import restrictions amounted to collective punishment of the population for the actions of their leaders, which is forbidden under international law. In UN eyes, Israel also remained the occupying power in legal terms, since it continued to control access to the territory, despite its withdrawal, and therefore had a particular responsibility for the welfare of the population.

During my visit, I was correspondingly critical to the Israelis in private about their policies towards Gaza and their effects on the population, as well as on the political situation inside Gaza. I urged them to find ways to allow in more humanitarian and commercial goods, without jeopardizing their security. I asked in particular that the supplies needed for various UN humanitarian and development projects, effectively frozen since the Hamas takeover, be allowed in, and that restrictions on humanitarians moving in and out of Gaza be lifted.

The Israelis cold-shouldered me at senior level, and gave little or no ground in response to my requests. However, my emphasis on practical measures, and careful balance in what I said and did publicly, did mean that we were just about able to maintain a working relationship. In public, while I set out my reasons for disagreeing with Israel's policies, I also made clear that the rocket attacks from Gaza amounted to terrorism, had no justification, and should stop immediately; and that the only result of them was misery for the Palestinians in Gaza, for whose welfare Hamas were supposed to be responsible.

My overall conclusion, reported to the Security Council on my return to New York, was that there was an almost complete disconnect between what was happening on the ground and the hopes and aims of the peace talks still going on at that stage. Unless the practical situation changed rapidly and radically, I was convinced that those talks could go nowhere, however well-intentioned some of the participants might be. Meanwhile, Gaza had become a giant open-air prison and a tinder box waiting for the right spark to explode.

The build-up to war

A six-month ceasefire negotiated between the parties in June 2008 somehow held for a while. A respite suited Hamas, to consolidate their power and increase their weapons holdings, while they also hoped international pressure would persuade Israel to lift the restrictions. For its part, Israel hoped the pressure of the siege would undermine Hamas and that the truce would help get Gilad Shalit back. German-mediated negotiations were under way, involving the swap of hundreds of Palestinian prisoners for him. But it became clear as the six months rolled on that neither side was gaining what they had hoped. As the ceasefire began to break down, Israeli pre-emptive operations intensified, but Hamas still steadily increased the rockets. A major Israeli response looked inevitable once the ceasefire expired on 19 December.

Operation Cast Lead

When it duly arrived on 27 December, the scale and intensity of the Israeli response – which would come to be known in Israel as Operation Cast Lead – were greater than anyone outside had imagined. The Israeli air force, backed up by naval bombardment, attacked simultaneously a large number of Hamas-controlled installations: command centres, bases, training camps, warehouses, tunnels, and police stations. In the succeeding days it extended bombing and shelling to the homes of Hamas activists and parliamentarians, and indeed all institutions which could be said to be under the control of Hamas, which meant virtually everything. In the days before the ground operation was launched on 3 January, reports suggested that around 430 people had already been killed and 2200 injured.

The ground operation itself involved Israeli forces entering Gaza from three separate directions, with around 10,000 troops in the initial phase. The aim was to go into the areas from which rockets had been fired, while surrounding, though not necessarily entering, the main population centres. Meanwhile, targets throughout Gaza continued to be bombed, including public infrastructure, businesses, and even structures such as mosques. The power was cut for the vast majority of the population, and water supplies became even more erratic. Raw sewage flowed in the streets. Some basic supplies did continue to enter via Israel, presumably to show that the aim was not to provoke a humanitarian crisis – indeed, ironically, the rate of trucks delivering supplies was greater than before the military operation, though still well below the needs of the population.

Despite a unanimous Security Council Resolution (SCR 1860) on 8 January, calling for an immediate cessation of hostilities, and immediate access for humanitarian goods and workers, Cast Lead continued intensively until 18 January. With the help of Egyptian mediation, a ceasefire was then declared by Israel, followed by Hamas a day later. Israeli forces withdrew from Gaza on 21 January. By that time, huge damage had been done to Gaza's infrastructure and basic services, as well as to residential homes – some 21,000 had reportedly been destroyed or badly damaged, and over 50,000 people displaced. According to the Palestinian Ministry of Health, 1326 Palestinians had been killed altogether, including 450 children and 110 women, and 5450 were injured. No Israeli soldiers died as a direct result of the operation, but three Israeli civilians were killed and 182 injured by rockets.

In practice, there had been relatively little direct fighting between Hamas and Israeli forces. Hamas were well aware that they were no match for the Israelis. Apart from a few hit-and-run attacks, their aim was therefore to lie low, wait for the Israelis to withdraw, and then re-emerge to declare victory simply by virtue of survival. They hoped at the same time that their position would also be strengthened by international criticism of the Israeli operation.

Quite apart from Security Council debate, the UN was deeply involved in this crisis from the start because of the size of its presence in Gaza. On the humanitarian side we were deeply concerned about the ability of agencies such as UNRWA and WFP to carry on their operations, including in UNRWA's case the ability to use their health facilities and ambulances, on which most of the civilian population relied. But it went further than that. Many UN installations in Gaza were themselves hit by bombs or shells, including the OCHA office. This constantly raised the question of whether they were being targeted or whether at the very least the Israelis did not care if they were hit or not. The Israeli military authorities certainly had all the coordinates of the UN buildings.

For their part the Israelis, long suspicious of UNRWA and its claimed bias towards the Palestinians politically, alleged that their buildings, including schools, were being used by Hamas to shelter their fighters, or even as cover for rocket launchers. This running dispute came to a climax when the main UNRWA headquarters in Gaza city was shelled for hours, despite desperate phone calls to the Israeli forces. Several buildings were set on fire, including a warehouse with hundreds of tonnes of food stocks. A much bigger disaster was only averted by brave workers who drove trucks laden with fuel away from the scene before they could explode.

The salience of the humanitarian issues, of both practice and principle, meant that I personally became deeply involved. For several weeks I was one of the main voices of the UN about the crisis on the world's media, together with John Ging, the UNRWA head of operations, who stayed in Gaza throughout. Inevitably, in such difficult and complex circumstances, this meant that I crossed swords repeatedly with the official Israeli version of events. But I was also regularly accused by the Arab media of soft-pedalling the reality to spare Israeli (and US) blushes. I simply tried to describe the situation as I saw it unfolding on the ground, and to stick closely to the facts as far as we could discover them.

Controversy

However, virtually every aspect of the military operation was highly controversial. Was Israel achieving her military objectives, described as changing the military situation along her border with Gaza, stopping the rockets and the weapons smuggling through the tunnels? Was she achieving whatever political objectives she had set for herself? Was she using excessive and disproportionate force, as well as banned weapons, in the military operation? How many civilians were killed, compared to Hamas militants/terrorists? Were Hamas deliberately using civilians and civilian installations as shields for their military operations?

The extent of civilian casualties was once again a particular controversy. It was clear from the nature of the operation – intensive bombing, shelling, and tank fire in one of the most densely populated areas in the world, with the people effectively trapped – that casualties were bound to be high. Israeli leafleting had given warnings in some cases, but these were not necessarily accurate, and in any case the people of the areas concerned really had nowhere else to go. All the media coverage supported the perception of high civilian deaths and injuries. But how were the true figures to be arrived at?

From the start of the operation the Palestinian Ministry of Health gave daily figures of dead and injured, compiled from the hospitals in Gaza. There was no way to verify these systematically, but from the start they looked plausible, unlike the wild guesses which often fly around in such circumstances. Those on the ground – UN representatives, other international observers and journalists who managed to get in somehow – said consistently that the figures corresponded closely to their impressions, and to whatever facts they could dig out from elsewhere. We therefore decided to refer to the Palestinian Ministry of Health figures as a rough guide to what might be happening. We did not treat them as anything like gospel truth; we spelled out that they were official Palestinian figures which we could not verify, but which looked to be of the right order of magnitude. The Israelis consistently said these figures were exaggerated for political effect and unreliable, and criticized us strongly for giving them credibility. However, when their own figures for overall casualties emerged after the end of the operation, they were, in fact, very similar – only a hundred or so less.

But the overall figures were only part of the story. How many of the dead and injured were civilians, i.e. not legitimate targets in the first place? Under international humanitarian law, combatants are usually defined as those belonging to security forces of one kind or another, who are armed, and threatening to use those arms. For Israel, anyone working for Hamas institutions, even institutions like the parliament, seemed to be defined as a legitimate target. The police were certainly seen as such: an attack on a police passing-out parade on the first day of Operation Cast Lead killed some forty recruits. What was obviously true was that those dressed in civilian clothes were not necessarily civilians. Most Hamas fighters did not wear uniforms, and were deliberately hiding among the civilian population.

This was tricky territory, which we did not want to politicize more than necessary. But making every effort to distinguish between combatants and non-combatants is a fundamental principle of international humanitarian law in armed conflicts. The fact that it is difficult in a particular situation, or that the other side make no such distinction themselves, does not reduce this obligation in any way. The other vital principle is proportionality, i.e. only using such force as is necessary to achieve the military objective in question.

There was no doubt that a large number of those killed and

injured by the Israeli attacks were women and children. The presumption that most of these were civilians seemed reasonable, though some women could of course be Hamas fighters, and some teenagers likewise. So the overall point that a large proportion of those killed and injured were civilians seemed hard to contest, however impossible it might be to put hard-and-fast figures to this. The use of force also looked excessive in relation to the military aim of stopping rockets which still caused relatively few deaths and injuries in Israel.

Even more difficult, and closely linked to the issue of proportionality, was the question of whether civilians killed in armed attacks constituted unavoidable collateral damage during reasonable military action, or had been attacked deliberately, or had been killed in the course of actions which were not proportional and where the risk of civilian casualties should have been known to be unacceptably high, compared to the military advantage likely to be gained.

A second area of controversy was the use of banned weapons. The Palestinians claimed that Israel was using cluster munitions, banned by most UN member states, though not by Israel, and flechettes (multiple darts released by tank shells). Both are inevitably highly risky for civilians if used in built-up areas. They also alleged that shells containing tungsten (DIME bombs) or depleted uranium, particularly damaging to human bodies, were being used. The evidence for these claims was and is hard to establish.

But the biggest issue was the use of white phosphorus shells. The phosphorus burns intensely on contact with the air, giving off plumes of white smoke. These shells are supposed to be used for smokescreens or as incendiaries/defoliants, not in densely populated urban areas. If the burning phosphorus comes into contact with human skin, it continues to burn down through the flesh, into the bone and internal organs, as long as there is oxygen to feed it. It cannot be doused by water and can also stick to and burn anyone unskilled and unequipped trying to help a victim.

From early in the Cast Lead operation, there were allegations that Israel was using phosphorus shells in urban areas of Gaza. These were strongly denied by Israel initially. When the evidence of spent shell casings and burn victims nevertheless became too strong to ignore, and especially after they were used against the UNRWA compound in Gaza city, the Israelis acknowledged that some had been fired, but only to create smokescreens. White phosphorus shells are not banned as such, but their use in areas with high civilian populations is certainly against customary international humanitarian law.

Even more seriously, allegations were made that Israeli soldiers had deliberately attacked and killed civilians in some incidents, ignoring white flags; used Palestinians as human shields themselves when entering houses they feared were booby-trapped; and deliberately refused to allow medical and other humanitarian assistance to reach wounded and trapped civilians. Hospitals were also shelled and bombed. The Israelis refused to accept any of these stories at the time, on the grounds that their forces were taking every possible precaution to avoid civilian casualties, and had a long record of being the most humane army in the world, a claim which had always looked hard to justify, but now looked particularly inappropriate.

On the other side, the Israelis accused Hamas and the other Palestinian groups of deliberately using civilian installations such as schools and mosques, and even hospitals, as locations for rocket firing and for storing weapons, in the hope that the Israelis would not dare to attack them. It was claimed, for example, that Hamas had deliberately placed a large bunker containing its command structure underneath the main Al Shifah hospital in Gaza city.

Israeli spokesmen also continued to allege that UN installations such as UNRWA schools were being used for military purposes, with the connivance of UNRWA staff, and that when shells and bombs were fired at or near these installations, it was because there were Palestinian fighters in or very near them. These allegations were fiercely denied by UNRWA, and the Israelis seemed unable to produce convincing evidence to back up their claims.

Maintaining a balance among these competing allegations, under fierce media scrutiny, was a considerable challenge. The propaganda battle was as intense as the ground fighting, and both sides were determined to win it. The only solution for us was to stick to the evidence and what could reasonably be shown to be the case – for example, the use of white phosphorus shells.

The aftermath

The ceasefire, when it eventually came, was a huge relief. At least the killing had stopped, and the task of providing humanitarian relief could resume properly, for both the victims and the wider population. Most Gazans had hardly been able to move for three weeks, despite occasional brief pauses.

Ban ki-Moon had already left for the region before the ceasefire, with the aim of stopping the fighting any way he could. He persuaded the Israelis to allow him to visit Gaza shortly after their withdrawal, though they did their best to discourage him by warning of unspecified serious security risks. He had been genuinely angered by the Israeli disregard for the UN, particularly UNRWA, throughout the military operation, and had already made clear that the UN would be expecting a full enquiry into attacks on UN property and personnel and, if necessary, compensation (which was eventually agreed). Six UN members of staff had been killed. He had also called for a full independent enquiry into the operation, though we all knew that the chances of the Israelis cooperating with any such enquiry were small.

The dramatic highlight of his brief trip to Gaza was a press conference, which he gave standing in front of the still-smouldering wreckage of part of the UNRWA compound. His passion about the unacceptability of what had happened made a significant impression, especially coming from someone who was normally seen as being close to Israel.

I followed up Ban ki-Moon's trip a few days later to see for myself the scale of the destruction, to look at how we could step up the humanitarian operation, and to launch an assessment of the reconstruction needs. Despite all the television pictures I had seen, I was still taken aback by the widespread devastation, including of many residential areas, and by the mammoth task of reconstruction which lay ahead. I saw the remains of the best school in Gaza, ironically the American school, entirely flattened by a missile, supposedly on the basis that it had been used for military purposes – a claim strongly denied by the school's principal. I visited badly damaged hospitals. Conversations with a wide range of Gazans brought out the psychological trauma, particularly for children, cowering in the ruins for three weeks with their parents completely unable to protect them: their drawings were all of planes, tanks, and destruction

But what made the biggest impression in some ways was the sight of an industrial estate, not bombed, but deliberately bulldozed flat. There were the usual claims that it had been used as a site of rocket launches, but they did not ring true. Rather, it seemed to have been singled out, like other key economic sites around Gaza, to demonstrate the costs of defying Israel. The owners of the squashed factories told me that they were not members of Hamas, or even supporters of the Hamas regime, but natural moderates and supporters of Fatah, who had worked closely with Israeli economic partners in the past, and wanted to do so again, given half a chance. The consequence of this piece of vandalism was bound to be lost jobs and further economic deprivation. How could this help?

In my talks with the Israelis, I appealed to them to grasp the opportunity of the terrible lesson they had just inflicted on Hamas and Gaza, whatever its rights or wrongs, and change the dynamic of the situation by lifting the restrictions. They were not interested, and our discussions were correspondingly difficult. It was clear that Israeli concerns about so-called dual-use materials such as cement, pipes and wire, all vital for reconstruction, would not change. For our part, we spelled out our view that a return to the status quo ante for goods going into Gaza would not be acceptable or workable.

Shortly after my return from Gaza, we launched an emergency humanitarian appeal for just over $600 million, to cover relief for 1.4 million people for nine months, as well as early recovery activities. The initial response was generous, both from the usual Western donors and many in the Middle East. But the major issue was still how aid could physically reach Gaza. In the short term, relief goods coming particularly from Arab countries had piled up at the Egyptian border town of Al Arish, mainly in a sports stadium. Much of this was perishable food or medical supplies, already rotting in the hot Egyptian sun. Much of it was also not really what was required – despite all our appeals to the contrary, and emphasis on the valuable flexibility of financial donations, Gulf donors in particular insisted on sending goods which were not actually needed. One of our first priorities was nevertheless to persuade the Israelis to allow in as many of these as possible, as well as allowing back in the humanitarian workers who had been kept out during the fighting.

We had a little success on the Al Arish front over the coming weeks, working in particular through Ban ki-Moon's special representative in Jerusalem, Robert Serry, and the UN humanitarian coordinator, Max Gaylard. But otherwise the extremely limited access, for humanitarian needs or for reconstruction, continued. The smuggling tunnels into Gaza had reopened almost as soon as the fighting stopped and the Israelis withdrew, but there were limits even to the ingenuity of the smugglers over what could be brought in by way of bulk materials such as cement. In any case UN and other agencies obviously could not buy from the smugglers, however great the temptation at times.

Much effort went into planning reconstruction. To ease this process, the Egyptians and others tried hard to reconcile the Palestinian factions. The argument that Hamas and Fatah could not afford to remain divided in the face of dramatic threats to the Palestinian people (like Cast Lead) clearly had resonance. Progress seemed close at times. But the personal and political divisions remained too deep to allow any meaningful breakthrough at that stage. Moreover, the Israelis and Americans had no wish to see reconciliation because they feared this might mean a de facto Hamas takeover of both territories.

The Fatah-dominated Palestinian Authority, though unable to access Gaza themselves, were determined to take the lead over reconstruction. They were desperate to demonstrate that, despite what was seen by many Palestinians as the heroic resistance of Hamas, the PA remained the legitimate government of both territories. Since this was also the view of the international community, the PA role had to be accepted, though they had no ability to put any of their plans into practice. A major international conference on reconstruction was held in Egypt at the beginning of March. Over $5 billion was pledged, on the basis of an outline plan from the PA, although there was the usual creative accounting in these numbers. The US alone promised $900 million, largely in support for the PA.

But the conference was a political gesture from the international community more than anything else, reflecting their guilt and frustration that they had not been able to do more to help during Cast Lead, and the wish to shore up the PA. Hamas was not present, and warned pointedly that it could not simply be ignored in reconstruction efforts. In any case, it was clear that any reconstruction plan would remain a dead letter as long as Israel did not reopen the crossing points in a meaningful way. Unfortunately, the US were never quite ready to put real pressure on the Israelis over this, preferring to reserve their fire for the big peace issues such as the West Bank settlements – where sadly their efforts also came to nothing in the following two years. Israel therefore continued to act as they chose, on the basis of their own views of their security interests, however short-sighted others might believe their attitudes to be.

Beyond the physical devastation of the infrastructure and the mental trauma of its inhabitants, the situation in Gaza after Cast Lead was little different from what it had been before the operation. Hamas was still fully in control, and probably more popular in some ways than before. It was seen as having successfully resisted overwhelming Israeli military force, however passive this resistance had been in reality. The crossings were still largely closed. The humanitarian community was still having to negotiate in detail the entry of basic supplies, and facing constant restrictions on the passage in and out of staff. The UN could hardly even begin to repair its own installations for lack of materials. The PA was still unable to visit the territory, still less exercise the administrative control it claimed. Gilad Shalit was still being held hostage in Gaza.

So had the Israeli operation been a waste of time? Many outside Israel thought so. The rocket attacks did at least stop for a significant period. Islamic Jihad continued to fire off the odd salvo. But for the next year or so, the scale of attacks was very different from what it had been. Hamas, whatever its outward defiance, did not actually want to provoke a repeat of Cast Lead.

However, Hamas and the other factions were busy rearming through the tunnels, and upgrading their weaponry at the same time, looking for longer-range and more accurate rockets than the old Qassam models, which were little more than flying drainpipes. The previous pattern has therefore gradually reasserted itself: regular rocket attacks – happily, still not very effective in terms of Israeli casualties, but traumatic enough for the cities affected – and Israeli retaliatory attacks, often successfully hitting the fighters they target, but sometimes killing civilians in the process. Both sides know the informal rules of this game. Hamas do not want to provoke the Israelis beyond a certain point. The Israelis do not want to repeat Cast Lead unless they absolutely have to. But the risk of miscalculation by either side is high. And the main victims continue to be the Palestinian civilians.

One year on

I returned to Gaza, and the West Bank and Israel, for the last time as ERC in February 2010, just over twelve months after the end of Cast Lead. It was not a cheerful visit. The worst of the rubble had been cleared, but little meaningful reconstruction had been possible. Palestinian ingenuity in recycling rubble was admirable, but was always going to be insufficient – and even dangerous in cases like bent and weakened steel reinforcing bars. Infrastructure such as water and sanitation remained in desperate need of major repair, impossible because of lack of materials and spare parts.

Some goods were in the shops, thanks to the tunnels, but few could afford them – 80 per cent of the population now depended on aid for the basics of life. The legitimate economy had shrunk even further, to the benefit of the gangster entrepreneurs who flourished through the tunnel economy. Moderates continued to be squeezed out. Even Hamas itself risked being outflanked by more extremist groups. Hamas was, meanwhile, increasingly inclined to interfere in humanitarian aid operations, in order to assert their authority, while any contact by international NGOs with Hamas authorities was enough to provoke the US authorities to withdraw support from the offending organization.

I met Gilad Shalit's father in Israel: he was a dignified figure, desperate for his son to be released. I sympathized, but had to tell him that while his son's continued detention was unacceptable and contrary to international humanitarian law, I did not believe that could justify Israel's restrictions on 1.5 million people. The German-led efforts to arrange his son's release failed again not long afterwards, although they did succeed eventually, eighteen months later, in October 2011. More than 1000 Palestinian prisoners were exchanged for Shalit, some of whom had been convicted of very serious crimes. However, hopes that this would somehow unlock the situation in Gaza and persuade the Israelis to relax the border restrictions proved predictably vain.

In meetings in Jerusalem and publicly, I again argued strongly that Israeli policy was counterproductive, as well as being unacceptable from a humanitarian point of view. It was not really protecting Israeli security, because of the tunnels, and was all the while fuelling despair and extremism, rather than the opposite. I thought I detected greater private understanding of this than previously. But the overall Israeli position remained the same.

I had tried again to persuade Ban ki-Moon that during this visit I should meet senior representatives of Hamas, to discuss humanitarian issues with them. This would have been entirely in line with the usual humanitarian policy of talking to anyone about getting aid through, and about their responsibilities under international humanitarian law. It did not imply any political recognition. But Ban ki-Moon remained firmly signed up to the conditions about dealing with Hamas originally set by the US/EU/Russia/UN Quartet, who purported to lead international policy on the Middle East peace process. He continued to believe, contrary to the views of many UN officials, that the Quartet had some influence on the peace process, and that membership of the Quartet could give the UN some leverage. The American under secretary-general for political affairs, Lynn Pascoe, also believed strongly in the boycott of Hamas. My pleas therefore fell on deaf ears. The Quartet remains in existence as I write, despite the collapse of the peace process, and the UN remains a member.

All in all, this was a deeply depressing visit. Not only had the situation in Gaza not improved materially, but Israeli policies in the West Bank and Jerusalem continued to make the lives of many Palestinians a misery, and to reduce the chances of a two-state solution. The wider peace process seemed to be headed for the rocks (and duly hit them a few months later). The international community did not really seem to care that much. Many governments seemed to prefer to cling to the illusion of a peace process instead of facing up to the reality that it was broken and could not now be fixed, certainly not by the continuation of the same policies. They were in effect waiting for something else bad to happen in Gaza, rather than trying everything to avert it.

The Turkish flotilla

Another crisis duly arrived in May 2010, in the shape of an attempt to reach Gaza with aid by sea by the so-called Gaza

Freedom Flotilla, and to break the blockade that way. A Turkish NGO, the Foundation for Human Rights and Freedoms and Humanitarian Relief, with humanitarian aims – but no doubt a political agenda too – chartered a ship, which was joined by others, including ships from the West, with a large number of activists from many countries (among them the US and UK). The Israelis warned that they would not be allowed entry, but the flotilla set sail from Cyprus anyway. It was intercepted by the Israeli navy, which boarded the main ship. Meeting violent resistance from some of the Turkish activists, Israeli commandos opened fire. Nine people were killed.

This caused a huge international outcry, and a particularly strong political reaction from the Turkish government, which had traditionally enjoyed good relations with Israel. They demanded an official Israeli apology and an international enquiry. The Israelis refused both. The resulting arguments deteriorated into a prolonged stand-off, with a profoundly damaging effect on Turkish–Israeli relations.

The Israelis claimed that their marines had been so violently attacked after boarding that they had had no choice but to respond with lethal force, and recalled their clear advance warning that the flotilla would not be allowed to reach Gaza. They regarded the whole thing as a political stunt organized by an extremist Islamic group in Turkey. The Turks accused the Israelis of callous disregard for the lives of the civilians on the ship, and underlined the genuine humanitarian intentions of the flotilla, faced with unacceptable Israeli restrictions on the lives of the people of Gaza.

Wherever the balance of these arguments may lie, it is clear that overall this was a PR disaster for Israel, and a blow to one of its few successful relationships with an Islamic country. The issues have rumbled on, as further flotillas have been attempted, and have been turned back by the Israelis, happily with less lethal consequences. More are still planned. However much there may be a deliberately provocative side to this, the underlying problem is still the unacceptable Israeli restrictions on Gaza.

Accountability

The controversies surrounding Cast Lead immediately raised the issue of whether there should be an investigation into the widespread accusations from the media and human rights organizations of large-scale abuses of international humanitarian law, even war crimes, by both sides. Israel rejected any suggestion of an independent international enquiry and mounted its own, the conclusions of which were not accepted as objective by the rest of the world. The UN Council on Human Rights commissioned its own enquiry, and turned to a Jewish judge from South Africa, Richard Goldstone, to carry it out. His 575-page report was published in September 2009.

Judge Goldstone pulled no punches. He concluded that there was evidence of serious violations of international humanitarian rights and humanitarian law by both sides, amounting to war crimes and possible crimes against humanity. Israel had used disproportionate force and breached the fundamental principle of distinction between military targets and civilians and civilian objects. The Palestinian rockets also constituted war crimes. He called for authorities on both sides to launch good faith, independent proceedings, or be referred after six months to the International Criminal Court by the UN Security Council.

The Israeli reaction was furious, denouncing the report as a pack of lies. They were particularly outraged at the idea of ICC action, and threatened dire consequences for any country attempting to arrest Israelis as a result. The US took a similar if less hysterical line, which immediately killed the chances of any

Security Council follow-up action. Hamas also rejected the accusations of war crimes against them. Judge Goldstone himself was the subject of a vicious campaign of personal vilification in Israel and the US. The following year he distanced himself from some aspects of his own report, saying that if evidence then available from Israel about not targeting civilians deliberately had been available to him when writing the report, it would have been a different document.

The UN Human Rights Council endorsed the report in a split vote, but the membership of that body confirmed their reputation for bias against Israel by focussing in their own resolution only on the accusations against Israel, and ignoring those against Hamas.

All this left Ban ki-Moon in an impossible position, facing strong demands that he take the Goldstone report further, and equally strong demands from some quarters that he leave it alone. The predictable result has been no further action. However, the Israelis, while not accepting the accusations against their forces, have pursued their internal investigations and established new practices to prevent future abuses. This could be seen as an admission of a kind that something had indeed gone wrong with the Cast Lead operation. Similar concerns emerged from evidence given after Cast Lead to Israeli NGOs by some Israeli soldiers horrified at what they had seen during the operation.

Judge Goldstone's report itself may not be perfect, but it is a serious piece of work by someone practised in the investigation of events such as these, from his experience with the International Court for the Former Republic of Yugoslavia. He had no political axe to grind, and no reason for bias against Israel. The report deserves to be read by anyone who wants to understand what happened.

My own broader take on Cast Lead is relatively simple. Israel was determined to inflict a lesson on Hamas and the Palestinians in Gaza that they would not easily forget – a show of force to overawe their enemies and deter further attacks. I doubt myself they deliberately set out to kill civilians. They had no good policy reason to do so. But anyone connected with Hamas, however remotely, was seen as a target, and if civilians or installations such as hospitals suffered in the course of the attack, that was not something over which they were going to lose too much sleep, especially since they were convinced Hamas were deliberately using the population as human shields. Moreover, in Israeli eyes, hitting the economic potential and infrastructure of Gaza was part of the lesson which Hamas and the people of Gaza needed to learn: in other words, that attacking Israel carried too many consequences to be worth it.

Underneath this was also something I found more worrying. It was natural that the Israeli population would react to Cast Lead by uniting behind the operation. But on this occasion their rejection of any criticism had special virulence. Anyone in Israel itself who raised doubts about any part of the operation was seen as more or less guilty of treason. This was not normal in a country where high levels of patriotism and awareness of outside security threats had not previously prevented healthy democratic debate and dissent. Israelis in general seemed to have convinced themselves that Gaza should be regarded as nothing more than a nest of terrorists, who deserved anything which might happen to them. They applied this not only to Hamas and its supporters, but to ordinary Palestinians too, since they had failed to reject Hamas. The effect was to dehumanize the people of Gaza to the point where normal empathy disappeared.

If you add to this the changing composition of the Israeli army, with increasing numbers of recruits from extreme orthodox communities, less tolerant recent immigrant groups, and the settlers, it becomes easier to understand how some Israeli soldiers and officers seem to have behaved during Cast Lead with such indifference to the fate of the civilians involved, and in ways not in accordance with Israel's own best traditions of a citizen army. I heard such fears strongly expressed by representatives of Israeli civil society whom I met in Israel and New York shortly after Cast Lead. Both groups were worried that something profound was changing in Israeli society: tolerance of dissent, respect for human rights – even of opponents – and acceptance that Israel should behave according to, and be judged by, higher standards than its opponents all seemed to be disappearing.

The future

As of mid-2012, the situation in Gaza has still not changed much in substance. Severe restrictions remain; rocket attacks continue, as does Israeli retaliation. But the dynamics beneath the surface are no longer the same. Arab-led attempts to bring about reconciliation between the Palestinian factions have resumed in earnest. The revolution in Egypt has removed official Egyptian concerns about the relationship between Hamas and the Muslim Brotherhood. There is much less Egyptian preoccupation now with Israeli reactions to the use of the crossing between Egypt and Gaza. Hamas has broken with Syria, where its leadership used to be based, and thereby indirectly with Syria's main local supporter, Iran, identifying itself more authentically as a Palestinian movement. Future crises may therefore not develop in the same way as in the past. Meanwhile, the smuggling tunnels continue to do a roaring business, which has enabled some reconstruction and even development to get under way, however expensive the raw materials. But this continues to contribute to the criminalization of business in Gaza, which cannot be in anyone's long-term interest.

The underlying question remains: why has Israeli policy towards Gaza developed in the way it has, if it has been as clearly counterproductive as I have suggested? I believe the answer lies mostly in the Israeli psychology I have just described which tends to see certain people purely as terrorists, reinforced in the case of Hamas and Gaza by Israel's fierce hostility towards Iran. Has there also been an element of political calculation, trying to ensure that the two territories of Gaza and the West Bank remain divided, and that therefore the issue of the two-state solution can go on being pushed down the road? Was there a more or less conscious attempt at times to push Gaza into the arms of the Egyptians, so that it could never be part of any Palestinian state? There may have been elements of both, at least in the minds of some Israeli politicians.

Be that as it may, the situation in and around Gaza remains unsustainable and dangerous, and policy towards it, on the part of the international community as well as the Israelis, short-sighted. We will finish up having to deal with Hamas, and to talk to them about peace, as we finished up dealing with the PLO and Fatah, despite decades of rhetoric about never dealing with terrorists. When we do, we may well find them more ready to do deals in a pragmatic way than we expect, even if they may remain reluctant to sign up explicitly to conditions we regard as eminently reasonable and justifiable, for their own psychological reasons.

At some stage, the question of allowing goods into Gaza in a normal way, ending the tunnel economy, and permitting the proper reconstruction and normalization of the territory, will also need to be resolved. The sooner we confront this, the better. Most people in Gaza are not terrorists or extremists, despite all they have been through. Many I spoke to on my visits recalled the time, not so long ago, when they had worked in Israel and traded with Israel, and looked forward to the time when this kind of relationship could resume. The international community needs to do all it can to hasten that day, rather than somehow pretending Gaza and its problems can be wished out of existence by ignoring them.

None of this can be considered in isolation from the wider issue of the future of the West Bank, and the prospects for a lasting peace settlement. I return to what I said to the Security Council after my first visit. As long as the disconnect between the rhetoric of peace and the realities of occupation on the ground is as wide as it is, there is little or no prospect of an enduring accord. The two-state solution may already have disappeared as a realistic prospect. This needs to be faced. Even as we all prefer to focus on the hopeful aspects of the Arab awakening, those developments are unlikely to help the Middle East peace prospects for now. They are simply convincing the Israelis that their own military muscle is all they can rely on, while increasing the chances of future Arab governments responding more to the anger about Israel on their own streets than to rational calculation about peace.

The worst does not always happen, but miracles are also rare. It will take a political miracle in present circumstances to align the local and international stars in ways which will allow progress towards the long-term settlement so desperately needed, where all the parties are simultaneously ready to do a deal, and their respective backers are equally ready to work together to bring this about. There is still no more explosive situation facing the world. Only the Americans can fix it, is the usual cry, because of their influence with Israel. But the truth is that the Americans can't fix it, because of their relationship with Israel. The rest of the world, starting with Europe, also has to step up to help. As I write, there is no sign of any such thing. We may all live to regret this.

Map Sources: UNCS, Europa Technologies. Map created in Dec 2011.
Dotted line represents approximately the Line of Control in Jammu and Kashmir agreed upon by India and Pakistan. The final status of Jammu and Kashmir has not yet been agreed upon by the parties.

Map Sources: ESRI, Europa Technologies, UNCS. Map created in Dec 2012.
Dotted line represents approximately the Line of Control in Jammu and Kashmir agreed upon by India and Pakistan. The final status of Jammu and Kashmir has not yet been agreed upon by the parties.

CHAPTER NINE

Afghanistan and Pakistan: safeguarding humanitarian space

Afghanistan and Pakistan are particularly dangerous for humanitarians, with their combination of conflict, natural disaster, and local hostility to outsiders. In both countries, in my time, we faced disputes about how humanitarian work should be led and organized, how to ensure safety for staff, and effective aid delivery. I only went once to each country, but both occupied a lot of policy time.

The wider political context after 9/11 is important. It seemed to me obvious, even from my short visits, that the international community was not getting it right in this area. In Afghanistan, the NATO security mission – the International Security Assistance Force (ISAF) – was increasingly fighting an unwinnable war, relying on a dysfunctional government and an inappropriate model of centralized democracy, and undermining its own position by making it clear that it would leave before long. In Pakistan, it was hard to imagine a worse combination than Western frustration over Pakistani policy and Pakistani fury at their treatment by Western interlocutors. The US in particular was furious at what they saw as Pakistani vacillation over its domestic Taliban threat and ambivalence over the Afghan Taliban. The Pakistanis believed their sovereignty was being

253

ignored by the American military and their drone attacks.

In circumstances like these, how can humanitarians find an operating space which allows them to do what they are there to do (including after the fighting has stopped), and does not put them and their staff at undue risk? How far can they differentiate themselves from the rest of the Western presence, and will the locals take any notice if they do? Can they work more safely through proxies, local staff, and local NGOs, without appearing to treat them as more dispensable than international staff? And can they find reliable methods to work more remotely, using new technologies to monitor aid delivery, rather than vulnerable monitors on the ground?

Afghanistan

There had been a significant humanitarian presence in Afghanistan ever since the withdrawal of the Soviet Union and the civil wars which followed. After the 1996 Taliban takeover, agencies and NGOs, coordinated by a large OCHA presence, surprisingly found a way to work with the authorities which they believed preserved their independence, while allowing them to help the sufferings of the population, however abhorrent the wider Taliban policies. This did not endear the humanitarian community to Western political actors, some of whom believed that the humanitarians were effectively supporting Taliban rule.

After the removal of the Taliban in 2001, the country was no longer perceived as being in humanitarian crisis. The focus instead was on political stabilization, reconstruction, and development. While the main agencies and NGOs continued some emergency relief operations, OCHA's separate humanitarian coordination structure was therefore not renewed. It was fully integrated instead into the UN Assistance Mission in Afghanistan (UNAMA), which was not a peacekeeping force, since this task had fallen to NATO, but a major political mission aiming to help the stabilization and reconstruction of the country.

By the time I took over OCHA in 2007, it was clear that this arrangement was no longer working on the humanitarian side, if it ever had. Insufficient effort was going into identifying humanitarian needs, raising funds, and coordinating. More seriously, humanitarians were simply seen by the locals as part of the overall US-led political and security effort, rather than as acting impartially on the basis of need. This complicated their ability to do their job and put them at increasing risk of attack, especially in remote locations where the Taliban was becoming stronger.

This was part of a wider problem of blurring of roles. The UN operation as a whole was seen by many as being too close to the ISAF operations. The UN depends on its credibility and impartiality to work successfully in conflict situations. It was hard to maintain these while working so closely with an organization conducting a major military operation. Of course, the UN's mandate from the Security Council was to support the government, which meant it could not claim to be neutral between the warring parties. But an approach could have been found to act and speak in ways compatible with that mandate, and with a broader impartiality, without giving the appearance of identifying with everything ISAF was doing. That would also have been helpful in establishing the UN as a more credible player for the future, after ISAF's withdrawal.

Meanwhile, the normally distinct roles of military and civilian presences were also blurred. Instead of the military focussing on providing security, including for development and humanitarian actors, they were engaged in their own development activities, and sometimes even in providing humanitarian aid. This was partly because US forces in particular had more financial and other resources than anyone else. But it was also because the Western allies had chosen a model of intervention through what were termed provincial reconstruction teams (PRTs), each led by a separate country, which deliberately put military and civilians together. The different actors gradually became mixed up in ways which could no longer be disentangled.

This posed an especially sensitive problem for the humanitarians, with their usual need to be perceived as separate from others' political and security objectives, and operating solely on the basis of need. The greatest difficulties came when the military either claimed that its whole operation was humanitarian, as they did at times, or, for example, offered humanitarian assistance to particular local communities only if they cooperated against the Taliban. The latter was completely contrary to humanitarian principles.

Of course there are times when only the military can deliver humanitarian aid, when security conditions are too bad for anyone else to operate, or when military escorts are indispensable. There were certainly examples of this in Afghanistan, particularly in the south. But it was far from always the case.

OCHA separation?

This mess was what lay behind the demand from the humanitarian community in Afghanistan, particularly the NGOs, that we should separate humanitarian coordination from the UN political presence again, and strengthen it significantly at the same time. The call was to re-establish an OCHA office physically and structurally distinct from UNAMA, and able to act and be seen to act autonomously. It would still be part of the overall UN operation in Afghanistan, would cooperate closely with other parts of the UN and the international community, and would certainly not run any kind of independent political operation, as humanitarians had been accused of doing before 2001. But it would be sufficiently independent to be accessible to local NGOs, to be seen as operating according to humanitarian principles of need, and to be able to talk to any actors – including if necessary the Taliban – about access to those in the need and the obligation of all concerned to show full respect for humanitarian principles. This was often known collectively as protecting humanitarian space, though this bit of jargon meant nothing to most people outside the aid community.

The demand was given greater urgency by rising relief needs. In early 2008, for example, food insecurity was growing rapidly because of drought in wheat-producing areas, the effects of the conflict on agriculture, and, above all, the rapid rise in global food prices at the time. Wheat imports from Pakistan were vital, but wheat prices had effectively doubled from early 2007 to April 2008. Forty-two per cent of Afghans were already living below the poverty line and were dependent on wheat flour as their staple diet. There was a gap of some 2 million tons of wheat for the year, which required hundreds of millions of dollars to buy.

But this was far from all. Almost 5 million Afghan refugees had returned to the country since 2002, mainly from Pakistan, and returns were continuing at the rate of hundreds of thousands every year – even if not always as voluntarily as they should have been. Many returnees had no means of support, since their original lands had been occupied by the rapidly rising population. There was also a burgeoning but largely hidden problem of internal displacement, as the conflict intensified. Finally, disaster-prone Afghanistan was also suffering a constant series of floods in the rainy seasons, and harsh winters when cold and snow blocked food deliveries, while the risk of a major earthquake was ever present.

Civilian deaths from the fighting were also rapidly increasing. In the first few months of 2008 alone, UNAMA reported that almost 700 civilians had been killed, some 60 per cent more than in the equivalent period of the previous year. Of these, 422 were attributed to anti-government elements, as the Taliban and related armed groups were described in the statistics, 255 to national and international forces, and 21 were unattributed. ISAF disputed these UN figures. But when I looked into how they were put together, with cross-checks of all reported deaths, and no inclusion in the statistics in the absence of a reasonable degree of certainty, they seemed to me an accurate reflection of the reality.

ISAF had already started to take action to reduce the number of civilian casualties its military operations were causing, recognizing the damage to its reputation from these deaths, however accidental. But casualties from insurgent action were steadily climbing, as the Taliban planted more improvised explosive devices (IEDs), many of which hit passing civilians rather than the military convoys presumably targeted, and assassinated more and more local officials seen as collaborating with foreign forces. At least ISAF worried about the civilian losses they caused. There was no sign that the Taliban did.

The expansion of the conflict and the displacement of civilians from their homes which went along with this meant that humanitarian needs were increasing rapidly just as aid delivery was becoming more difficult. Specific threats to humanitarian workers were also growing. In the first six months of 2008, seven humanitarians were killed and eighty-eight abducted, mainly World Food Programme drivers. Large parts of the country, particularly in the south, were becoming too dangerous for international personnel. Even local staff usually able to understand the local dynamics and keep out of trouble faced significant risks. Nevertheless, the humanitarian requirement was clear: step up capacity; put together a proper humanitarian action plan; raise more funds from international donors unused to seeing

Afghanistan as a humanitarian crisis; and create a capable and autonomous OCHA office.

A visit to Afghanistan in June 2008 brought home these realities. Like so many before me, I was stunned by the beauty of the country's arid mountains and lush valleys. But that was about my only positive impression. After sobering talks in Kabul with the government, ISAF, and UN and NGO colleagues, I went to Nangahar and Kunar provinces in the east. They were not then as threatened by Taliban action as southern provinces such as Helmand, but were already becoming increasingly dangerous. The US outposts I visited were under rising threat of attack from across the nearby Pakistan border, and were struggling to maintain security while roads and other vital infrastructure were built. The American soldiers I met, many on their second or third year-long tour, were dedicated and knowledgeable. But it was hard not to conclude even then that they were fighting a losing war, no matter how many local military engagements they won. The safe haven across the border, the difficulty of distinguishing friend from foe, the obvious weakness of the official army and police forces, the persistence of the Taliban threat, and the resentment against ISAF whenever they made mistakes in their raids, all boded ill for ultimate success.

What struck me most, talking to local Afghan officials and villagers, was their helpless feeling of being caught between opposing forces. They could afford to offend neither, but could not please both simultaneously. ISAF and the government were there during the day, and the Taliban or their local equivalent at night. How could they maintain their balance and survive? Sadly for ISAF, the locals knew who would be there longer, even at that stage, and made their calculations accordingly, even though they had no love for the Taliban. As the local saying had it, NATO had the watches, but the Taliban had the time.

In my meetings in Kabul, it was clear that all concerned had little interest in the humanitarian part of the story, preoccupied as they were with the deteriorating political and security situation, and the large but struggling development effort. The government itself did not want to admit that there was a humanitarian crisis on top of everything else. I was therefore, essentially, an unwelcome visitor, though I was able to see the vice-president. Meanwhile, the main embassies had few if any humanitarian aid experts.

Kai Eide, the recently appointed Norwegian head of UNAMA, understood the humanitarian need in principle, but my efforts to persuade him that OCHA needed to separate itself from UNAMA to meet that need unfortunately fell on stony ground. He took the view that the international effort was quite fragmented enough. He already felt that he was not receiving the support he deserved from New York, and saw my request as one more demonstration of this. I pointed out in vain that it helped no one if a key part of the international effort was not effective, and that the main humanitarian staff inside UNAMA simply would not stay in any case if the set-up were not changed. Unfortunately, he took this last point as a threat rather than the simple statement of fact it was.

My arguments found little or no support in New York either. Head of UN peacekeeping Jean-Marie Guehenno, in charge of UNAMA, did not buy the humanitarian arguments about the need for separation. He persuaded the secretary-general to take the same view, though I think Ban ki-Moon hated having to choose between us. I had some allies, notably the wise head of the UN refugee agency (UNHCR), Antonio Guterres, always concerned to preserve humanitarian space. But key ambassadors in New York, as in Kabul, found it difficult to understand why the UN should not be united, and did not bother to examine our arguments too closely. In Western capitals, aid ministries could see our point, but could not prevail over their political masters.

And yet what we were recommending was no more than what was commonplace in other difficult conflict areas. There were separate OCHA offices in DRC and Darfur which were not structurally integrated into the wider UN peacekeeping presence. Instead, they reported into the overall UN command structure, i.e. the special representative of the secretary-general (SRSG), through one of his deputies, a triple-hatted figure known in the jargon as the DSRG/RC/HC, combining the jobs of deputy special representative of the secretary-general, resident coordinator, and humanitarian coordinator. While an almost impossible job for the incumbent, this set-up did at least combine the required degree of humanitarian separation with the necessary overall coherence with the rest of the UN.

This 'one foot in, one foot out' model worked well in situations where there was neither full-scale war nor proper peace. In a full-scale war case, where there was a particular need to work with all sides, we favoured a totally separate structure ('two feet out'). Where there was real peace, we were generally happy to be fully integrated into the UN ('two feet in'). All this no doubt sounds arcane. But, as I have suggested in other contexts, these arrangements were practically crucial for the humanitarian community in difficult and dangerous situations, particularly for the NGOs, and for the effective delivery of relief.

In Afghanistan, the DSRSG/RC/HC role already existed, and worked reasonably well. Most in the military and diplomatic worlds therefore simply could not see why we were making a fuss about the OCHA office: surely everything which could be brought to bear in the struggle against the Taliban was justified, and any idea that the humanitarians could somehow distinguish themselves from the rest of the international community was naive. How was the average villager or Taliban fighter going to make meaningful distinctions between foreign organizations, all of which were alien to them?

In fact, there was plenty of evidence that Afghans *did* distinguish between different foreigners and different organizations. The Taliban regularly blew up schools which were tainted by military money or too close ISAF involvement, but left alone others less marked in this way. We understood that we could not be entirely separate from the rest of the UN, and that getting the arrangement we wanted would not solve all our problems. But we believed that effectiveness on the ground was at stake, and that it was important not to give up key principles just because their application was difficult.

In the end our arguments carried the day in late 2008, after it became clear to all, including Kai Eide, that the existing humanitarian coordination arrangements within UNAMA had indeed become unworkable. But the struggle had not helped relationships in Kabul or New York.

The separate OCHA office was established in Kabul, with sub-offices in other main cities, in early 2009. I wish I could report that this made a quick and dramatic difference, but in practice it took us a long time to get the right people there, in the right premises, with the right relationships with the government, the international and local NGOs, UNAMA, and ISAF. We wanted to begin a dialogue with the Taliban, to improve access, and persuade them to respect their own humanitarian and human rights obligations, but this was slow progress at best.

By this stage in the Afghan conflict, like many other organizations, we were in fact bedevilled by recruitment and office-management difficulties. Few middle-level OCHA staff members with families wanted to leave them behind and work in such a dangerous and unrewarding place. From late 2009 onwards, just when our complement was getting up to speed, we were also badly hit by wider moves to reduce the UN 'footprint' because of rising attacks on UN workers and compounds. We therefore struggled to make the difference to humanitarian needs analysis and delivery we desperately wanted, and to establish an effective relationship with non-state actors. That struggle continues as I write.

We were, nevertheless, able to produce a much better Humanitarian Action Plan from 2009 onwards, to help improve capacity on the ground, and to raise badly needed funding from the donors. That helped to keep the humanitarian situation from degrading too much further. We are also better placed to help on a larger scale in future, as I fear we may have to, once ISAF pulls out most of its troops in 2014, and the government is left facing the Taliban again.

Most international attention naturally remains on the political and security challenges before 2014, and on whether the development aid poured in has made enough difference to ordinary Afghans. But we should not forget the basic humanitarian needs. Population growth rates are among the highest in the world, in a country where habitable land is strictly limited. Maternal and infant mortality rates are dreadful, and most educational and health facilities still appalling. The conflict has also prevented real progress in strengthening national disaster-management capacity. In the rush for the exits in 2014, we will neglect all this at our peril.

Pakistan

It would be good to turn to Pakistan for a more encouraging story. But that would not reflect the reality. The humanitarian community had already had plenty of experience there. The relief operation for the major earthquake in Kashmir in 2005 had been tough to deal with in such a remote area, but an overall success. This had created a degree of familiarity and mutual trust between international humanitarian actors and the authorities, including the military.

However, working in Pakistan was never easy. The dominance by the military of every aspect of life, including humanitarian aid, made for great sensitivities. The advantage of the military in Pakistan was that they were relatively efficient and had resources they could mobilize. They were much less likely to be driven by partisan politics, or corruption, than the civilian authorities.

But their control inevitably came with its own political and security strings attached. These issues were manageable in a natural disaster like the earthquake, but became a much bigger problem in spring 2009 when a major government offensive against the Pakistan Taliban in the north-west led to one of the biggest and most rapid population displacements in the world in recent years.

Crisis on the north-west frontier
Military operations against the Taliban had started the year before in some of the so-called tribal areas. This was partly a response to insistent US pressure to do something about the safe haven enjoyed by the Afghan Taliban in these no-go border areas. But the Pakistanis themselves were also increasingly aware that long years of inaction had created an internal Taliban threat which could overwhelm them if left unchecked.

In April 2009, over 500,000 people who had fled the area in the previous months were already internally displaced persons (IDPs). In the next three weeks, as the military began a new major operation in the Swat and neighbouring valleys, over 2 million more joined them.

This extraordinary exodus came from a combination of fear of being caught up in vicious fighting between the well-entrenched Taliban and the better-armed Pakistan army, and clear orders from the army to the local population to leave. These instructions were, no doubt, meant to save civilian lives, but they also gave the army a free field of fire – their automatic tendency was to see anyone still left as being either Taliban themselves or at least supporters. These orders proved a major problem later, when it came to distributing humanitarian aid: the military took the view that only those from areas officially evacuated on their orders were entitled to aid, whereas the reality was that many others from nearby areas had also genuinely fled for their lives.

The IDPs mostly fled south-east to a province called Mardan. The situation there was unusual: only about 10 per cent went into the camps hastily set up by the government and the international agencies working with them. The rest rented accommodation if they could afford it, found shelter with so-called host families (sometimes relatives, but by no means always), or took over buildings such as local schools, luckily on holiday at the time. Some Mardan families took in IDP groups greatly exceeding their own number for months at a time, at major sacrifice to themselves. This spontaneous solidarity and generosity was striking and humbling.

But why did the vast majority of the IDPs avoid the camps, despite the ready availability of aid there? It was partly traditional self-reliance and distrust of the government. But there was also a real cultural fear of exposing women who lived in purdah to open camp conditions, with common latrines and little possibility of privacy. The heat in tents was also particularly difficult for women confined inside almost twenty-four hours a day.

Camps are never pleasant, but they have one major advantage for humanitarians: giving aid and providing basic services such as clean water and health care to a lot of people is far easier in a camp setting. The effort can be concentrated. People can be registered and have their needs assessed in a regulated and predictable environment. In this case, how were we going to help over 2 million people when they were scattered over such a wide area?

The innovative answer was to set up twenty-five hubs where people could come to register and collect aid, in locations which were advertised widely and were reasonably accessible. These hubs proved remarkably effective, especially when combined with mobile teams in sectors like health, who could identify and help the most vulnerable groups wherever they were.

Everything is sensitive
Meanwhile, scaling up humanitarian expertise and experience as fast as possible meant attracting rapid and substantial support from the donors, to supplement the quick money we could release from our own Central Emergency Response Fund (CERF), set up in 2006 for just this reason and funded annually by a wide range of international government donors. On 22 May we therefore launched a flash appeal. We had to call it a humanitarian response plan, not an appeal, to respond to acute Pakistani sensitivities about terminology they thought demeaning. We asked for some $550 million, to help 1.5 million people for the rest of 2009. This was less than the number of people displaced, and was also optimistic about the duration. It was partly our best guess about the average number of people to whom we would have access and the capacity to help over the period. But it was also a reaction to Pakistani insistence that the displaced would be going home very soon, since the Taliban would be defeated and security restored quickly. We doubted this in private, but could not challenge it openly.

The Pakistanis were likewise adamant that no humanitarian provision should be made beyond the end of 2009. They feared that humanitarian aid would interfere with what they were more interested in, international funding for reconstruction and redevelopment of the areas hit by the fighting. We explained in vain that humanitarian and development funds came from different donor pots of money, and that more of one did not necessarily mean less of the other.

Other Pakistani sensitivities, primarily from the military, led them to insist that we should not refer in any public statements or documents to 'armed conflict' in the area of fighting, but simply to a law-enforcement or terrorist clean-up operation. This became a tricky stand-off. We had no wish to offend or confront the government, but could not simply adopt their terminology either. Recognition of a state of armed conflict has a particular significance in humanitarian law, and has to be a matter of fact, not political opinion. Moreover, blatantly taking sides in the words we used would have further complicated delivery of aid in areas where the armed opposition was powerful, and put humanitarians even more at risk. The extent of the risks we were already running was to be tragically illustrated later in the year. We therefore put our collective foot down over the words we chose to use ouselves, and the Pakistanis had no choice but to acquiesce, however reluctantly.

There were initial concerns that the Pakistan army were using disproportionate force, causing many civilian casualties, and needlessly destroying property and infrastructure. Since we had no presence in the areas of the fighting, it was almost impossible to verify these accusations. We certainly believed the army to be ready to act ruthlessly when it came to rooting out the Taliban. We reminded the Pakistanis regularly of their obligation to respect international humanitarian law, in terms of the degree of force used, and the distinction to be made between combatants and civilians. They took note politely, but did not seem likely to make much of this in what they actually did.

Nevertheless, when we were able to return to the affected areas afterwards, the general impression was that, though civilian deaths and destruction of property had been significant in some places, overall they were not as bad as had been feared. The evacuation of civilians in advance, however crudely carried out, had undoubtedly helped.

Seeing for myself

I managed to get to Pakistan in early July 2009. The situation had moved on by then. While new military action was starting in parts of Waziristan, the government were claiming victory in key areas elsewhere and were pushing the population to go back, with a significant cash inducement for those who agreed to do so, paid through a specially supplied smart card. The humanitarian operation was working reasonably well, though funding was fragile to say the least. When I talked to the government, including President Zardari, they said the right things, but I felt that their heart was not in the relief operation. Few if any central government ministers had bothered to visit the camps or the affected areas, and they knew little of the real situation on the ground.

Buner, one of the recently 'liberated' areas I visited, next to the Swat valley, had already seen some returns, but was still a long way from anything approaching normality. The population there were naturally more hostile to the Taliban than in other areas where the resentment against the underlying feudal system was stronger. But economic activity, particularly agriculture, was clearly going to take a long time to restart. The government had, for example, banned tall crops like maize, for fear of the Taliban hiding in the fields. The main industry of stone-quarrying was likewise stalled, because the government had forbidden sale of explosives.

The next-door Swat valley was far from liberated, outside the main towns, but here too the government were saying people should go home. We shared the government's determination to avoid aid dependency. But it was important at the same time that the principles of consultation and voluntariness were respected, and that a time limit on the government's card-based cash grant was not used as a form of blackmail. We urged the government to organize visits by representatives from the communities concerned, to check in advance whether the areas they had come from had genuinely been stabilized. But the military had their own agenda, and it was an uphill struggle at best.

I also went up to Peshawar, despite the fears of the UN security people, to talk to the local authorities. An IDP camp visit on the way was rather surreal, with a four-lane motorway swishing past. It was also the only camp I ever saw with mains electricity. But conditions were still tough for those inside, with temperatures reaching 45°C in the tents, and high humidity too, as the rainy season approached.

In Peshawar I discussed the real problems we had about aid eligibility with the local authorities. The military insistence that IDPs from areas not officially declared to have been conflict-affected should not be entitled to aid was disqualifying far too many of them. Others – for example, female-headed households – did not have the right ID cards, and were being refused help on those grounds. Such issues affected hundreds of thousands of people. However, although the civilian authorities were sympathetic, once the military had decided how something was to be organized, it was the devil's own job to get them to change their minds or be more flexible. The best we could do in the end was to persuade them to set up an appeals system, which at least helped in some cases.

Security threats

By and large we got on reasonably amicably with the Pakistani military on the practical side, helped by the familiarity from the Kashmir earthquake. However, the fact that they were simultaneously conducting the military attacks on the Taliban causing the displacement, and running the relief operations to help those displaced, was hardly ideal. In some cases, the same general was directly in charge of both. This was a problem in two ways. The military distribution of aid was hardly likely to be neutral when it came to giving to groups seen as being sympathizers with the Taliban, compared to others regarded as government supporters. It also greatly increased the risk that in the minds of the Taliban humanitarian organizations were inextricably associated with the military. We could expect to be targeted accordingly. A well-respected local staff member of UNHCR had already been killed in what appeared to be a bungled abduction attempt.

When the WFP headquarters in Islamabad was subsequently attacked by a suicide bomber at the beginning of October 2009, killing five members of staff, security issues inevitably came to dominate thinking. This was one of a wave of attacks, mostly on official Pakistani targets, which were aimed at demonstrating that government claims of victory over the Taliban were unfounded. But the WFP deaths also represented implementation of a Taliban propaganda assertion we had been hearing more and more, that the UN was an enemy of Islam and a tool of the West. It sent a chill through all UN staff in Pakistan.

The attack also revealed the UN's woeful lack of security preparation in Pakistan. The dangers to staff were becoming almost as great as they had been in Afghanistan, but our readiness to meet them bore no relation to what had been put in place there. Most of the 3000 international and national staff were poorly trained in security precautions; premises were scattered and generally not proof against determined suicide bombers; vehicles were too easily identifiable; intelligence was poor; and there was only a tiny full-time security presence to pull the necessary precautions together. This prompted a root and branch look not only at the security set-up, but also at the whole UN footprint in Pakistan.

Late 2009 therefore saw a so-called programme criticality survey for Pakistan, to identify which UN activities in the country were really essential and urgent for the local population. Those which were not would be cancelled or postponed in order to reduce the staff at risk. Since life-saving activities were presumed to be essential, humanitarian operations were not directly affected. But everything else had to prove its worth. Each UN agency's local office had to rate its own projects. Most agencies were naturally inclined to defend their own activities – the argument was that if they were not essential they would not be doing them in the first place! The team on the ground was therefore unable to make the necessary choices.

In the end, Ban ki-Moon had to impose an arbitrary 25 per cent cut in staff numbers to force the necessary decisions about cancelling projects. The outcome was no doubt imperfect, but the process did at least show that the UN could take tough decisions when it really had to. It was also a valuable precedent for future similar situations, sadly increasingly likely, where the UN is under attack in a particular country and has to decide collectively on its fundamental priorities. As well as WFP in Pakistan in 2009, we had already seen the terrible attack in Algiers in November 2007 which left seventeen dead. An attack on the

UN building in Abuja by the Islamic group Boko Haram in August 2011 killed twenty-three people. There will be others.

UN leadership

Questions about the size of the UN presence in the country were linked to a wider argument about how the UN should deal with Pakistan, a country in which it had a big development stake. In other conflict-affected countries, there was usually a leading UN figure in the shape of a special representative of the secretary-general (SRSG), with more status, seniority, and clout than the ordinary UN resident coordinator. The Pakistanis had absolutely refused to consider such an appointment because they regarded it as a signal that they were seen by the outside world as a basket case. There was a UN representative appointed to help a group of countries known as the Friends of Democratic Pakistan, mostly key donors, but that was not the same thing.

Pakistani policy was, in fact, to restrict the UN role as far as they could. They would accept humanitarian aid if necessary, but do all they could to control it. They would try to maximize reconstruction funding, but retain a total veto over where it was spent. And meanwhile, they would ensure that the UN got nowhere near the big questions of politics and security, regarded as essential to their sovereignty.

The Americans had a different view of this, keen as they were to share some of the burden of dealing with the Pakistanis. When the 2009 crisis in the north-west hit, they quickly began one of their characteristic campaigns in favour of a 'bigger figure' as head of the UN locally, in order to pull together the UN and wider international effort. This campaign was led by then US special representative for 'Af-Pak', Dick Holbrooke, a strong and charismatic diplomat who tragically died in 2011. The Americans saw one of the roles of this bigger figure as coordination of the humanitarian aid effort, because they did not believe that the UN resident coordinator had the time or the qualities to do it effectively himself. But part of the American motivation was also a wish to share some of the difficult issue of international coordination with Pakistan, given their own close but fraught bilateral relationship. There was an element of hypocrisy in this. As in other similar situations, including Afghanistan, where the Americans said that the UN should coordinate the international effort more, everyone knew that they were never likely to accept UN coordination of their own activities in practice.

I agreed about the inability of the then UN resident coordinator to run the relief operation, but was unwilling to see humanitarian coordination entrusted directly to an SRSG with important political responsibilities. This would inevitably blur roles and responsibilities in ways which could jeopardize the effectiveness of the aid operation and put humanitarian staff even more at risk, in the way we had seen in Afghanistan. I therefore pressed for the able and experienced UNICEF representative in Pakistan, Martin Mogwanja, to be made UN humanitarian coordinator, separating this remit from the existing resident coordinator tasks. This was welcome to the humanitarian community, both for practical reasons and because some believed that a separate HC always had more ability to criticize the government and to preserve humanitarian space.

When the crisis was of the magnitude and sensitivity of that in Pakistan, there was a clear logic for a separate HC. But I was not in favour of this separation for all situations, since it too easily led to confusion and competition for UN authority at country level. It also gave a great opportunity for the local government to play divide and rule between the two, or more likely to marginalize the humanitarian coordinator in favour of his resident coordinator development colleague – the latter's position always made him or her more ready to stick close to government views, rather than rocking the boat with criticism of human rights or humanitarian abuses.

In any case, Martin Mogwanja's appointment did not, unfortunately, make the question of a 'big figure' go away. Eventually the Americans persuaded Ban ki-Moon to appoint as 'special envoy' Jean-Maurice Ripert, a French diplomat who had been permanent representative in New York, and convinced the Pakistanis not to stand in the way. Ripert's terms of reference gave him overall oversight of UN activities in Pakistan, but not the mandate or resources to micromanage humanitarian aid, which just about kept us happy.

All this may seem to the reader to be obscure bureaucratic infighting. It was certainly very tiresome to live through, when the priority was to get help to the people suffering on the ground. But these arguments reflected the real difficulty of deciding exactly how international efforts in sensitive, conflict-affected countries are to be organized, and the tricky dynamics of the relationships between international organizations and big member states trying to throw their weight around for their own reasons. We have already seen how delicate this was in Somalia and Sudan. We will see it again in Haiti.

In the Pakistan case, the government proved more than equal to the task of playing the international community at bureaucratic games. Despite their apparent acceptance of Ripert's appointment, in practice they froze him out, to the point that he was eventually taken out by Ban ki-Moon and replaced, after only just over a year, in the even more fraught context of the floods of autumn 2010. Martin Mogwanja, on the other hand, who knew the local authorities well, and how to handle them, continued to do a good job as HC, in very challenging circumstances.

How to operate safely

Behind these organizational questions was the problem of how to maintain life-saving operations in difficult and dangerous contexts such as Afghanistan and Pakistan. Humanitarian organizations were, as always, desperate to keep their activities going if at all possible because the very complexity of the context meant that the needs were correspondingly high. However, they also owed a duty of care to their own staff which could not be ducked. Different agencies dealt with this in different ways, though transparency about the risks, opportunities for staff members to opt out, good local security, and proper evacuation and insurance arrangements were common essentials. But that still left the contentious issue of how to operate effectively when international staff could not reach the areas of operations, except perhaps on occasional rapid and highly protected visits.

The obvious solution was to rely on local staff. But this raised questions of both principle and practice. On the principle side was the unacceptability of transferring risk to locals and appearing to value their lives less highly than those of international staff. No one did this intentionally or consciously, but sometimes it was hard to escape the impression of double standards. Figures about deaths and injuries among humanitarian workers – for example, in the press – tended to focus on international staff only; and the public fuss about the death or abduction of an international worker tended to be much greater than that for a national staff member.

From a practical point of view, it was, of course, true that a national of the country concerned could blend into the local environment much more easily than an outsider, knew the local dynamics and risks much more readily, and had his or her own ways of mitigating these risks. But this was absolutely no guarantee of safety. Sometimes locals working for international organizations, even humanitarian ones, were specifically seen by armed insurgents as traitors collaborating with the enemy, and therefore as particular targets in their own right.

Similar considerations applied to transferring activities to local NGOs, so that they did the hard and dangerous work of delivering the aid at the sharp end. All agencies and international NGOs do this to some extent in any case, as part of good practice in developing local capacity, and working with those who understand local conditions best. But transferring all the risk to local NGOs, even if they seem happy to accept it, and the funding which goes with it, raises awkward questions of principle and propriety which cannot be ignored.

There is no obvious right answer but, while each case needs to be looked at on its merits by each humanitarian organization, bearing in mind its traditions, there is a lot to be learned about best practice from those who have spent years trying to work out the right approaches, such as the ICRC. In any case, transparency about the risks has to be part of the answer, rather than leaving such things unsaid. This is an issue with which the humanitarian community will have to continue to grapple.

Talking to terrorists
Operating safely also depends on relations with those with power and guns. As we have seen in previous chapters, humanitarian contact with the non-state armed groups operating in a conflict zone is often controversial. The ideal for humanitarian organizations is a constant and open dialogue with such groups to explain what is being done and why, and to gain their acceptance of these activities for the benefit of the people, with no political motive or agenda. This has often worked. For example, it has allowed humanitarian agencies such as the International Committee of the Red Cross or Médecins Sans Frontières to

move with relative freedom between government- and insurgent-controlled areas, and operate safely in both. This doctrine of 'consent' is at the heart of humanitarian policy wherever possible.

However, it is far from always possible. Some armed groups are unwilling to make any promises to outsiders. Some have no recognizable command and control structures, making agreements difficult to reach, and unreliable as between different factions. And sometimes the government concerned, or parts of the international community, have strong objections to any contact with such groups because they fear that this will confer on them a measure of respectability and recognition they do not deserve.

In the Pakistan case, the government made it clear in 2008 that they would take a very dim view indeed of any humanitarian organization making contact with the local Taliban or other armed rebel groups operating on their territory, such as those in Balochistan. We did not accept in principle that they had the right to ban such contacts, but clearly their objections had to be factored in as a matter of practical politics. The government would certainly come to know of any contacts, and could well react by expelling the organization concerned. This would be counterproductive from all points of view, especially that of the people we were trying to help.

In Pakistan, once the attacks in the north-west started in earnest in early 2009, it became in any case almost impossible to contact the scattered Taliban leadership. The issues therefore remained moot. But the suspicions of the authorities, and our wish to resume contacts when we could, were still there, and no doubt still are. There is no easy answer, but it is up to the humanitarian community to explain more clearly and convincingly to politicians and diplomats why the doctrine of consent is so important, and that talking to terrorists is not only vital for humanitarians, but also has no automatic wider political implications.

Floods

The crisis in the north-west was still rumbling on in summer 2010 when Pakistan was overwhelmed by the largest floods in living memory, caused by astonishingly heavy downpours in the same north-west area. As the massive volumes of water made their way down the river system towards the sea, they wrecked huge tracts of farmland, destroyed vital infrastructure – roads, railways, bridges, dams, power lines – and ruined the lives of at least 20 million people. Deaths were relatively few, at a few hundred, but the humanitarian needs were overwhelming, dwarfing those of the conflict with the Taliban and, indeed, most other humanitarian crises. The health risks from water-borne diseases were frightening, and the requirements for food, clean water, and shelter mind-bogglingly large.

Unfortunately, the international reaction, including from the public, was not commensurate with the scale of the disaster, and was completely different from that which had accompanied the Haiti earthquake earlier the same year. Then the world had reacted with sympathetic horror, and instinctive and massive generosity, helped by twenty-four-hour media coverage.

Why the difference? The Pakistan floods started in late July/early August, when many in the West were on holiday. Disaster was, no doubt, not what people wanted to see or respond to at that moment. Floods do not, in any case, have the same television impact as an earthquake, with the drama of collapsed buildings, thousands of bodies, survivors being pulled out from the rubble over several days, and the shocked population wandering the streets. An aerial shot of lots of water can be impressive, but thereafter the images tend to be repetitive. The number of dead did not have the same capacity to shock.

But there was something more at work too. Was it compassion fatigue about the subcontinent? Had there been too many recent disasters altogether? Was it a feeling that a country which could afford to have nuclear weapons should be able to deal with its own disasters? Was it a reaction against Pakistan as a source of terrorism? It may well have been a combination of all these things. But the fact was that the global public seemed unmoved, with the partial exception of the UK. This relative public indifference then, inevitably, had an impact on the willingness of donor governments to loosen their humanitarian purse strings too, especially when those purses had already been stretched to breaking point by Haiti.

It was, therefore, a real struggle to mobilize the necessary resources. We launched a first emergency appeal for $460 million in mid-August, knowing the needs would in the end be much greater than that. But reaching even that figure proved a major challenge.

I accompanied Ban ki-Moon on a rapid visit in late August 2010, a few days before I was due to leave the job of ERC. We were horrified by the extent of the suffering, and indeed of the floods themselves. There was water as far as the eye could see and as far as our helicopter could reach. The Pakistani government had taken on the main immediate responsibility for relief, while the international agencies tried to scale up their efforts, and switch from the continuing IDP issues in the north-west to this much bigger drama. The Pakistan army did a good job in many ways, which helped their reputation in the country. But they too were overwhelmed by the sheer scale of the disaster.

The catastrophe unfolded over a relatively long period, and in an odd fashion. As the flood waters made their way south, their arrival in particular areas could be foreseen weeks in advance, and preparations made accordingly, at least in theory. However, it was not so clear exactly where the water would overwhelm the flood defences, or where it would finish up flowing. This was sadly not just a matter of chance and the solidity of particular embankments. Local politicians and warlords battled it out as the water approached to see who could open or close crucial sluices, or even make deliberate breaches in the earth levees which lined the main rivers, in order to divert the water away from their own lands. It was a dirty business where those with the most goons and the most guns won out. The poorest communities were, as always, the main victims.

The government, meanwhile, struggled to give the impression of being in charge. President Zardari was heavily criticized for leaving the country for a visit to Europe just after the floods started. When Ban ki-Moon and I met him, he still gave off an air of general detachment, as he had during the earlier crisis in the north-west. But he was sufficiently concerned by adverse reaction to his European foray to decide that he had better accompany us to the flood-affected area. His advisers were not at all sure that this was sensible. They feared a backlash from the disgruntled local population. We feared for our part that our visit would be even more heavily controlled by the security agencies than it would have been otherwise, to make sure we only met people who could be trusted not to boo him. In the end, it passed off not too badly. If there was certainly a Potemkin element to part of our tour, it did at least force the president to confront some of the ground realities, and there were not too many unpleasant scenes for the media to rake over.

I handed over the reins to my successor, Valerie Amos, just as the Pakistan floods were reaching their height. I was sorry to land her in the middle of such a mess, but there was probably never going to be an ideal moment to leave. There was always a new crisis somewhere. She sensibly decided to get to Pakistan herself as soon as she possibly could. It was a sobering start to her mandate. But it was perhaps as good a place as any to learn about the problems of dealing with a massive emergency which threatened to overwhelm international capacity, and of working with a difficult and sensitive government.

Eventually, the waters did recede, though they took months to dry up in southern Sind, nearest the sea. Almost two years on, as I write, a lot of progress has been made in helping people to return to their lands and rebuild their lives. Crops have been replanted and reconstruction of the key parts of the infrastructure is under way. But it will take many years before the damage can be finally undone. And there is no guarantee that another flood will not have come along in the interim to set all these efforts at naught. Disaster risk-reduction measures are still sadly lacking.

Back to the future

Meanwhile, the conflict in the north-west, though reduced in intensity, has by no means gone away. The political and security situation in areas like the Swat valley remains fragile, while most of Waziristan is still bandit country. In mid-2012, fighting in the Khyber region once more displaced hundreds of thousands of people into Mardan province, to add to the half a million who had never gone home from 2009. The regular US drone attacks on the Taliban, in the meantime, may seem to be effective from a military point of view, but accompanying civilian casualties and the challenge to Pakistan's sovereignty inevitably exacerbate American–Pakistani differences.

The truth is that little is likely to change the underlying tensions in the area while some of the fundamentals remain. As long as the conflict in Afghanistan goes on, and as long as Pakistan remains so fragile and poorly governed, with an essentially feudal society in the north-west, and so little investment in economic and social improvement for the people, the seeds of violence will still be evident. The need for humanitarian aid is therefore likely to remain. We may also be doomed to repeat the same cycle of difficulties with the government, the military, and the non-state armed groups unless some of the basic lessons from the past can be learned. I wish I could be more optimistic about this, but it is hard to see Pakistani politics changing radically in the next few years, or the baleful influence of Afghanistan reducing.

For now, I wish Western governments could come to a more nuanced view of local security and political issues, rather than a Manichean perception of good and bad actors, over-influenced by the war on terrorism. This would give them a better chance of influencing events effectively, and understanding the inevitably complicated local dynamics. But I am not confident of that either.

Map Sources: Europa Technologies, UNCS. Map created in Nov 2011.

CHAPTER TEN

Earthquake horrors in Haiti

The most dramatic natural disaster of my time as ERC was the earthquake which devastated Haiti's capital, Port-au-Prince, in January 2010. At 7.0 on the Richter scale, it was the biggest tremor to hit the country in 200 years. The relief operation which followed illustrated in full the practical and policy challenges which accompany any such catastrophic event. However, making the basics happen quickly and efficiently in Haiti was unusually tough, for a host of reasons. Managing personal frustration under intense media scrutiny was also a major challenge. I hope the details of the operation will be instructive from all these points of view.

I had already seen something of the problems of helping in Haiti when the country was hit by four successive tropical storms in 2008. The massive flooding left the port city of Gonaïves under several feet of mud, and ruined 70 per cent of Haiti's agriculture. Despite the scale of the devastation, getting the aid effort moving then was a huge logistic and political struggle. I therefore knew a little of the dysfunctional government and alienated society in what was habitually and rightly characterized as the poorest country in the western hemisphere. But nothing had prepared me for what was to happen after the earthquake.

The context

The problems of this western half of the island of Hispaniola (the Dominican Republic occupies the rest) cannot be understood without a look at its sad history. A slave revolt secured the country's independence from France as early as 1804. However, this was only the beginning of a long series of political crises, military coups, and episodes of foreign interference. US occupation of the island from 1915 to 1934 helped Haiti's infrastructure, but did not bring lasting stability.

The country's recent history has been particularly tragic. Repressive dictatorship under Papa Doc Duvalier, his son Baby Doc, and their dreaded Tontons Macoutes thugs, from 1957 to 1986, undermined Haiti's institutions and fragmented its society. Jean-Bertrand Aristide, elected president in 1990, but quickly driven out of office, was first helped back to power by the US in the name of democracy in 1994, then effectively ousted again with their help ten years later. Aristide had abolished the army and a UN peacekeeping force, known as MINUSTAH, had to be established by the Security Council after his departure, to try to restore order and, in particular, bring the powerful criminal gangs under control.

René Préval had been elected president for the second time in 2005, and was nearing the end of his term on that fateful January day. Despite his good intentions, he had not succeeded in reforming the Haitian body politic either. Society and the economy in this country of 10 million people were still dominated by a few feudal families, poverty and unemployment were widespread, and criminal gangs were still powerful, especially in the extensive slums of Port-au-Prince. Meanwhile, political infighting and rampant corruption prevented effective governance, to the extent that international NGOs working in the country (mostly American) had created an alternative network of services which came to be known as the 'Republic of NGOs'. This disempowered the government further.

The country's other huge problem was environmental degradation. Forest cover had been reduced almost to zero by poor practice and exploitation. Satellite pictures of the border with the Dominican Republic showed green tree cover on one side and bare brown earth on the other. All attempts at reforestation seemed doomed to fail: whatever grew was immediately cut down by people trying to scratch a living by making and selling the charcoal universally used for cooking. The denuded hillsides brought devastating soil erosion and flash flooding from the frequent tropical storms.

Haiti's chronic exposure to hurricanes and flash floods had distracted attention from its vulnerability to earthquakes. The island straddles two major and active seismic faults, linked to the clash of the North American and Caribbean tectonic plates. Port-au-Prince had been badly shaken in the eighteenth and nineteenth centuries. Other cities had been hit in the twentieth century. The potential for another major event was known. But it had been shunted into the background by Haiti's many other ills. Preparedness for an earthquake was low. In any case, a country as poor and as poorly run as Haiti was never likely to enforce the planning and building codes necessary to cope with a major shock. The overcrowded capital, with at least 3 million inhabitants (no one was counting), was particularly vulnerable.

Cataclysm

In the late afternoon of 12 January 2010, I was with other senior UN staff in New York when all our mobile phones began to buzz. The first news of a dramatic event in Haiti had begun to filter through. The signs that we might be facing something really big quickly accumulated. Back in my office, I was able to speak briefly to the humanitarian coordinator and the head of the OCHA office in Port–au-Prince before the phones went dead. They were standing in the darkness in the car park of one of the UN buildings, trying to decide how far they could go back into the partly destroyed building to rescue colleagues. The OCHA head did not know what had happened to his wife and two small children because he could not get through to them on the telephone or physically. He continued working on the response anyway, despite the agony of uncertainty, until it was tragically confirmed a couple of days later that they had been killed when their apartment building collapsed.

By the following morning the talk was already of huge destruction and hundreds of dead. We knew that the main UN building had partly collapsed, with the leadership inside, their fates unknown. The airport was closed and the government seemed to have, in effect, disappeared under the rubble. But it was even worse than we imagined. Hundreds of thousands had died – the eventual government figure of 300,000 plus may be a bit over the mark, but it is not implausible. Large parts of Port-au-Prince had collapsed, particularly where poor-quality houses were piled together on the hills which make up much of the city. The devastation was symbolized by the collapse of the main dome of the presidential palace itself. The city echoed to the screams for help of thousands of people trapped. Outside the capital, the town at the earthquake's epicentre, Léogâne, was almost completely destroyed. Most organizations, including the humanitarian agencies and NGOs, had themselves lost staff, could no longer use their headquarters buildings, and were in chaos.

Friends and neighbours pulled out survivors as they could – they are always the most effective, but least appreciated, responders

– but there were limits to what they could do without specialized equipment in the midst of so much collapsed concrete. International teams flooded in to help. Over the following days around 130 people were pulled out, a few after hope had been more or less abandoned. This was a considerable success for international search-and-rescue teams, who often only arrive after most chances of finding survivors alive have effectively gone.

Getting the basics right

However, these were rare positive moments in a bleak and chaotic picture. Even many of those rescued had to have limbs amputated, with all the risks of infection in the post-earthquake chaos and Haiti's steamy climate. Indeed problems of medical care loomed largest in the first few days, as the international community struggled to mobilize and get to Haiti, even though it was only less than two hours flight from the US mainland. The local hospitals were doing their best, but had themselves been badly damaged, while many doctors and nurses were desperately trying to find members of their own families. In time, a combination of the military from the US and Canada, and agencies such as the Red Cross and Médecins Sans Frontières, were able to provide decent emergency treatment. A few excellent field hospitals arrived from elsewhere, including Israel. But aftercare remained a big problem, except for those lucky enough to stay on a US hospital ship for a few days. Many had little choice but to return to the rubble and take their chances.

After medical care, the basics of water, food, and shelter were what worried us most, with so little capacity on the ground and such limited access. Some 3 million people were thought to have been badly affected. The airport was back in partial operation after a few days, thanks to US military expertise, but the port was closed for the foreseeable future. There were few trucks and even less fuel on the spot. In order to bring in the large quantities of aid required, road links from the Dominican Republic were the only immediate option. Organizing the necessary transport capacity became a top priority. Fortunately, the authorities in the Dominican Republic quickly took a very constructive attitude, setting aside decades of hostility.

Water proved less of a problem than initially feared. The capital's main treatment plant had not been badly damaged, miraculously, and was back working after a few days. This was a great relief: bottled water is expensive and hard to transport, while the bottles themselves quickly become an environmental hazard. Large amounts of bottled water were still imported in the early stages, particularly by the American military, but once distribution by tankers could be organized, drinking water became much less of a life-or-death issue.

Feeding people was trickier. The capital had largely depended on imported food even before the earthquake. Local agriculture had been undermined by decades of neglect and disasters, as well as years of cheap supplies of US rice. Global price rises in 2008 had already plunged millions of Haitians into food insecurity, provoking riots. After the earthquake, all commercial supply arrangements broke down. The airport, even once patched up, was clogged with military flights. Air transport was, in any case, too expensive for bulk food. How were we to feed the survivors for the next few months, especially when most people had no means of cooking? The first thought was ready-to-eat meals (MREs). The World Food Programme worked out how many would be needed, and how to get them to Haiti. But this proved a blind alley. The tens of millions of MREs required did not exist, even in US military stocks. Thousands of tons of rice and grain would be needed instead, despite the problems of cooking it for many survivors.

WFP did an excellent job in standing up the road-based supply chain from the Dominican Republic, and also beginning to ship bulk food to nearby undamaged ports. The problems of overall supply began to look soluble. But this still left the delicate question of distributing food effectively in a city where rubble made many roads impassable, there were no organized camps, truck capacity and fuel were scarce at best, and there were fears about insecurity in a notoriously volatile environment. It took a while to establish an effective system.

This led to a lot of criticism from the international media, particularly the US TV networks. They were reporting from Haiti 24/7, notably CNN, looking constantly for new angles, and unwilling to understand the problems of organizing a sustainable and fair system for well over 2 million people. It was the scale of the tonnage needed every day they could not grasp. If they were there with their cameras, why couldn't enough food be there too?

This almost led to some poor, and highly risky, decisions by the US aid authorities. Under fire from their own media and desperate to show they were being effective, they started to drop supplies of food and water directly out of helicopters in one or two places, causing a mad scramble. We had to explain to the decision-makers in Washington that this was not only unnecessary, since people did not die of starvation after a few days, but also seriously dangerous: the chances of supplies hitting people waiting underneath were high, and the lack of discrimination about who got the food would lead to bad outcomes: the fittest and strongest, rather than the neediest and most vulnerable, would get what fell, and probably sell it for a huge mark-up to the rest. Fights, even deaths, were likely. Random food drops could only be justified in the most extreme famine circumstances, and we were nowhere near those, whatever CNN might think.

In the end, while it remained tough and slow, WFP and their partner NGOs did a good job. No one starved, though many were hungry. Storage and distribution points were identified and made safe at different points in Port-au-Prince and outside – no easy task when so few major buildings were still standing and usable. Trucks and fuel were scraped together. Secure(ish) ration cards were given to the females of each household, to maximize the chances of the food reaching the rest of the families. Help for the women to get the food home was arranged, in case they were robbed on the way. MINUSTAH and the US and Canadian forces were engaged to provide overall security.

There were one or two potential riots where distributions had to be suspended, but remarkably little trouble overall. Violence had been a big fear immediately after the earthquake, not helped by the escape of the capital's worst criminals when the walls of the main jail cracked open. Happily, such concerns proved largely unfounded. We were able progressively to relax security requirements for humanitarian workers, which had otherwise been proving increasingly onerous and bureaucratic.

Shelter

After food, emergency accommodation remained the most difficult problem for many months. In the capital alone, well over 100,000 houses and apartments had been destroyed or rendered uninhabitable. Aftershocks were frequent, large, and terrifying to an already traumatized population. Many who could have gone back to their homes were too frightened to do so, while those who rented had no money to pay since their jobs had disappeared with the earthquake. Up to 2 million people needed shelter.

The first thought was to establish large camps just outside Port-au-Prince. Services would be much easier to provide there, away from the rubble and traffic nightmares, and the environment would be much safer, particularly for women and children. But it quickly became clear that there was no space: the city is squeezed between the sea and the mountains, and the local experts were unanimous that any apparently free flat land was only unoccupied because it was flooded during the monsoon season. In any case, people were unwilling to move away from their neighbourhoods, despite everything: their lives and livelihoods had been there, and their possessions – even if stuck in their collapsed houses – were there too.

We therefore quickly decided we would have to help people wherever they were. That meant in the so-called spontaneous settlements which had already sprung up. Every available bit of space, including the main square in front of the collapsed presidential palace, had been quickly covered with rudimentary shelters made from rags and sticks and anything people could lay their hands on. There were hundreds of such sites all over the city and in the towns outside. It said something about the underlying poverty that such camps, however poor the conditions, became a magnet for many not made homeless by the earthquake but just hoping for a little aid to get them through the days.

People could survive in such camps for a little while. The weather at the beginning of the year was mostly warm and dry. But the monsoon would be upon us in not many weeks, and it was imperative to get something more substantial over people's heads. There was no way of rebuilding anything in the time available, even if the countless tons of rubble could somehow have been miraculously cleared. The only possible solution was hundreds of thousands of tents or, better because more flexible, plastic sheets/tarpaulins, timber and ropes. That may sound relatively straightforward in this day and age. After all, when we could send a man to the moon, how difficult could it be to get tents and tarpaulins to Haiti, which was more accessible than most disaster sites?

The answer, we were to discover, was very difficult indeed, though we never succeeded in convincing the media that this was anything but a cover story for our incompetence. There were some stocks of tents and plastic sheets available in humanitarian stores around the world, but nothing like enough. There were some available for purchase worldwide, but again not nearly enough of the quality we needed – anything thin and insubstantial would quickly be in shreds in the heat, rain and wind of Haiti. Even when ordered and bought, getting them to Haiti was a huge logistical challenge, as long as the port was out and truck capacity was monopolized by food and medical supplies. Air transport for such heavy items was largely unaffordable, even with the sums so generously donated by individuals and governments alike for Haiti. We therefore struggled to get the necessary materials to Haiti in a timely way. Complaints mounted.

Did we make mistakes in the area of shelter? Without doubt. Under the post-tsunami humanitarian reforms introduced in 2006, each major relief sector, or cluster, was organized, coordinated and led separately. One agency was given the lead locally for each crisis, and was responsible for effective aid delivery. Even though they were not the normal 'cluster lead', we entrusted shelter in Haiti to the International Organization for Migration (IOM), because they had a lot of local capacity on the ground.

It soon became clear that they were struggling. This was not entirely their fault. In addition to the supply problems, it took time to get the right strategy agreed. A couple of key donors were guilty of trying to implement strategies of their own before rallying to the majority approach. Nevertheless, IOM had after a few weeks lost the confidence of other agencies and NGOs. Not enough progress was being made on the ground, key decisions were not being taken quickly enough, and communication was poor to non-existent. I therefore had to take the virtually unprecedented step of taking the lead away from them, and giving it to the International Federation of the Red Cross/Red Crescent. They were the global cluster lead for shelter, but had had very little presence on the ground at the start of the crisis. This was the right move, but still took some time to have an effect.

All told, it took about six months of effort, amid great frustration and criticism, to break the back of the task of putting a decent cover over most heads. Some 150,000 tents and tarpaulins were procured, delivered, and distributed in that time. However, the issues by no means ended there. Even good-quality materials only lasted six to nine months in Haitian conditions. Procurement had to go on at almost the same rate for many months more to ensure adequate replacements were available.

More seriously still, since it would be years before what had been destroyed could be fully rebuilt, we needed an intermediate housing solution. That meant designing temporary dwellings for the conditions, bringing in huge amounts of building materials, and, above all, finding land. Here we ran into further big trouble. It proved virtually impossible to find decent areas for construction which were close enough to the capital for people to be prepared to go there, that were not on a flood plain, and had owners willing to release them. Land tenure was a delicate issue in a country with no proper cadastre, little written proof of ownership, and a lot of deep feudal and business interests. The government was very reluctant to commandeer land, fearing endless problems from powerful landlords and local authorities, ever ready to exploit the situation for political reasons. Landlords were even more reluctant to see their land used for longer-term camps, fearing that these would become permanent settlements, even slums.

As I had repeatedly found to be the case in Haiti, each step forward therefore took a long time, and involved multiple frustrations and steps backwards or sideways on the way. Eventually, sites were identified, and some temporary houses built. But they were further from Port-au-Prince than was desirable, and in the absence of good basic services, easy transport, and locally available jobs, they were not popular. Many preferred to take their chances where they were in the central areas of the capital. Shelter remains an issue as I write.

Sanitation

Our waking hours were also dominated by the provision of toilets. Even before the earthquake the proportion of the capital's citizens with access to adequate sanitation was unconscionably low, especially in the big slum areas of Cité Soleil, fortunately largely untouched by the earthquake. Trying to provide it for the homeless now proved a massive headache. Digging latrines, the usual humanitarian solution in rural areas, was not possible in a city – most landlords flatly refused to allow it, even if there had been enough soft ground available to make it physically possible. The number of spontaneous camps also made economies of scale difficult. In the end, portable toilets had to be imported by the thousand from all over the world, reliable arrangements made for them to be emptied frequently, and places to dispose of the waste safely identified – which took us straight back to the land issue. All this took vast amounts of time, money, and effort to put together, particularly daily cleaning and waste disposal.

Protection

Keeping the vulnerable safe was a major priority, and threw up some awkward dilemmas. There were many street children and orphans before the disaster, and even more after. The TV crews did a lot to highlight their plight. But this had unfortunate and unforeseen results. Some groups, particularly from the US, took it upon themselves to fly in and take children home for adoption. But they consulted no one and made some terrible mistakes. They even took some children who were not actually orphans, but had been handed into care by parents unable to look after them. This caused an understandable outcry. The process had to go into hasty reverse.

Women in the spontaneous camps were also at great risk, in a country where respect for women's rights was never high. My visits to the camps were punctuated by women and girls tearfully recounting their experiences and well-justified fears. Allegations of appalling sexual violence circulated, along with claims that gangs were taking control of the camps, and practising extortion and other abuses on a large scale. It was not easy to get to the bottom of such claims, and even harder to provide on-the-spot security for the hundreds of camps. Neither MINUSTAH nor the Haitian police, who had lost a lot of men and equipment in the earthquake, had the capacity to do much, despite our urgings. We therefore had to do what we could ourselves; for example, by providing lighting in the camps and ensuring in particular that the latrines were well sited and lit, to minimize risks. We also organized local camp-management structures. But we were very conscious that this was not enough.

Frustration

Because Haiti was such a big crisis, so much in the spotlight, and because everything seemed so difficult and time-consuming, I found myself not only leading – as usual – overall coordination and policy-setting, acting as global spokesman, and raising international relief funds (we appealed for $1.5 billion dollars for the first year alone), but also increasingly dragged down into the details to try to get things moving. I was in Haiti shortly after the earthquake, with Ban ki-Moon, and at regular intervals thereafter. It was a thankless business, trying to get the government to take decisions, pressing the agencies and NGOs to move faster, keeping restless donors pointing in the right direction, and managing the media.

It was made worse in the early days by the struggle to know exactly what was happening. Reliable information, for the media and donors, but also for the humanitarian community themselves, is a major requirement. Who exactly needs what, and where are they? Who is providing what, and when and how? Once an operation is up and running, this information can start to be collected reliably. But at the beginning – when the press are screaming to know how many people have been fed that day, donors are demanding to know what aid is most needed, and there are a myriad organizations on the ground, struggling to cope, who cannot be expected to prioritize collection of statistics – getting a clear picture can be difficult. Haiti illustrated this in full measure.

My own frustrations boiled over after a further visit to Haiti in early March. I sent a stiff message to humanitarian partners and cluster leads, telling them in no uncertain terms that given the magnitude of the crisis they had to do better on strategy, information, and delivery. This email was leaked to the press (not by me), and led to a lot of questions. Was I saying that we had failed?

The reality was more complex. We were making progress despite everything. However, there were real problems of coherence and leadership on the ground. The 'cluster' system of coordination functioned well at the beginning in kick-starting the response, but struggled thereafter. Cluster-lead agencies who were trying desperately to get their own operations moving were reluctant to put the resources necessary – specifically, enough good senior people – into coordination of cluster aid delivery and information. Agreeing and implementing coherent strategies in key areas was taking longer than it should have done.

Practical limitations had a lot to do with these shortcomings. Getting anything done in the crowded urban environment of Port-au-Prince proved an unexpected headache for organizations used to working in spacious rural environments, however remote. Accommodation for humanitarian workers, for both office and living purposes, was a nightmare for the first few months. No safe buildings were available except the UN logistical base near the airport. This was quickly overrun by humanitarians sleeping wherever they could find a space, and fighting for power and internet connections. For many weeks, until large living tents and a ship moored off the port arrived, conditions were terrible, with little food and water and virtually no showers. This was more than the displaced of the capital had, I hear you say. True – but working effectively in such conditions, with little sleep, for more than a few weeks at a time, was almost impossible. Burnout was rapid, and the consequent high turnover of staff a real problem.

This exacerbated a recurring 'surge capacity' problem in such crises, namely the difficulty of maintaining the number and quality of staff as the first wave of emergency responders move out after a couple of months. Haiti exposed the frailty of the systems for OCHA and many other organizations. OCHA had gone from four staff in Haiti to more than fifty in a couple of weeks. But as many of these began to rotate out to go back to their regular jobs, having done their emergency stint, we did not have enough permanent staff ready to take their places – identifying enough

French-speakers to work in francophone Haiti was a particular problem. Finding the necessary further fifty temporary staff with the right experience was extremely challenging. This issue of surge capacity requires more work and imagination, given that the organizations concerned cannot afford to have large numbers of staff just waiting around for the next emergency.

In the Haiti case, these problems were further compounded by the urgent need to move out staff who had been working in the capital at the time of the earthquake. It took us a couple of weeks to realize the immediacy of this requirement. Like the rest of the population, the staff concerned had been traumatized by what they had lived through, a trauma deepened by every aftershock. Many had escaped death themselves by a hair's breadth. Most had close friends who had been killed. The UN itself had lost under the rubble of its headquarters the head of the MINUSTAH stabilization mission, Hedi Annabi, and his deputy, as well as many others. Grief at these deaths was never far away. Most survivors were desperate to stay, to help the people they had known so well before, and perhaps to expiate the unreasonable guilt they felt for surviving. Many did an amazing job in incredibly difficult circumstances. But they could not, in practice, work effectively for long. Moving them out quickly was vital, even if it also aggravated the lack of local experience and knowledge.

The sheer number of humanitarian organizations who had arrived was also impossible to manage. Hundreds of NGOs were trying to attend coordination meetings, for example in the health cluster. This is not the norm for disasters – usually there are not enough actors on the ground, rather than too many – but it had happened in the media-intense Indian Ocean tsunami too. Driven by a range of motives, from a genuine desire to help to the need to be seen to be there for credibility and fund-raising purposes, far too many NGOs try to get in on the act when there is a major 'television' emergency. Some are too small and inexperienced to assist, and can even make things worse since they, in turn, need help in terms of accommodation, communications, food, and how to operate in an emergency.

Meanwhile, local organizations and NGOs, which had a lot to offer, but were too knocked sideways to be included in the initial stages, continued to be left out as the relief effort developed. Coordination meetings were held in the UN logistics base which had impossible security arrangements for the locals, and were mainly conducted in English, which was no good for local Creole or French speakers. We got better at this as time went on, but ignoring local capacity and wishes is a recurring problem. It is regularly highlighted by evaluations of crisis response, but correcting it remains more of an aspiration than a reality.

Humanitarian leadership

Kim Bolduc, the UN resident and humanitarian coordinator when the earthquake struck, was a tough and experienced former Vietnamese refugee from Canada. She was determined to carry on with what she had been appointed to do, despite the changed circumstances, and her own traumatic experience – when the walls of her office had opened up she thought her end had come. I supported her, while urging an early break. Continuity and local knowledge were important. But the strain was very great. She had had to take overall charge of MINUSTAH until a temporary replacement for Hedi Annabi could be appointed. She had also lost her own immediate support staff.

Instinctively more at home in development than in humanitarian relief, she was slow to set up mechanisms which would have helped unite the humanitarian community around her. Criticism started early, as did, once again, US-led calls for the appointment of a 'bigger figure'. When she was finally persuaded to take a decent leave break a few weeks in, she resigned without warning, complaining that she was being made a scapegoat for problems with the relief operation.

I regretted her departure, but hoped a fresh start might help. However, any thought of finding an effective and consensual successor quickly proved vain. Instead, we ran into a long argument about leadership structure. This was a rerun of disputes we have come across before. Was it possible to combine the roles of resident coordinator and humanitarian coordinator, when the pressures on the emergency and reconstruction sides were simultaneously so great? Was an overall supremo, as once again pushed for by the US, the right answer?

The United Nations Development Programme argued that splitting the RC and HC roles was a recipe for rivalry and inefficiency, and for lack of coordination between relief and reconstruction, a besetting sin in previous crises. Others said the task was simply too great for any one person, no matter how talented. They were supported, as we have also seen before, by more purist humanitarians opposed to combining the roles because they thought RCs were, by definition, too close to the government to be independent.

My own view was that a separate HC made sense in the circumstances of Haiti, as in Pakistan. But I favoured a team player rather than the high-profile banger-of-heads-together the Americans wanted. In the hothouse atmosphere of Haiti, personality clashes were the last thing we needed. We went round these circles for too long while we sought the perfect structure and the individual or individuals who could keep everyone happy. As an emergency measure I brought in Dan Baker, who had done such a good job in Myanmar, as deputy HC. His calm and sure touch immediately began to make a difference.

Eventually, Nigel Fisher, a Canadian brought in to help with the reconstruction planning, but who also had humanitarian experience, was appointed to do both RC and HC jobs. This worked reasonably well, even though I would have preferred to give a separate HC role to Dan Baker. But time and effort spent arguing could have been better devoted to the ground operation.

How much of this was my fault? I was urged by colleagues as soon as the earthquake struck to insist on the removal of the then RC/HC and appoint a tried-and-tested leader. With hindsight, perhaps I should have done so. But there were powerful arguments against this at the time, besides worry about the potentially disruptive influence of a large ego: UNDP were fighting tooth and nail to keep Kim Bolduc in place; I could see the arguments for sticking with someone with local knowledge; and she undoubtedly had many qualities.

In any case, this experience brought to a head the arguments about UN leadership on the ground in a major crisis. It was subsequently agreed by the humanitarian system in 2012 that the resident coordinator in place, whether or not already double-hatted as humanitarian coordinator, should automatically be replaced in the event of a major humanitarian disaster. He or she had obviously not been selected with such a huge role in mind. It should therefore be assumed that someone with different skills and experience was needed.

This helpfully creates a presumption of change which is easier to handle in personal terms than trying to decide whether the incumbent will really be able to rise to the occasion. However, it is far from guaranteed that experienced leaders will be available when they are needed. They are thin on the ground to start with, and also, by definition, unlikely to be waiting around to be called, unless they happen to be already retired. Moreover, there may be cases where keeping the incumbent is, in fact, the right solution. That should not be ruled out, or we are in danger of throwing the baby out with the bathwater.

Working with other players

I have focussed on these details to show what problems can lie behind the scenes of any similar crisis. But there were other more specific Haitian dynamics too. Former US president Bill Clinton has a real commitment to Haiti, ever since he and Hillary spent their honeymoon there. After the earthquake, he immediately volunteered his services, which we welcomed. It made a lot of sense to use his advocacy and convening power. But integrating him and his organization with the rest of the operation was easier said than done. He wanted an overall leadership role which others in the UN were reluctant to concede, not least because they feared that he would not actually devote the necessary time on the ground to such a role.

Moreover, his office was a complicated machine to understand, never mind work with successfully. This was more of a problem on the reconstruction side, but President Clinton's involvement was a mixed blessing for the humanitarians too. He could mobilize resources and people better than anyone else in the world and express the big-picture needs brilliantly. Some things would never have happened without him. His habit of plunging into the minutiae of detailed issues could be less helpful, however – and some of those around him tended to over-promise and under-deliver.

Another preoccupation was how to coordinate with the military, particularly the Americans. We had good reason to be grateful to them. Their deterrent presence helped ensure that no one tried to take advantage of the earthquake for the wrong reasons. They took over the airport and made it function again quickly, notwithstanding some legitimate criticism from the humanitarian community that they unduly favoured their own military flights in the early days. They helped with security for food distributions and other sensitive aid delivery operations. They provided heavy equipment for tasks such as drainage ditch clearance with which we were struggling otherwise. Our relations with both them and the Canadians, doing an excellent job in the devastated towns outside Port-au-Prince, remained good throughout. All concerned recognized that we were in the same boat and could not afford to argue among ourselves.

Nevertheless, there were frustrations on both sides. The Americans found the UN baffling, not surprisingly, and took time to understand that we really did have worthwhile expertise on aid delivery in desperate circumstances. For their part they had a habit of trying to second-guess our strategies in key areas. The reality was that neither of us could find quick fixes for massive problems such as rubble removal or land and property rights. We therefore had to find ways for our very different structures to interact and sort out the right division of labour. The result was a set of liaison committees which were more bureaucratic than any of us wanted, but at least got the basic job done.

The media, constantly looking for a story that wasn't there, did not help. Many American journalists assumed that the US military really wanted to take over leadership of humanitarian relief or indeed already had. The truth was that the military on the spot were far too sensible to want any such thing (though there was a moment when some hotheads in Washington were definitely thinking about it). Why risk getting the blame for something they knew they could not fix and were not qualified to take on anyway? The military also had a strong interest in not staying around too long, both for political reasons (some in Haiti were suspicious of their role for historical reasons), and because they feared that the costs of the operation would simply come out of their regular budget and result in cuts elsewhere.

Meanwhile, dealings with the Haitian government were a constant challenge. It took months to get back on its feet after the earthquake. Most ministries had physically collapsed and many senior officials had died. Ministers had nowhere to work or meet, and no one to advise them. President Préval was personally devastated. He could not and would not address his people publicly for many days. When he did start to operate more effectively, he often seemed more concerned to protect Haitian sovereignty than facilitate the aid operation. Some of his interventions were positively unhelpful – for example, his insistence that food aid should stop after a month, long before this was sensible. We shared his anxiety to avoid aid dependency, but knew that people were still not ready to stand on their own two feet. His prime minister, Jean-Max Bellerive, was able and intelligent, but lacked a political base to give him authority and a decent administrative structure to make things happen. His relationship with the president was also difficult. None of this helped.

Building back better

Problems with the government also reflected a more fundamental dilemma. Everyone agreed that the national and international responsibility was to build Haiti back better than it had been before. Going back to the previous dysfunctional mess would not be good enough. There was also agreement that no reconstruction plans would work unless they had full Haitian ownership – 'no return to the Republic of NGOs' and 'Haitian solutions for Haitian problems' were the watchwords. This was sincere. We all knew that solutions imposed from the outside would never work sustainably.

However, this was easy to say and hard to stick to, when fears of a return to old corrupt ways were still so strong. The World Bank and UNDP, despite their rivalries, did most of the serious work on the early reconstruction plans. This was followed by a long-running dispute about how implementation of the plans should be managed. The Americans, with the support of President Clinton's organization, were keen to put in a ginger group of hundreds of expert outsiders to get things moving quickly. The government, with support from elsewhere in the international community, were determined to keep the key decisions firmly in their own hands. The outcome was a messy compromise which satisfied no one. Slow decision-making on projects also gave a pretext to drag their feet for donors who had promised more than they were really willing or able to give at a New York reconstruction conference in April – $9 billion was pledged, but very little was received or spent in the first two years.

As of mid-2012, what progress has been made? The number of displaced people is about a quarter of what it was. A good proportion of the rubble has been cleared. Some private-sector investment has come in – the crucial requirement if real jobs are going to be created for the future in areas like tourism, agriculture, and textiles. But Port-au-Prince is still far from being in vibrant health and we are still a long way from the objective of 'building back better', to avoid just going back to the previous vulnerabilities. Sadly, international interest has been steadily on the wane for a long time.

There is also an underlying concern, which most people are reluctant to articulate openly: the chances of another major earthquake around the capital remain very high. As always, there is no way of predicting the timing, but the seismologists are clear that the faults running through Haiti, including right through Port-au-Prince, remain active. In a strictly rational world, the capital should probably have been moved somewhere else. The idea was floated in the weeks immediately after the earthquake. But it was always likely to be a political bridge too far. So it quickly proved.

The risk of a further shock means that disaster risk-reduction measures must be centre stage, including strict codes for rebuilding with the latest earthquake-resistant technology and designs. This will probably happen for public buildings. But the chances of it being applied to private housing in the context of Haiti are sadly poor.

Cholera

Tragically, after I left OCHA, in October 2010, just at the point when progress was beginning to be visible, the country was hit by cholera. The death rate was appallingly high in the early stages. The first six months saw more than 250,000 cases, and 5000 deaths. The weakened condition of the population after the earthquake was undoubtedly a factor. But Haiti had also previously been cholera-free for many years. There was, therefore, no natural immunity and no popular experience in dealing with it.

Where did the disease come from? Suspicion fell quickly on the Nepalese contingent of MINUSTAH: the outbreak started near their base, the strain of cholera was from South Asia, and Nepal had just had an outbreak when the contingent left the country. The UN has never admitted responsibility, and it is almost impossible to prove. But it is certainly widely believed in Haiti that MINUSTAH was to blame. Their failure to acknowledge this, even though doing so would have made no practical difference, has certainly contributed to the force's unpopularity among the locals.

Lessons

Did Haiti demonstrate that the overall humanitarian model, despite the 2006 reforms, was inadequate? A major lessons-learned report was produced to coincide with the six-months anniversary of the earthquake. Its conclusions were balanced, but sobering.

We had got more right than wrong: 4 million people had received food assistance, 1.2 million safe water supplies, 1.5 million emergency shelter, 1 million cash-for-work, and so on. But there were many areas where we should have done better: stronger early leadership, resources for cluster leaders, continuity and quality of surge staff, speed of response on shelter, engagement with local civil society, communication with the affected population, working with the military and the private sector, operating in an urban setting.

I think this overall judgment of the report is about right. There was no big second wave of deaths from hunger or disaster-related disease in the months immediately after the disaster, though the conditions were there. The shelter and sanitation problems were just about managed. Fears of another major catastrophe from a hurricane hit on the camps were not in the end borne out. Enough money was raised to keep the humanitarian show on the road, at least for the first year. Coordination on the ground just about did its job, though the system creaked badly at times. Not much to be proud of, but nothing to be too ashamed about either, in the difficult circumstances of Haiti.

Nevertheless, there is no doubt we need to improve the system further. Unfortunately, ideas which have been put forward for a fresh start after Haiti, such as a standing humanitarian force of some kind (to be called the red helmets, on the analogy of the peacekeepers' blue helmets), may seem superficially attractive, but do not stand up to scrutiny. They would almost certainly complicate rather than simplify the task of responding quickly and effectively in emergencies. I will return to this question at the end of the book, in Chapter Fourteen.

Meanwhile, the focus should remain on how to improve the lives of the long-suffering Haitian people. Like most peoples around the world, all they need is a half-decent chance from a half-decent government, and they will manage the rest. Will it be different this time? The chances of a better Haiti in five or ten years' time still look fragile. The political situation is unhealthy, with Baby Doc Duvalier back in the country again without being prosecuted for his crimes, and former president Aristide still lurking in the wings.

For its part, the international community is not as fundamentally committed to helping Haiti as it should be, despite all the fine words in the wake of the earthquake. They have little confidence in the Haitian government turning the situation round, and are still not sure the money they are ready to put in will be well used. This is understandable. Governments have to be wary of what they are doing with their taxpayers' money, and past experience in Haiti naturally leads to scepticism. However, I am convinced that, albeit with all the monitoring and due diligence we can manage, international donors have to take risks in this case, for the greater good. Going back to a situation where the Haitian government is disempowered will be fatal. They have to lead, take responsibility, and be accountable for what they do, above all to the people of Haiti.

In any case, Haiti will remain highly exposed to further disasters, beyond the earthquake risk, because of the island's position on the traditional tracks of destructive Caribbean hurricanes and the environmental degradation – which will not be fixed as long as the people continue to rely on charcoal for cooking. Whatever the state of the economy and redevelopment, there is no excuse for not putting in place now the best disaster-impact-mitigation measures available, to make the population much more resilient to both floods and earthquakes, and the best disaster-management system that can be devised. The techniques are known and the expertise is available, as we shall see in Chapter Twelve. That is one priority the government and the international community must not neglect.

Map Sources: ESRI, Europa
Technologies, UNCS.
Map created in Sep 2011.
*Final boundary between the
Republic of Sudan and the republic
of South Sudan has not yet been
determined.*

Map Sources: ESRI, Europa
Technologies, UNCS.
Map created in Nov 2011.
*Final boundary between the
Republic of Sudan and the republic
of South Sudan has not yet been
determined. Final status of the Abyei
area is not yet determined.*

Map Sources: ESRI, UNCS.
Map created in Nov 2011.

CHAPTER ELEVEN

Food Insecurity: country lessons and the 2008 food crisis

For people of a certain age, humanitarian catastrophe and the response to it are indelibly associated with the Horn of Africa in the mid-1980s. Prolonged drought in parts of Ethiopia led to mass starvation. Emaciated babies dying of hunger in front of our eyes dominated the television screens. The Western public and its governments eventually responded, provoked by Bob Geldof and Live Aid. But it was too late for many. At least 100,000 are thought to have died.

Everyone said never again. However, the underlying conditions which led to this and similar disasters did not change much as a result. Recent major droughts in West Africa and in the Horn have once again put the issues centre stage. Are we condemned to witness endless such tragedies, worsening as climate change and desertification bite deeper, and populations continue to rise?

The wider background is the scandal of world hunger. The UN estimates that some 950 million people, almost one seventh of the world's population, go to bed hungry every night. This figure has been rising again in recent years, particularly following the food-price crisis of 2008. More shocking still are the children dying every day from the effects of malnutrition. Estimates vary from 10,000 to three times that. Whatever the exact figure, this is a massive failure of international action and compassion. Malnutrition has a horribly insidious impact on children, particularly those under two. The physical and mental stunting can never be reversed.

Africa is not the only region of the world to suffer. There are by some estimates more people below the poverty line in India, for all its emerging economy status, than in the whole of Africa. Hunger is a daily reality for many of them too. But parts of Africa are still where the issues of poverty, climate unreliability, conflict, and poor governance most often come together to such tragic effect.

Some governments have learned lessons and put in place measures to mitigate the worst effects of drought. Donors, agencies, and NGOs also know how to respond more quickly and effectively, using products such as Plumpy'Nut – a peanut-based miracle paste which can bring children back from the direst malnutrition in a few days. But the cycle of serious drought seems to be shortening steadily: twenty years or so in the early part of the twentieth century, ten years towards the end of the century, and as little as five now.

A brief account of experiences in three countries facing food-insecurity disasters may help to illustrate the ground complexities, before I look at the food-price crisis of 2008 and the particular issue of food aid.

Ethiopia

Ethiopia is not unique in the Horn in suffering badly from drought. It is not even necessarily the worst-affected country. Somalia has been regularly hit with great severity, as have Djibouti and northern parts of Kenya and Uganda. But Ethiopia's population of over 80 million, in a huge and diverse territory, means at least one region is usually suffering from failed rains. Desperate food shortages in one part of a country can coexist with plenty, or at least sufficiency, in other parts. Market failure and lack of infrastructure to move supplies around are key elements of most food crises. Ethiopia is no exception.

Ethiopia was frequently on my itinerary as ERC, and never far from my thoughts. General concern about food insecurity was compounded by worry about the humanitarian consequences of the conflict between the government and the Ogaden National Liberation Front (ONLF) in the country's ethnic Somali region. The Ethiopian government, led by Prime Minister Meles Zenawi from 1991 until his death in August 2012, was relatively strong and competent. Its introduction of the Production Safety Nets Programme (PSNP), a system of cash transfers to around 8 million of the most vulnerable people, to enable them to develop their assets and protect them in lean times, had made a real difference. Loan possibilities for poor families and government grain reserves were important complementary measures.

This certainly helped people to cope when the rains failed once. But when they failed several times in succession, disaster was still likely in the absence of rapid food aid and other emergency help: therapeutic nutrition, supplementary water supplies, fodder for herds, and extra medical care. The problems were brought home when I went to Ethiopia twice within nine months in 2007 and 2008.

In the south, following prolonged drought in the exotically if bureaucratically named Southern Nations, Nationalities and Peoples Region (SNNPR), action by the government and relief agencies was already well under way. But I still saw hundreds of undernourished children and mothers receiving treatment at the nutrition centres. The personal shock for me of those babies with wasted limbs and heads out of all proportion to their bodies was not reduced by my familiarity with similar images on TV screens.

I was also struck by the still rudimentary nature of most agriculture in the area, with little or no irrigation, and by the dramatic effects of rapid population growth. Inheritance rules meant that family plots were being divided further and further, so that even in good years what each family farmed was hardly able to provide a bare subsistence, never mind surpluses for local markets. Part of the problem was also a strict government policy which did not allow people to own land outright, or sell their surpluses freely. Whatever the wider ideological or political reasons for this policy, it was a major disincentive to investment and higher productivity.

Much time on these visits was taken up by policy arguments with the government in Addis Ababa, not least with Prime Minister Meles himself. Not an easy interlocutor, though outwardly friendly, he had clear views about what he wanted, and a built-in resistance to being told what to do by foreigners, however well-meaning. Two basic problems were on our agenda: government attempts to play down the seriousness of the food-security situation, and the Somali region.

By 2007/8 Ethiopia was a successful and fast-growing economy. The government was determined to keep it that way and particularly anxious to improve Ethiopia's international image in order to go on attracting foreign investment. The last thing they wanted was reassociation of Ethiopia in international minds with drought and starvation. This led them to interfere regularly with estimates of food aid needs produced by international agencies like WFP, FAO and UNICEF. For 2008, for example, while agency figures were showing 8 million people in need of food aid, double what it had been a few months previously, the government claimed the true figure was still more like 4 million.

Their argument was partly that the international figures were not reliable, since they did not correspond to what they were hearing from their own regional governors (who had their own reasons for manipulating the truth); and partly that, as the international community never supplied all the aid requested in any case, there was little point in putting out high figures!

In response, I supported the local humanitarian community, stressing both the principled need to stick to the facts, and the requirement in donor terms to make clear the full gravity of the situation. We underlined that we had no desire to exaggerate the situation, and no self-interest in doing so. The latter point was important because governments like Ethiopia's often accused humanitarian organizations of painting a bleaker picture than necessary just to keep themselves in business (and, as I have commented earlier in the book, this was not an unknown phenomenon in the humanitarian world).

In the end, a compromise was struck. The government did not really want a head-on collision with the international aid community, and were clever enough to avoid it. They accepted most of the caseload, but whittled the numbers down to 6.5 million people in need of food aid, while we insisted on a further joint review later in the year to check the figures. The international appeal for emergency funds went out on that basis.

Internal humanitarian critics pointed out, correctly, that the idea of a political compromise on the figures for suffering was bizarre and unacceptable in principle. But we had our own reasons for not wanting a total break – the usual humanitarian imperative: the most vulnerable people would be the ones to suffer most if we pulled out or were expelled.

Should we have taken a more principled stand, and forced the issue? I thought our practical approach was best in the circumstances. But it is certainly debatable. The arguments for staying to help in any particular case tend to look compelling. But, as we saw with Sri Lanka, if the humanitarian community never draws any red lines, are we not inviting governments to treat us badly?

The second issue was the conflict between the government and the Ogaden National Liberation Front (ONLF) in the Somali region. This had been going on for many years but occasionally flared into new life. The Somali region was also badly drought-prone. The government were even more anxious to minimize the problems here than elsewhere, and to keep international noses out of what they saw as exclusively their own business. They were strongly inclined to deny access to international humanitarian and human rights organizations. In essence, they did not want a foreign presence, media or humanitarian, to see what they were doing, including what some outside observers claimed were scorched-earth tactics.

Their approach was that the problems were not as serious as we were saying, and that, in any case, they could not assure our security because of terrorist attacks. They also believed, or purported to believe, that some NGOs and their workers were politically sympathetic to the ONLF and were helping them; or that at the very least that the NGOs were being exploited by the ONLF, with aid stolen or diverted from its intended recipients. This was indeed a potentially serious issue but, as we pointed out to the government, we could only assure ourselves that aid was reaching those intended if we had better access for international staff to monitor this. Meanwhile, the government regularly tried to insist on delivering the aid themselves in the more dangerous areas, creating the opposite risk that they were diverting the aid – for example, giving it only to 'loyal' villages.

The visits I paid to the region in late 2007 and 2008 were particularly alarming. The combined consequences of drought and conflict were creating a truly desperate situation on the ground. Some areas already resembled giant dust bowls. But international presence and access were extremely limited. Prime Minister Meles assured me solemnly that the government would always act to prevent famine from happening again anywhere in his country. But he was also unyielding in his view that not only did we not really understand the situation, but in addition there was collusion, deliberate or unwitting, between aid agencies and ONLF rebels. He pointed out that he had been a rebel himself once and had personal experience of how easy it was to con aid NGOs and divert what they were giving!

This was not an easy argument to deal with. My response was that even if he was right about his own experiences, we had become much more professional since then; and that if aid agencies had contacts with the ONLF, it was only to make sure that the aid got through, and to urge them to comply with humanitarian principles and law, in line with our usual practice. We had to agree to disagree. But my pleading may have had more effect than was obvious at the time, together with the subtle pressure applied by the effective RC/HC in Addis Ababa, Fidele Sarassoro. The government did eventually accept the proposal for more aid delivery. They also allowed OCHA to open local offices and gave permission for more NGOs to work in the area. But it was all grudging and fragile. Debate about the twin problems of needs and access in this sensitive area continues as I write. It remains to be seen whether the successors to Prime Minister Meles Zenawi will take a different approach.

The problems in the Somali region reinforced wider donor doubts about the Ethiopian government; for example, about political and human rights abuses driven by a prime minister determined to stay in power. We were able to convince donors in 2008 that they should continue to fund emergency assistance, given the depth of the needs, but their willingness to go on doing so outside the most critical famine situations was clearly under increasing pressure.

I go through all this to bring out the political sensitivities of dealing with food insecurity, in case anyone is tempted to think it is just a technical issue: just work out where the problems are, get the food in, and all will be well. Government sensitivities and sovereignty concerns remain major issues even when people are dying.

Of course, if the situation deteriorates beyond a certain point, the politics can often be more easily set aside. This happened in Ethiopia in the renewed Horn food crisis of 2011, as it did in the case of Somalia. The alarm was first raised in the autumn of 2010. A further poor rainy season in early 2011 caused the situation to worsen dramatically, including large price rises for staples. A full-scale emergency appeal was launched in the summer of 2011 – 13 million people were said to be at high risk across the region, including parts of Ethiopia, though famine was not officially declared there, as it was in Somalia. Questions about the extent of vulnerability and about access were set aside, though no doubt only for the time being.

Better rains towards the end of 2011 gradually eased the situation. But as I write there are still far too many people on the edge of disaster. The hundreds of thousands of nomads/pastoralists of the area are particularly susceptible: so many of the animals on which they depend have died. Replacing these herds is a long business at best, raising further questions about the viability of the pastoralist way of life in the region, already under severe threat from modern administrative boundaries and habits, as well as the vagaries of the climate.

Although the 2011 aid operation succeeded in saving many lives, some major NGOs were very critical of the failure to heed the early warning signs once again. They lambasted the continuing propensity to wait to act in earnest until the TV pictures of starving children are all over our screens. By that time it was too late for many, and the help needed was also that much more expensive – for example, having to truck in water at vast expense, rather than drilling more boreholes.

These points are sadly valid. However, the more fundamental issue still is how to avoid the crisis in the first place. Drought cannot be prevented, but famine can. I will return to this later in the chapter.

Niger

If the challenges in the Horn remain huge, the prospects are just as frightening in parts of West Africa. Populations are rising even faster, and the effects of climate change and the southward creep of the deserts are even more pronounced. These problems came to one of their periodic heads in 2010, especially in Niger, a country twice the size of France, firmly rooted at the bottom of the UNDP Human Development Index – 182nd out of 182. A previous food-security crisis there in 2005 had been a subject of considerable controversy between then President Tandja and my predecessor, Jan Egeland. The president accused the BBC and Jan of making up a famine story, and largely refused to allow access for humanitarian aid agencies. Many probably died needlessly as a result, though it was hard to be sure in the absence of meaningful access at the time. Even after 2005, NGOs such as Action Contre la Faim and Médecins Sans Frontières were still expelled or prevented from working properly at different times.

The alarm was sounded again in late 2009 after the rains failed across much of the Sahel. Prices of whatever food was available were rising rapidly, and stocks were almost exhausted.

Malnutrition was once more on the march – 8 million people (half the population) were seriously affected. The prospects looked bleak indeed.

President Tandja was still there and still in denial mode, but fortunately he was deposed in the nick of time by a military coup in February 2010, after he had tried to extend his rule unconstitutionally. Whatever international disapproval of their method of taking power, the new ruling military junta were not only apparently committed to the return of democracy, but were also clear that the drought crisis was a top priority, and international aid was welcome.

With this green light, we were able to mobilize the key agencies and NGOs, reinforce the network of nutritional clinics, and engage the international donors. We were late, but we hoped not too late to prevent what was already a major crisis turning into a full-scale catastrophe. When I visited in April 2010, the picture was nevertheless alarming. Water holes were drying up rapidly. Men were moving in large numbers to look for work and food in neighbouring countries. The national herd was losing animals at a frightening rate. Levels of acute and severe malnutrition, particularly among children, were well over international emergency thresholds. In villages I visited, women with seemingly endless small children at their knees pressed me desperately on how they were supposed to survive. They were already walking extra miles each day in search of dwindling and ever deeper sources of drinkable water, and boiling unpalatable local berries to keep off the worst of the hunger pangs. Large numbers of bony animals were crowding around muddy wells, waiting the turn of their owners to drag up a few bucketfuls of dirty water. The next harvest, even with normal rains, was still many months away.

My job in this case was to make sure agencies and NGOs were stepping up their efforts to meet the huge needs, and to ring the international donor alarm bells even louder. The response was, in the end, reasonably good: a combination of targeted food assistance, nutritional help for children and fodder for the animals did succeed in averting the worst. The situation was stabilized just long enough to last until the next rains arrived, mercifully decent this time.

What struck me most forcibly once again, however, was the inevitability of further such crises, at ever shorter intervals and with ever greater intensity, unless the underlying causes were tackled with the same urgency as the immediate symptoms. In a country mostly desert to start with, the sands were advancing south inexorably and visibly. Climate change could only make this worse. Meanwhile, the country's population of 15 million, compared with only 2 million in 1950, was projected to reach no fewer than 50 million by 2050. Most of the women I met had families of ten or more. The national herd, thought to be around 31 million animals in 2010, had been growing at similar rates to the human population, exhausting grass and fodder ever more rapidly, even when rain was more or less normal, and contributing further to desertification. This was quite simply, and obviously, unsustainable in one of the poorest and least developed countries in the world.

What can be done? Effective measures to help with drought are known. Massive investment is needed in water retention schemes, in water-saving irrigation, in new agricultural techniques and drought-resistant crops, and in rural infrastructure of all kinds, to increase harvests, enable stocks to be held securely, and improve the workings of the local markets. Nothing like enough effort is being made in these areas.

However, all this will be in vain if there are no serious efforts at the same time to moderate the rate of population growth. This is a huge task in a deeply conservative Muslim country where women's views and rights are not valued, access to contraception is very limited at best, and the government does not have the issue of population on its priority list at all. But the results will be all too predictable otherwise: recurrent famine killing many, and driving mass migration to neighbouring countries, struggling themselves with similar problems, as well as further afield. Domestic political instability will contribute to wider regional volatility.

As I write in 2012, yet another food-security crisis has struck Niger, as rains have once more been poor across the Sahel. Neighbouring Mali has been hit particularly hard. The politics and economics of the region are, meanwhile, deteriorating from the spill-over effects of the fall of Libya's Colonel Gaddafi. Well-armed Tuareg former mercenaries are returning to give fresh life to old rebellions, helped by Al Qaeda-affiliated groups, while remittances from those working in Libya have dried up. This is an explosive mixture, with Mali again suffering the worst effects.

Chad

Niger was not the only Sahelian country badly affected in 2010. Even Senegal struggled, despite the denials of then President Wade, perennially optimistic and sadly out of touch with the real difficulties of his country. But the problems were particularly acutely felt in Chad too, another huge, terribly poor country with a climate and geography only just able to sustain human life. Chad had been suffering from long-running internal conflict, as well as 250,000 refugees from the war in Darfur. I had already been there in 2007 and 2009 to pursue the humanitarian consequences of these conflicts. The original reason for a third visit in 2010 was to lobby the government against their demand for the withdrawal of the MINURCAT UN peacekeeping force from the east of the country. They said that improving relations with Khartoum had transformed the security situation. We worried that MINURCAT's withdrawal would be the last straw for the humanitarians, already facing severe security threats, and for the people depending on their help.

But when I got to Chad, the effects of drought in the western half of the country had become an even bigger concern: millions affected by desperate shortages of food and water, high rates of child malnutrition, increasing vulnerability to disease, and rising death rates among the herds. As in Niger, many men had already left to try to find work elsewhere, leaving the women to fend for themselves and their children.

The humanitarian team in the country were desperately working to switch their geographic focus, previously almost exclusively on the east. I saw more dreadful sights of emaciated children arriving at nutritional centres in Mao, one of the main towns in the west. The view among the local experts was that the situation was much worse in remote rural areas where there were no nutritional centres, indeed virtually no official or international presence at all, and no transport for people to get themselves or their children to towns.

As in Niger, my role was more to make sure that the world did not forget about what was happening in this isolated part of a little-known country than to battle with the government about principles. But there was still an element of fatalism and complacency about the government's own response, which I tried to counter.

As in Niger, the problems in Chad are long-running and deep-seated. Both countries provide examples of a wider phenomenon with which we have yet to come to grips: the existence of large populations living on the edge of catastrophe on a quasi-permanent basis, with climate change as a major aggravating factor. We cannot divide these situations into humanitarian or development problems, as if these categories meant something useful in reality, or had any significance for the people themselves. These crises have no easily identifiable trigger points which mark their beginnings or ends, and therefore when the humanitarians should be arriving or leaving. We have to address the immediate humanitarian needs and the underlying issues simultaneously, and with exactly the same degree of urgency, if we are to have any chance of breaking out of these vicious circles. That means humanitarian and development actors burying their traditional divisions and genuinely acting together. I will come back to this theme later in Chapters Twelve and Fourteen.

The 2008 food crisis

Besides these country-based food disasters, my time as ERC was also marked by a period of acute global anxiety about food supplies. I was drawn into a significant role in understanding what was happening and proposing solutions. This may be of interest particularly since similar conditions are bound to recur, and indeed are doing so in 2012.

In early 2008, prices of key food commodities, especially rice and wheat, soared dramatically. Bread riots spread, and fears grew of a new era of starvation and instability across the world. Ban ki-Moon decided to bring the key global institutions together to face this. He therefore set up a High Level Task Force (HLTF) composed of the relevant UN agencies – the World Food Programme, Food and Agriculture Organization, UNICEF, etc. – together with the World Bank, International Monetary Fund, World Trade Organization, Organization for Economic Cooperation and Development, and others. This may seem an obvious move, but in fact system-wide coherence had never been attempted before in quite this way.

Rather to my surprise, Ban ki-Moon asked me to be the HLTF coordinator. I was hesitant because, while there was obviously an immediate requirement for extra food assistance in some countries, this was to my mind less a humanitarian issue than a question of global development and agriculture policy. I also had more than a full-time job already. But the SG would not take no for an answer: he wanted a credible and neutral figure, not identified with any of the often competing institutions or with particular solutions.

My first step was to set up a small team of bright thinkers to help me, headed by Hans-Joerg Strohmeyer, then in charge of OCHA's policy department. We also established an advisory group representing the main international players to make sure we had access to all the right knowledge and expertise. We decided that while the world was hardly short of reports, most ignored and unimplemented, a new short analysis of the reasons for this particular crisis, with a list of recommendations for action, was the best contribution we could make. For international institutional coherence to be possible, we needed a core consensus around which all relevant organizations could coalesce, and a peg on which to hang outreach to other big players: governments, the private sector, the farmers themselves, and the NGOs.

The process proved more fraught than I had anticipated, partly because of the complexity of the issues at stake, but also because of the politics of the food and agriculture world. The UN heart of this sector was the so-called Rome institutions: WFP, FAO, and the International Fund for Agricultural Development (IFAD), set up at the end of the 1970s to channel surplus revenues from the first big oil price rise into agricultural investment. IFAD was a relatively technical organization, with good expertise and no particular axe to grind. WFP and FAO, on the other hand, had a difficult mutual history, including political and personal rivalries.

FAO had been set up in 1945, before the UN itself. Its director general was elected by its members, without the involvement of the UN secretary-general. This gave him a certain status, above the heads of the other UN Specialized Agencies. Certainly, the then FAO head, Jacques Diouf, saw himself as more or less the equal of Ban ki-Moon, and behaved accordingly. Unfortunately, FAO was not well regarded by the donor community after more than ten years of Diouf's stewardship. He was seen by Western governments as more political than operational, cultivating carefully his constituency of developing country voters, while not doing enough to improve FAO's base skills in the food and agriculture sector. FAO was therefore increasingly starved of funds by Western donors, and faced an ever louder clamour for fundamental reform. This was particularly unfortunate in 2008: the messages FAO and Diouf himself had been preaching for years about the need to invest more in agriculture were finally being listened to, but they were not well placed to lead.

WFP was more of a Western, particularly US, preserve. It was highly regarded by most donors, whatever doubts there might be from time to time about food aid. Its executive director, Josette Sheeran, was a formidable operator and advocate, particularly in Washington. Unfortunately, FAO regarded WFP as trying to usurp its own role in the area of food and agriculture. They were also envious of WFP's ability to attract relatively generous funding. The fact that WFP was historically an offshoot of FAO, only established in 1961, added insult to injury.

These tensions, and the differences in the FAO and WFP mandates, inevitably played into the work of the High Level Task Force. WFP were constantly underlining the need for more emergency aid, while FAO stressed the underlying problems of agricultural production. Finding the right balance between the two, and avoiding the infighting, was a constant preoccupation.

Unfortunately, this was not the only minefield around. As we have seen in other contexts, the relationship between the UN and the World Bank had long been uneasy and even competitive. The UN tended to see the World Bank as well funded, well staffed, and good at writing position papers, but not so good on the ground, while the World Bank looked down its nose at the UN in the economic area as being poorly funded and disorganized. The World Bank was an important part of the HLTF, but Bob Zoellick, then head of the Bank, rarely attended the monthly meetings, even telephonically. His body language suggested that he regarded the exercise as likely to be a bureaucratic waste of time, and that the Bank was going to pursue its own policies whatever the HLTF said.

This was the somewhat unpromising background to the preparation of the report, which we decided to call the Comprehensive Framework for Action (CFA). It was aimed in the first place at a food summit in June 2008 in Rome under the auspices of the FAO. This meant that we had about five weeks to produce a meaningful and mutually agreed document.

Our collective analysis of the dramatic state of food prices in early 2008, overall more than 50 per cent higher than a year earlier, was that this reflected a significant imbalance between supply and demand, not just the effects of market speculation, as some observers had suggested. The imbalance came from a mix of short- and long-term factors, including crop failures in some key producer countries, changing diets in the big emerging economies, and use of land for biofuels. Rising input costs, notably of fertilizers and transport, driven by higher oil prices, had also been a big contributor. Prices had then been forced up further by panic buying and by a beggar-my-neighbour reaction from several key supplier countries, banning exports for fear of not having enough for their own populations.

While prices could be expected to stabilize or even reduce somewhat after a few months as markets adjusted, our expectation was that the long-term trend would still be upward. World food production would have to increase by at least 70 per cent by 2050 to cope with a global population of at least 9 billion by then, many demanding much better diets than now. And this would have to happen against the background of climate change and environmental degradation affecting food production negatively in some areas.

These trends posed particular risks for the poorer countries and the poorer people in them, in both urban and rural areas. Poorer countries faced steeply rising import bills, well beyond their capacity to finance. For individual families on or below the poverty line, food would become an even bigger part of their expenditure than it is now. This would have significant knock-on effects, not only on their nutritional status, but also on education and health, as these services became even less affordable. There could be major setbacks to human development, as children were taken out of school, for example, as well as the potential for violent political change and large-scale migration from populations with no safety nets.

High food prices ought, in theory, to benefit all farmers, and therefore bring widespread advantages in a world where most people still lived in rural areas. In reality, while commercial farmers in developed countries would do well, and respond by increasing supply, the vast majority of smallholder farmers in developing countries profited little from increased global prices, since they remained net buyers overall, and had no credit available to finance planting more themselves.

Overall, we argued that 2008 represented a turning point in the international food market. There had been an assumption for the previous thirty years that production would always be sufficiently elastic to meet demand, and that global prices would remain generally stable, despite temporary blips up and down. Countries, including poor ones, would therefore always be able to buy the staples their people needed on world markets. This had led many developing countries to ignore their own agriculture. It had also encouraged changes of eating habits which were not necessarily sustainable – for example, consumption of imported rice, rather than long-standing local crops like cassava, in places such as West Africa. This was manageable while prices were low, but not when they shot up. It also led to encouragement of inappropriate crops, like the cultivation of rice where there was simply not enough water.

One of our main conclusions was, therefore, that the thirty years of neglect of agriculture and agricultural investment had been a big mistake. Many big international players, including the World Bank, had underplayed its importance for development and encouraged developing countries to focus on other areas of economic development – industry or services. The proportion of overseas aid going to agriculture had fallen from 19 per cent in 1979 to 3 per cent in 2006, while expenditure by African governments on agriculture had fallen similarly. Extension services had been cut or disappeared. Productivity in Africa had stagnated.

Our principal recommendation was, therefore, that this historic error had to be reversed urgently. In particular, a major effort was needed to increase smallholder productivity and production in developing countries. Investments and public interventions should be stepped up to provide better access to crucial inputs such as fertilizer and seeds, improve the rural infrastructure (transport, credit, storage), and provide new techniques and varieties. More fundamental issues, such as land tenure problems in many countries, also needed to be tackled, not least the right of women to own land.

More than 2 billion people were estimated to be smallholder farmers or their dependants, one third of the world's population. Measures like these would not only boost yields, therefore, but could also be win–win–win, with a positive impact on poverty reduction and on the exodus of small farmers to the already bulging cities. We also argued that it should be possible to do this in ways which did not increase environmental damage and the risks of climate change and crucial scarcities in the future – for example, by using new tillage methods – although we were not able to go deep into these issues ourselves in the time we had available.

This long-term action on the agricultural front should be underpinned by provision wherever possible of social safety nets to build resilience and increase people's ability to absorb shocks, as well as by increased food assistance to address the needs of the most vulnerable. It should also be accompanied by long-touted reform of agricultural trade, reducing subsidies, improving access to key markets, and outlawing unreasonable export bans when supplies became tight.

Hidden in these recommendations were individual controversial issues. What should be done – if anything – to rebuild global, regional, or national grain stocks? They had been run down over the years, meaning there were few buffers in the system in the event of a sudden spike in prices. Holding and managing stocks, preventing them from rotting, was an expensive and tricky business. Nevertheless, some kind of new strategic grain reserves, real or virtual, seemed to be a good idea as a necessary buffer. But who should run them and how?

Meanwhile, how far had biofuels really contributed to the dramatic price rises by taking land which could and should have been more productively used for food? There was a view that

US subsidies for corn for ethanol had had an overall negative impact, but that the same might not be true in all cases – for example, sugar cane in Brazil. These were highly charged political questions, with no easy technical answers. There was a hope that so-called second-generation biofuels, using the biomass of food crops (leaves and stalks) rather than the crops themselves, might resolve some of these questions, but this was still speculative.

Finally, what role should there be for genetic modification (GM) technology in increasing future productivity? Here scientists tended to line up against environmentalists, the former arguing that this was a technology vital for the next green revolution in Africa, and the latter that its effects on the environment were at best unknown, and that in any case poor developing country farmers could never afford to buy the GM seeds every year, just to make profits for the international seed companies.

We did not pretend to have all the answers to such fundamental and difficult questions, but tried to set out the issues in a fair-minded way, while encouraging more research and analysis, instead of emotional arguments based on little evidence.

Overall, our aim was not great originality, but an agreed approach, and a bridge over traditional humanitarian/development and other divides, through a single document belonging to key players in and out of the UN system. We hoped that setting out clearly and comprehensively the short- and long-term policy options would help spur the necessary action.

The CFA was not a fund-raising document. But we could not entirely dodge the issue of how much what we were recommending might cost, and over what period. This was more than a technical question, since agencies' own funding strategies and successes would be affected, and many of them already had major appeals out there. The humanitarian agencies were anxious to see money raised quickly for immediate needs, or people would starve. The agricultural development experts tended to think that humanitarian causes already did quite well for money, and that the more important and urgent need was to increase investment in agriculture in all its forms.

Previous estimates had suggested that the overall cost of effective action might be some $25–40 billion per year. We did not challenge these figures, but pointed out that real costs would depend on so many variables that they were more or less impossible to calculate. The sources of funding were also multiple: international aid, national governments, local authorities, private companies, farmers themselves, communities, and civil society as a whole. We took the view that, whatever the figures and the sources, one third of the money should go to immediate requirements (food aid, inputs for small farmers, and temporary budgetary support) and two thirds for building longer-term resilience (food and nutritional security, agricultural productivity, rural infrastructure, and so on). Irrespective of the exact calculations, a major increase in funding was needed from all sources. It was also vital that official finance for food and agriculture was genuinely additional to existing funding, not robbing Peter to pay Paul.

We debated long and hard about whether a new international fund was needed to assemble contributions and focus fund-raising efforts. The balance of opinion was against: there were already too many funds out there, and individual agencies were keen not to disrupt their normal campaigns. So while the World Bank did set up a new global facility, FAO continued to appeal for vast sums for its own projects, and WFP upped its usual annual appeal from around $3 billion to twice that. In retrospect, I am not at all sure that the decision not to go for a single new fund was the right one.

The CFA was generally well received, despite grumbles from UN member states, the private sector, and international NGOs that they had been insufficiently consulted in its preparation. It had a useful impact on the policy debate. But we were well aware of the risk that it would join all the other agriculture reports gathering dust on the shelves. I therefore encouraged all parts of the international system to take responsibility for implementing it. We kept the HLTF going and meeting regularly to operate as a ginger group, and created a follow-up mechanism to coordinate implementation. The latter was not straightforward, since FAO and WFP remained nervous about anything which could seem to infringe their independence. Nevertheless, they did eventually agree to a small Coordination Unit, partly based in Rome.

By this time, in late 2008, I was trying to extricate myself from the role of HLTF coordinator in any case. It had proved hard to combine with my day job, as predicted. Donors and my own staff were concerned that I could not give enough time and energy to emergency relief. I was also still concerned that my presence suggested that the core of the issue was humanitarian, when it was much more agricultural. Fortunately, a natural successor was at hand in the shape of David Nabarro, an able and experienced international civil servant who had already been appointed deputy HLTF coordinator in May 2008. He is still there as I write, working to encourage the local, national, and global partnerships which we saw from the beginning as the heart of future action.

What did we achieve in the end, beyond helping the policy debate? Food and nutrition have certainly remained higher up the international agenda than they were before, as demonstrated by the number of high-level meetings still devoted to them. Donors have made significant promises of extra resources for agricultural investment and related programmes, including a promise of $20 billion dollars over three years from the G8 Summit in Italy in July 2009. However, follow-up action on such pledges has been limited and hard to measure.

Governments around the world, particularly in Africa, seem to have understood the need to take agriculture and rural development seriously again. The World Bank has been able to do more in this area than for many years previously. More funds are flowing into vital research into new crop varieties and technologies. The FAO has a new Brazilian head and is in the middle of a major reform programme.

But a more rapid than forecast end to the 2008 global price spikes, and a respite from food-driven unrest, quickly reduced the international sense of urgency. Attention inevitably switched to the economic and financial crisis of autumn 2008. The great food scare appeared to be over almost before it had started. This was, I hardly need to say, an illusion. Prices on global markets did not fall back to their previous levels, and were not necessarily followed by price reductions on local markets. Prices have also been edging steadily back up again. In mid-2012, they are more or less at the same levels as in early 2008, except for rice, not least because of major drought in the US. This is a long-running crisis, not a one-off event.

We are also still far too complacent about this most basic of challenges – how to feed the world, sustainably. The technology exists to provide enough food, even for a population double that of today, but can it be done without causing unacceptable damage to the global environment, given growing scarcities of land, water and energy, and the worsening effects of climate change? Not without major changes – to our diets (more cereals, less meat), our agricultural practices (fewer chemicals and fertilizers, better crop varieties), our spending patterns (more help for small farmers and rural infrastructure, less subsidies for unsustainable developed country crops), and our trade policies (more access, less barriers).

If it were politically and practically easy to fix these problems, we would have done so already. There is no silver bullet, in either institutional or policy terms. It is not even easy to define our overall goal beyond sustainable food supplies. Do we want cheap food? That might not encourage production enough, and would certainly leave huge numbers of smallholder farmers still struggling to make ends meet, even if we could ensure improved productivity. It would also encourage further waste and obesity in the developed world, both already serious problems in their own right. Do we want to incentivize agricultural production by the big commercial producers who can make most difference to overall food availability? That would tend to squeeze out the small farmers even further.

The truth is that we need differentiated policies for different groups, and action in a wide range of areas, on many levels, to start to make a difference, including in unfashionable areas such as urban agriculture and vegetable production. Sadly, it may take another, deeper crisis than that of 2008 before the international community takes the issue seriously enough to make a real difference. How many more children will have to be stunted for life, physically and mentally, before we wake up?

Food aid

Let me finish this chapter with some reflections on the perennial debate about food aid. This has long been controversial. It was a running theme throughout my time as ERC, and underlay much of the tension about how to deal with the 2008 food crisis. There are many situations where food aid is essential and needed with the utmost urgency. It can also be used to great effect in school feeding programmes, not least as an incentive to parents to send their children to school. WFP is extraordinarily effective at procuring food, organizing the logistics, and mobilizing local partners to deliver it. It works closely with major international

NGOs on these programmes. I always admired WFP's profes-sionalism, dedication, and efficiency, and got on well with Josette Sheeran, its executive director.

However, food aid is well known to be a two-edged sword. It too easily creates aid dependency, stifles local initiative, and erodes personal responsibility. Free or cheap food quickly undermines the livelihoods of local farmers and shopkeepers once immediate emergency conditions are over. And food is a very expensive commodity to transport, especially to remote and dangerous places in the middle of Africa. The logistics can easily represent more than half of the overall cost.

The case for alternatives wherever possible is therefore very strong. If food is available in the local markets, provision of cash or vouchers to enable those in need to buy for themselves is less expensive than providing food, involves less risk in terms of secure delivery, is more flexible for the recipients, and avoids problems of food aid unsuitable for local diets. There are issues of potential corruption and diversion about using cash, but these are neither exclusive (food can also be sold or diverted) nor insoluble. Handing out smart cards is a way forward in some situations (for example, urban areas), if the local government and the aid agencies can collaborate on how this should be done. Meanwhile, if food aid is genuinely necessary, procurement from as close to the area of delivery as possible also makes a lot of sense, to minimize delivery and other costs, encourage farmers in the same country or region, and help economic growth and jobs there.

WFP is already pursuing all these ideas, particularly local purchase. The days of being a machine for the disposal of surplus food from the US and the EU are long gone. They are experimenting with cash and vouchers. But I would say they still need to go further in weaning themselves and their beneficiaries off the drug of food aid. One way of encouraging this is more help for the local private sector immediately after a disaster, with the view of getting them back on their feet again as quickly as possible. Restarting local shops and small businesses provides jobs, a sense of normality, and the basis for recovery. Combining this with cash for the affected population to buy goods is a better investment than aid in kind. There will always be cases where supply chains and infrastructure have gone, and there is no realistic alternative to food aid in the short term. But recovery can be faster than we imagine if we apply help in the right places, and let natural entrepreneurism do the rest.

CHAPTER TWELVE

Prevention is better than cure: acting before disasters happen

Previous chapters have concentrated on the response to natural disasters and conflicts. This is natural: it is where the drama and dilemmas of the reaction to human suffering come together – the essence of humanitarianism. The international community must always be ready to help a country struck by a catastrophe that is beyond its resources to cope with.

However, most humanitarians are also aware that response is far from enough. We need to focus much more than we currently do on reducing the risks of disasters and helping vulnerable countries prepare themselves. The international community is failing to get the balance right between spending on responses to humanitarian crises and investment in mitigating the impact of disasters before they happen. We are also guilty of not doing what we should to build local capacity. We urgently need a new 'business model' for humanitarianism which puts these two challenges squarely up front.

Disaster risk reduction

We cannot anticipate all disasters, especially when they strike in places with no history of such events. But there are places which we know are going to be hit regularly, and types of disaster we know are going to happen, even if we cannot be sure exactly when or where. We know, for example, that Central America and the Caribbean will be hit by severe hurricanes every year. Parts of South and South-East Asia will suffer catastrophic tropical storms and floods. Drought in North-East and West Africa is predictable, and increasingly frequent. Many cities are on earthquake faults which we know will shift disastrously again. Undersea earthquakes will produce devastating tsunamis, as we saw again in early 2011 in Japan. Meanwhile, climate change is a current reality for hundreds of millions of people around the globe. Over the past thirty years the number of weather-related disasters – storms, floods, and droughts – is estimated to have increased threefold, affecting five times as many people as a generation ago.

The world's megacities are particularly vulnerable. Eight of the world's ten most populous cities are earthquake-prone, and six of them are on or near the coast. One billion people live in unstable and overcrowded slums, a figure rising steadily as urbanization increases. The combination of decaying infrastructure, land erosion, crowded conditions, and poor or non-existent rescue and disaster-management services could lead to catastrophes on an unprecedented scale.

We cannot stop natural hazards arising. Our ability to control nature may never reach that stage. But we *can* stop the hazard from becoming a disaster. Whether or not a natural cataclysm becomes a human catastrophe is mostly down to what people have or have not done in advance. The most obvious example is ensuring that buildings in seismic zones are earthquake-proof, or at least earthquake-resistant. But it goes well beyond this. Flood defences can be built, and people can be persuaded to stop living in flood-prone areas, especially in big cities, where such areas are likely to be taken over by poor squatters with inadequate and vulnerable housing. Natural barriers such as mangrove forests can be restored on coasts liable to tidal surges and tsunamis. Key infrastructure such as bridges and roads can be built with resilience to potential disaster in mind. Hospitals and schools can be protected by sound construction standards and good design; important facilities such as cold stores can be sited where floods are least likely to reach. If such measures are included in the design from the start the extra cost may be no more than a few per cent.

Improving preparedness for disaster can also make a huge difference. It starts with effective early-warning systems. There is sadly little we can do yet to predict earthquakes. But meteorologists can warn us when hurricanes and tropical storms are approaching, and track their progress so that those in their paths can protect themselves. Good forecasting and good international cooperation can save many lives. Improving weather forecasting in Africa is probably the single most effective investment we can make in reducing the impact of disasters there, and is relatively inexpensive. Tsunami warning systems are now in place in the Indian Ocean, and elsewhere.

However, such systems are only as good as the arrangements to get the key information to those at most risk on the ground. This is where many break down, a phenomenon usually described as the syndrome of the 'failure of the last mile'. TV and radio can be used where people routinely watch or listen to them – for example, in Florida. Generalized text messages can be extremely effective where most people have mobile phones. But the most vulnerable of all, such as impoverished inhabitants of threatened fishing villages, usually do not. This is far from insoluble. Bangladesh has, for example, established over the years a highly effective system of bicycles and bullhorns (loudhailers) which are used by local officials to warn villagers along its extremely vulnerable delta coast against the arrival of tropical cyclones. This, together with the provision of shelters, and education of the population about what to do if a cyclone is arriving, has dramatically reduced the death toll from hundreds of thousands in the 1960s and 1970s to the low thousands today (as in Cyclone Sidr in 2007). Contrast this with the experience of Myanmar during the similar Cyclone Nargis, when 140,000 died in circumstances of virtually no warning and no preparedness.

Disaster risk reduction (DRR) is not really a humanitarian issue. It is about sustainable development practice, and should have been adopted accordingly long ago by governments and the development community. So why have humanitarians been in the lead on the subject for many years now? First, humanitarians are constantly confronted by the impact of disasters, and are reminded with distressing frequency of the human misery they cause, and the way in which they can set back development of a country by years. They therefore understand automatically the value of trying to reduce the damage. Second, the apparent minnow of disaster risk reduction is always too likely to be ignored next to the whale of development priorities as a whole. That is largely what has happened in the past. And third, humanitarians sometimes find it easier to generate money for particular causes than development actors. There are so many other competing needs in the development field, as well as scepticism about results.

Whatever the reasons for this humanitarian focus, DRR now needs to be mainstreamed into all development decisions as a matter of course, particularly – but not only – in poor, disaster-prone countries. Governments and local authorities should do this for themselves, but international institutions should encourage and help them to do so. DRR measures built into the design and planning of infrastructure or developments of any kind can cost nothing or relatively little. Retrofitting DRR is often likely to be impossible and is certainly the more expensive option.

A lot of international effort has already gone into this agenda. A separate UN body, the International Secretariat for Disaster Risk Reduction (ISDR), is devoted to promoting DRR. As ERC, I supervised UNISDR, though this began to change after the 2008 appointment of a special representative of the secretary-general for disaster risk reduction, Margareta Wahlstrom. A former deputy head of OCHA, and a tremendously experienced actor in this field, she has done a lot to raise international awareness. But ISDR remains small and underfunded.

There is also an agreed international DRR strategy, the Hyogo Framework for Action (HFA), endorsed unanimously by the World Conference on Disaster Reduction in January 2005. The conference took place in the Japanese city of Kobe, in Hyogo Province, the site of a major 1995 earthquake which killed more than 6000 people and caused damage worth 2.5 per cent of Japan's GDP – it is no accident that the Japanese are the greatest experts in disaster risk reduction. Fortuitously, the Kobe Conference also took place shortly after the Indian Ocean tsunami of 2004, which killed more than 200,000 people – an event which dramatically, if temporarily, focussed the minds of governments, media, and the public on the risks of natural disasters.

The HFA is an excellent action programme for ten years, up to 2015, aimed at substantially reducing loss of life and economic and social damage from disasters. Its strategic goals are to ensure that disaster risk reduction is integrated into all development policies and planning, to strengthen the mechanisms and institutions which build resilience to natural hazards, and to promote the incorporation of risk reduction into emergency preparedness and response programmes. The idea is to create risk-reduction lobbies and platforms around the world at local, national, and regional levels, and to force the issue on to the agenda of short-sighted politicians and decision-makers.

The Mid-Term Review of the HFA in 2010/11 concluded that progress had been made. The knowledge about how to make a difference was now there. But the commitment to use this knowledge, and the determination to mainstream disaster risk reduction, were still insufficient.

This is the striking feature of DRR. Everyone can see the point of it. Everyone is in favour of it in theory, especially just after a disaster, when it is obvious that better precautions would have saved many lives. But memories are astonishingly short. The political impetus and will rarely last long enough for presidents, prime ministers and finance ministers to agree the necessary priorities and sign off the necessary spending. Democratic politicians find it difficult to look ahead beyond the length of their mandate, and non-democratic governments are often too focussed on their own survival to prioritize the threat to their citizens from natural disasters.

In other words, DRR is a worthy cause but not one which is naturally sexy or media-friendly. We should perhaps not be surprised that governments behave like this. It reflects the human condition. We all know in our personal lives that an ounce of prevention is worth a pound of cure, a stitch in time saves nine, but we rarely behave accordingly. Dentists would be out of business otherwise.

Like others involved in humanitarian response, the more disasters I saw and the more I thought about this, the more convinced I became that the international community had to put much more emphasis on DRR. But I was frustrated by the difficulty of generating serious interest. Every two years, for example, UNISDR organized a Geneva Global Platform on DRR for practitioners and politicians. These were significant events, well attended and attracting a lot of enthusiasm from DRR champions around the world. Developing country officials and ministers came in numbers to testify about what was happening in their countries, not least the impact of climate change, as rains became less and less reliable, and floods or droughts caused devastation in places and ways never seen before. They were desperate to do more to mitigate the risks to which they were subject. They wanted help from the international community both to convince their own ultimate bosses of the importance of rapid action, and to help them implement real measures.

Developed country ministers, on the other hand, were usually only mildly interested, and rarely present at these meetings. Above all, we struggled heavily to get the international press to write stories. The issue remained in the realm of the specialists, with little sign of serious public pressure, or the key governments or institutions increasing their readiness to devote more money to it. One or two aid ministries, like the UK's Department for International Development (DfID), have made commitments to put 10 per cent of the total that they spend on humanitarian response towards DRR. The International Federation of the Red Cross have promised to go up to 20 per cent. But these examples have not been widely followed.

What we know, but don't do

I decided early on in my time at OCHA that we needed new ways to persuade governments of the wisdom of investing in DRR. One way was to put together the compelling economic arguments for doing so, along the lines of Nick Stern's seminal 2006 report on climate change, to give authoritative weight and hard figures to the DRR narrative. The World Bank, which already had an effective fund to help qualifying countries – the

Global Facility for Disaster Reduction and Recovery – agreed to take the lead, working with UNISDR and others.

The resulting report was published in 2010: 'Natural Hazards, Unnatural Disasters – The economics of effective prevention'. It is not just pious platitudes. It starts, for example, from the proposition that not every investment in DRR is necessarily worthwhile. Proper cost-benefit analysis is vital to establish this. There is little point in investing to reduce the risks of a once-in-a-thousand-years event – better to spend on the clean-up, if such a black-swan disaster actually takes place. But it also makes clear that there are so many things which *can* be done to improve prevention. Not all cost money, and not all of them are obvious. Most are for governments, but by no means all.

The authors point particularly to the importance of good governance in all its aspects, arguing that what a disaster and its aftermath expose above all is the cumulative effect of many earlier decisions. Symptoms should not be mistaken for causes. Transparency about the risks is also the key to enabling citizens to make informed choices about where and how they should live. But there are some areas where what is needed is obvious and effective. For example, as I have already suggested, spending on early-warning systems can produce huge dividends, as can investing in good infrastructure, and maintaining it properly once built. Managing cities better is also crucial, especially as the numbers of people exposed to major risks in them rise.

The report is a good read for a document of its type, illustrating its points with examples and anecdotes of all kinds. How far do building codes make a difference? Not much, if no one enforces them or the codes are wrong – indeed, they can easily be counterproductive. Why do people choose to live in hazardous areas, not only poor fishermen in Bangladesh, but also the wealthy Americans along Florida's hurricane-prone coastline? What can we learn about people's assessment of risk by looking at where they live in earthquake-prone Bogotá? Why do public buildings seem to collapse more in earthquakes than private ones, in both rich and poor countries?

The conclusion that it is the overall impact of many decisions which makes the difference between a safe and a vulnerable population is a crucial insight. Governments which are sensitive to the concerns of local people, and operate in an accountable and consultative way, are far more likely to make the right cumulative decisions. The people of developed countries with relatively effective governments tend to be much less vulnerable to disaster than those from poor and undeveloped countries. There can, of course, be exceptions to this rule, as Hurricane Katrina demonstrated in the US in 2005.

The World Bank study is far from the only report in the field. UNISDR produce an excellent global assessment report on DRR every two years. Data on disasters are published on an annual basis by several organizations, including the Centre of Research on the Epidemiology of Disasters (CRED), a Brussels-based independent research unit specializing in humanitarian emergencies.

In other words, there is plenty of excellent information and analysis available. Governments have no excuse for not knowing the extent of the risks their countries and peoples face, and the measures they can and should take to reduce these risks. They should be held accountable for the decisions they make accordingly. There has been progress in recent years in reducing the lives lost in disasters. But the toll is still far too high – and the economic costs are going up rapidly.

Climate change may, in the end, propel DRR once and for all to the forefront of national and international consciousness. Adaptation to the effects of climate change, including the extra risk of disasters, is as important in many ways as trying to fix the underlying causes of global warming, since the latter will take so many years to have the required effect. Many in developing countries are more aware with every passing year of the dramatic impact on their lives and economies. Farmers in many parts of Africa no longer know when to plant or harvest because the rains no longer arrive with any consistency, if they arrive at all. It is impossible to attribute any particular event to the effects of climate change. But the frequency, location, and intensity of droughts, floods, and storms are increasingly different in degree from what has been known before, whatever comfortable climate-change deniers in the West may say. The consequences for hundreds of millions of people are already devastating.

We can no longer afford to keep our heads in the sand. Developed countries will be affected too, directly through changes in their own climate, and indirectly through the heightened risks of migration and conflict. Investing more now to adapt to the realities of climate change, and more widely to mitigate the impact of natural hazards, is essential and no more than common sense. The world needs to face up to this reality.

Building local capacity

The second element of a new model is the systematic creation of greater local capacity. International help should be reserved for the very large crises which leave any country, even the richest and most developed, struggling to cope. International resources are more and more stretched in any case, as disasters increase and austerity bites in normally generous places. Local response is always likely to be quicker, cheaper, more sensitive to local circumstances and more culturally appropriate. Building local expertise and local jobs is self-evidently worthwhile.

White men in shorts

But there are wider issues too. It is sometimes suggested by politicians or journalists, in developed as well as developing countries, that humanitarian organizations and workers are interfering in a damaging way in the countries in which they are working, acting counterproductively, rather than helping, either through ignorance or by imposing inappropriate views, values and standards. Some journalists and authors have made very public claims along these lines, and some governments of developing countries have seized on these to run campaigns against NGOs, questioning in particular their lack of accountability: who do these people think they are and who gave them the right to pontificate about my country?

I hope I have already made clear my conviction that humanitarians are overwhelmingly in the business because they are driven by a desire to make a difference, to save lives and help others. Many of those working for me in OCHA or whom I came across in other UN agencies, the Red Cross movement, or the NGOs were bright and able and would have done well anywhere they chose to work. Coming from the outside, I was consistently impressed by the dedication and commitment of the organizations and individuals I came across in the field. The narrative sometimes seen in the British tabloids and one or two books that they spend all their time dining in fancy restaurants in the main cities and driving around in flashy white 4x4s, while the local people starve and struggle around them, has, in my experience, no serious basis in reality. Most humanitarians work, by definition, in uncomfortable and dangerous places, with poor financial rewards and worse career prospects, at great personal sacrifice to themselves and their families. Even those in the bigger UN agencies, where conditions of service are usually better than

351

in the NGOs, could readily find easier jobs and lives elsewhere.

I see no merit either in the accusations – for example, from the Sudanese government at times of tension over Darfur – that NGOs are staffed by Western youths who can't find jobs at home and have a built-in incentive to exaggerate and prolong humanitarian needs. The humanitarians I met were always rightly anxious to work themselves out of that particular job: by meeting the needs and then leaving.

Humanitarians are, of course, human too. They occasionally relax over a local meal if they find themselves in a large town, and have a few drinks in the process. Some are young and like to party when they get a chance. There will always be the odd bad episode. But in my experience, stories of regular wild and inappropriate behaviour are largely unfounded, given the strict guidelines and the sense of responsibility of those concerned.

Likewise, many humanitarian staff do drive 4x4s, as a simple necessity given the state of the roads in the field where they do most of their work. The ability to get to places and see things, to carry equipment and aid, and to have radio communications is crucial for the job and the safety of those doing it. I understand that international presences can be offensive to local opinion where they become oppressively heavy, and where half the vehicles on the roads are 4x4s from international agencies, with little apparent positive effect on local conditions. I have seen examples myself. But that is usually the cumulative effect of peacekeepers, embassy staff and development aid workers too. The problem should not just be laid at the humanitarians' door.

More serious are concerns that Western-based humanitarians arrogantly push solutions which betray ignorance of local traditions and dynamics, and are both inappropriate and likely to be ineffective. It would be foolish to say this does not happen. There are plenty of examples of projects with little or no local buy-in whose effects do not survive the departure of those running them. Communities are not always involved, as they should be, in the design and implementation of projects. International humanitarian workers arriving from the outside in an emergency can seem to have their own agendas, especially when they are angered by the suffering they see and apparent local indifference to it. They can be desperate to apply the experience they have gained elsewhere, but take insufficient account of the authorities with whom they have to deal, and the contexts in which they are working.

Most aid organizations have long recognized these risks and the problems of seeming too white and Western. Increasingly, the overwhelming majority of their staff are locals of the countries concerned. This is not just good PR, but also practical sense. Local staff speak the language, are much closer to the local culture and environment, and are less likely to make crass mistakes. More cynically, they are also often much cheaper to employ than expatriates. Even where the top layer of the staff of local operations of international agencies is from outside, international staff these days are progressively more from other developing countries, which can help to reduce sensitivities.

There are, nevertheless, reasons for retaining international staff in some key posts. While the days may have gone when the finance officer was always an expatriate for fear of local corruption, someone with experience of the wider culture and nature of the international agency or NGO is helpful to ensure common standards and common policies. In politically difficult countries, international staff can also be vital in speaking out over issues where locals fear to tread because of well-justified fear of intimidation or persecution of themselves and their families by local governments or non-state actors.

In any new emergency, especially in a country which is not

normally disaster-prone, the first responders from major organizations are bound to be international: the knowledge and experience required to get through the first few difficult weeks are unlikely to be available locally. It is impossible to recruit and train enough local staff instantly. Humanitarian organizations are always likely to employ more international staff for emergencies than development organizations do for working on long-term projects.

But in practice, the biggest issue is not the number of international staff, but perceptions. Most NGOs inevitably risk being seen by some local governments and groups, in places like Somalia or Afghanistan, as pursuing a Western political and security agenda because they come originally from the West. They were established in the West because that is where the money to help and time to reflect on the imperative of helping others happened to be. In practice, most of these organizations tend to be highly critical of the governments of their countries of origin, and are certainly not any kind of tools or proxies for them. They are the last people willing to be used for political purposes. But that does not prevent the damaging perception that they are somehow part of a Western strategy. This is precisely why humanitarians are so keen to establish some space between themselves and other Western/international presences.

Natural suspicions about Western-based NGOs cannot in any way justify the actions of governments who use accusations of arrogance, spying, and insensitive behaviour to conceal their wish to stop outside organizations discovering and publishing unpleasant truths. As we have seen, the risks of this are high when humanitarian organizations are not only providing basic aid, but also involved in protection of civilians. The Sudanese expulsion of international NGOs from Darfur in 2009 was a classic example of a desire to cover up sensitive realities such as sexual violence, dressed up as defence of national sovereignty and protection of local values against alien Western ones.

This issue of values is always tricky. International NGOs tend to defend rights and values which are those espoused generally in the West. They can be seen on occasion as insensitive to local traditions – for example, over the position of women. Personally, I believe that the rights and values which the NGOs and agencies seek to promote are for the most part essentially universal, not Western, including those which concern the basic rights of women to live free from the threat of sexual violence. No amount of bluster from upset governments or use of anti-Western rhetoric should be allowed to obscure that.

Humanitarian organizations nevertheless need to adapt their behaviour and temper their criticism to take into account local sensitivities and cultural attitudes. They should engage and try to convince local authorities, rather than run straight to the media to complain about real or supposed problems. They should not denounce publicly if they have said nothing privately, or engage in counterproductive and shrill lobbying about issues not central to their own business. As always, a reasonable balance needs to be struck between advocacy and operations. Nevertheless, NGOs should not be expected to abandon their core values and beliefs just because ill-intentioned local actors do not like them.

There can be particular problems where NGOs are faith-based, as many are, particularly from the US. Fortunately, the majority of such organizations are careful not to carry out any proselytizing activity to accompany their aid work, recognizing the need to keep these things strictly separate. Nevertheless, their presence is always sensitive, especially in Muslim countries only too ready to believe that they are subject to Western efforts to convert their populations and turn them away from the true faith. Faith-based NGOs need to make a special effort to ensure that they are operating solely on the basis of humanitarian need, to allay suspicions.

Go local

If I have gone – in some detail – into what may seem obvious to many, it is to set the record straight at a time when NGOs are under pressure in countries inclined to see them as a nuisance. At the same time, NGOs have to recognize that they *are* unaccountable in important ways, however responsible and transparent they may be. Localization of both jobs and attitudes is therefore vital. It has still not gone far enough. Locals still tend to be too concentrated at the lower ends of the structures. Career opportunities for them outside their own country are often too few. Consulting and involving local opinion is still not an automatic habit, as it should be, as we saw in Haiti.

There is also a need for Western-based NGOs to move towards authentic federal structures for their international operations, to ensure that in developing countries they are creating and working through genuinely local organizations with local leadership and local faces, while still ensuring that they adhere to central standards. This can be done. Indeed, it is already happening, at least for many of the major European NGOs. But it needs to go further.

International NGOs should also help to create, mentor, and maintain truly independent local NGOs with serious capacity, not just franchised examples of their own brand. These can then become vehicles for delivering aid, not only in their own countries, reducing the need for the 'international fire brigade', but also in other developing countries, in a more acceptable way than Western-based organizations sometimes can. Examples such as Mercy Malaysia, a local NGO originally set up to deal with emergencies in Malaysia, which has, over time, expanded to be able to work in many other countries of the world, are already showing the way.

Many Western-origin NGOs pay lip service to this, but do little about it in practice. Perhaps they are nervous at some level about creating more competition for themselves. But this kind of help is essential. It can be very difficult otherwise for local humanitarian NGOs to grow and stay in business over time. When there is no immediate disaster in their country, they have no depth of local support and no core funding to keep themselves going against the day when they are next called upon. These problems are not insoluble if there is a real will to solve them, from both international NGOs and international donors. Otherwise, the mantra about international humanitarians having to intervene to help because there is no local capacity will always be a self-fulfilling prophecy. There is a significant agenda for change here.

Building disaster-management capacity

Strengthening local NGOs is doubly desirable because strengthening civil society in many of the countries concerned has wider political and social benefits. But improving government capacity, at central and local level, is also crucial. Disaster-prone countries need an effective disaster-management set-up, with the right skills, training, and experience to react when disaster strikes, and the ability to scale up operations with great speed when necessary. These skills need to be tested regularly, with pre-trained 'surge' staff, i.e. those ready and able to go at a moment's notice to any new emergency, automatically available from other parts of the government, civilian or military. Some countries already have or are developing this capacity. Indonesia, for example – possibly the most disaster-prone country in the world – has made huge progress in developing strong disaster-management institutions following the Indian Ocean tsunami, and looks more and more capable of handling its own problems with each disaster that comes along.

Organizations like OCHA and some large donors have long been investing in this kind of capacity building and training. The UN Disaster Assessment and Coordination unit, run by OCHA, is a good example of how this can be done. UNDAC teams are a vital element at the beginning of new disasters. They are first in from the outside with tried-and-tested procedures and equipment, to kick-start the international relief effort, and provide initial needs assessments and coordination.

But UNDAC also have a significant capacity-building role. They train volunteers from developing and disaster-prone countries for participation in their own emergency teams. These experts then automatically spread within their own countries the knowledge and experience they have gained. UNDAC also lead specific training missions to advise and help countries establish and improve their own institutions and arrangements. Investments like this are gradually beginning to bring dividends. But once again, much more is needed.

A new business model

The fact that there is still such a long way to go underlines the case for the new 'business model' for humanitarian assistance, one which properly reflects the primordial importance of DRR and local capability. Such a model relies on bringing governments, the private sector, and civil society together, in order to put the emphasis on increasing local resilience. This should mean resilience to disasters of any kind, economic and social as well as those caused by natural hazards. New partnerships between these three actors are urgently needed at every level – local, national, regional, and global – to look at where the greatest vulnerabilities are and to establish mechanisms to increase the ability of affected peoples to survive and bounce back from disaster.

Involvement of the private sector is particularly desirable. They are key actors in the aid process, with huge skills and resources, but are too often ignored by both governments and aid organizations. The latter tend to engage with the private sector only on their own strictly defined and hard-to-understand terms. This needs to change. I have already brought out, in the context of food aid, the need to help small businesses and shopkeepers after a natural disaster has hit their premises and stocks. This speeds up the return of local jobs and income, encourages self-reliance, and strengthens the prospects of a rapid return to normality, while discouraging aid dependency and reducing the time and resources spent on aid relief. But small businesses can also be engaged *before* disaster strikes to ensure they have looked at the risks they face and put in place mitigating measures wherever possible, with the help of local authorities and civil society.

Large companies have a major role to play in thinking about their own vulnerabilities and taking appropriate action to reduce them. They can also help by mentoring small businesses, both before and after disasters, setting up mechanisms and relationships which can kick in quickly if the worst happens. They inevitably depend on the community around them for workers and services of all kinds, and have a clear enlightened self-interest in ensuring wider resilience.

This can lead to genuinely win–win situations, including in the happy event that there is no disaster. The partnerships improve community acceptance of companies' commercial activities. They also provide an extra interest for companies' own employees, who have no commercial stake in emergency relief but can see the need for contributions to particular crises. They are almost always keen to help on issues which go beyond simple money-making, especially when they involve the future health of their own communities.

The thesis is therefore simple. International humanitarian response is necessary, but not sufficient. Reducing the risks of disasters and increasing local capacity go together. They should attract more commitment and investment from the donor community and both humanitarian and development organizations. That is the best way of improving resilience and response in the face of the rising challenges of the future, particularly from climate change. It should be adopted as a basic policy aim. Many actors around the system agree. Now is the time to start to put it into practice in earnest.

CHAPTER THIRTEEN

Humanitarian Intervention, and protecting civilians in armed conflict

I have described specific crises to bring out the policy dilemmas for humanitarians operating in highly charged political contexts. This chapter takes a wider look at the principles behind protection of civilians in armed conflict, and at perhaps the biggest single challenge: the case for so-called humanitarian intervention. It also draws together the threads on accountability, and the role of the International Criminal Court, including the real tensions between peace and justice.

What does protection of civilians (POC) mean?

Civilians are overwhelmingly the victims of today's internal conflicts. Pitched battles between armies are increasingly rare, and military casualties in low-intensity warfare limited. Civilians, by contrast, are killed, wounded, and assaulted by all sides, either accidentally when they are caught in the crossfire, or deliberately when combatants use them to make political points. They are forced to flee their homes in huge numbers, and become vulnerable to abuses of all kinds, including sexual violence, recruitment of children as soldiers, and use of indiscriminate weapons, such as landmines and cluster munitions.

Humanitarian organizations have therefore devoted increasing energy and resources to protecting those innocently caught up in armed conflict. Protection has become the watchword behind many programmes. A new breed of humanitarian workers called protection officers has been born, causing endless confusion with bodyguards in the minds of suspicious governments in the countries in which they are operating. So what does protection of civilians in armed conflict actually mean?

The official definition, agreed collectively by humanitarian organizations in 1999, is as follows: '... all activities aimed at ensuring full respect for the rights of the individual in accordance with the letter and spirit of the relevant bodies of law, i.e. human rights law, international humanitarian law, and refugee law.'

This covers anything which can help ensure civilian populations survive with dignity and return to their normal lives as soon as possible. Protection is sometimes seen as an ivory-tower concept. But it is, or should be, highly practical. To understand its importance requires a leap of imagination for people living comfortable lives in the West, in order to comprehend the depth of despair for individuals from normally peaceful communities: your relatives and friends killed, often brutally, your home destroyed, and you yourself a long way from anything familiar, under imminent threat of death or rape, hungry and exhausted. Even the most resilient individuals can give way in such apparently hopeless circumstances. That is why the need for practical help is so stark.

Clearly the best solution is to get civilians out of harm's way entirely. Once across a border into another country they become refugees and can avail themselves of all the physical and legal protections which flow from that status. UNHCR takes responsibility for them. The responsibilities of host governments are clearly set out in the 1951 Convention, and widely understood.

However, when conflicts are internal within states, involve armed guerrilla groups, and are unpredictable in their impact, civilians often do not cross borders. They flee particular outbreaks of fighting when they have no choice, sometimes finishing up in camps and sometimes not, but do not want to go too far. Their hope is to return as soon as they can, to carry on tending whatever is left of their crops and animals, or to resume their city lives.

These internally displaced persons (IDPs) are now much more numerous than refugees – more than 26 million in 2011, compared to around 15 million refugees, according to UNHCR official figures. They are also much harder to look after. They are not in a place of safety and do not have the same defined legal rights, although there are now widely accepted guiding principles about their treatment.

In these difficult and dangerous circumstances, protection workers are trying to make sure that governments and militias alike are aware of their responsibilities; that civilians are not only receiving basic services, but are aware of their rights; that their sufferings are documented and brought to the attention of all concerned; that they are given psychological and legal support as well as medical treatment when they are victims of abuses or sexual violence; and that aid organizations and others trying to help them are able to operate in as safe an environment as possible.

Most of this assistance is after the fact rather than before. Unlike armed peacekeepers, protection officers cannot physically intervene to protect civilians from armed groups, and are often helpless to intervene when large-scale abuses are taking place. This mismatch between what protection officers appear to offer and what they can do in reality frequently left me frustrated, and calling for a different word from 'protection' to make the gap between promise and delivery less obviously yawning. At the same time, the very fact that there are expert witnesses on the ground in the areas where abuses are being committed does provide deterrence by presence. This is not to be underestimated.

Protection work brings those involved into greater risk of confrontation with governments and armed groups because they are engaging in politically neuralgic areas where humanitarian operations and human rights overlap. Revealing the extent of sexual violence and treating its victims can be especially sensitive, as we saw in the case of Darfur. Denial is often the response of governments, and sometimes non-state actors too, accompanied by attempts to take out anger and frustration on the messengers. Risks to humanitarian workers escalate accordingly – of physical assault and harassment, as well as expulsion.

Protecting the protection workers is therefore a priority, not least by emphasizing that protection work is an indispensable element of modern humanitarianism. Governments cannot in this day and age just opt for the basic services of food, water, shelter, and medical care without accepting at the same time the protection aspects. This is not always an easy message. In my time as ERC, governments like those of Sudan and Sri Lanka resisted it strongly in different ways, as we have seen. We did not always win such battles, but we made advances wherever we could, relying on time, increasing acceptance of norms, international support, and attrition by constant argument to help us move forward.

POC and the Security Council

One of the ERC's tasks is to write the secretary-general's annual report to the Security Council on the protection of civilians in armed conflict, under Resolution 1265 of 1999, which had recognized for the first time the responsibility of all member states to ensure protection of civilians. I also briefed the Security Council in person twice a year on implementation of the resolution on the ground. These were great opportunities to remind member states of their responsibilities and to draw attention to some of the worst infringements in the previous six months – the thousands of civilians killed and wounded, the countless victims of sexual violence, the violations of the rights of children, the millions of displaced. I usually managed to upset several member states by including their actions or omissions in my list – not only the usual suspects from the conflicts of the day, but also, for example, the US over civilian casualties from NATO actions in Afghanistan.

These occasions were also highly frustrating: a large number of member states spoke in each debate, reaffirming the prime importance they gave to protection of civilians in armed conflict and their commitment to act accordingly. This was a good example of the UN's role in shaping norms of behaviour and setting the bar in the right place for states and non-state actors alike. Having the major states of the world line up to endorse the rights of civilians to protection from the effects of armed conflict was certainly better than the other way round. But the gap between rhetoric and reality in many of the states making speeches was wide, to say the least. I increasingly felt that for some, if not most, making the speech was a substitute for action, and I pointed this out with growing insistence.

The reports to the Security Council were also an excellent opportunity to highlight specific policy concerns and to attempt to advance thinking on them. In my time, for example, we focussed on what we saw as several key interrelated issues:

- the necessity for effective protection of civilians of free access for humanitarians to areas of conflict – we carried out an analysis of the factors preventing or restricting access in 2009, demonstrating the extent to which lack of access was often the result of deliberate obstruction by governments and other armed actors

- the requirement for greater security for humanitarian workers, against the background of the alarming trends in killings, assaults, and abductions during my time as ERC
- combating sexual violence, and the need for concerted action not only to treat its victims, but also to stop it happening in the first place
- the need for humanitarians to talk to all sides, including unofficial armed groups, even those widely regarded as terrorist groups, in order to improve access and remind them of their responsibilities towards civilians
- making protection of civilians a meaningful part of the activities of UN peacekeeping forces, not just in the military sense, but as central to everything they are doing; a joint OCHA/Department of Peacekeeping study in 2009 had revealed major weaknesses in every aspect of this from leadership, through training, to the absence of standing instructions for the troops on the ground on how to respond to particular situations involving civilians
- accountability, and the importance of ending the culture of impunity for abuses and atrocities which characterizes so many recent conflicts.

One of the innovations during my time as ERC was the establishment of a Security Council Expert Working Group on POC. This was an informal mechanism to brief Security Council members about protection issues in the geographical crises on their agenda, and to suggest ways in which they could be addressed in the Council's deliberations and resolutions. It was resisted by several Council members at first. Some feared a new heavy procedure in an already over-bureaucratic environment. Others such as China and Russia tended to regard such talk as idealism not much connected to hard reality. However the Working Group has become a valuable forum to help Security Council members make sure that POC issues do not slip between the cracks – for example, when peacekeeping force mandates are being established or reviewed.

Some member states, such as Israel and Sri Lanka, argued in the bi-annual debates that traditional legal requirements for protection of civilians could no longer apply. When war was being waged against illegal armed groups deliberately using civilians as human shields, old norms of distinction between civilians and combatants and of use of proportionate force were impossible to respect and unduly favourable to the 'terrorists'. Our response was that, while these issues had undeniably become more and more difficult, that could not be a reason for ignoring human rights and humanitarian law. Extra care needed to be exercised, rather than the opposite, however frustrating this might be. But there was, nevertheless, a recognition that the norms and standards might need to be looked at again, not to weaken them, but to adapt them to current reality.

Accountability

Probably the most difficult question linked to protection was accountability for abuses. Member states were always in favour of this in theory. Many made eloquent speeches about the need to end impunity. But when it came to specific situations, these principles generally went out of the window in favour of political selectivity. Thus the US was unwilling to agree to any kind of investigation of Israeli practices, while the Arab countries ignored the many abuses and barbarities in their own camp in order to press for an exclusive focus on Israeli policies. Western countries were willing to agree to proposals of investigations into Sri Lankan behaviour in the last days of the war against the LTTE, but the Russians and Chinese, and indeed the vast majority of developing countries, would not hear of it. And so on.

Although the secretary-general had theoretical powers to set up investigations into allegations of serious violations of human rights and international humanitarian law, in practice he was unwilling to use these powers without strong political backing from the Security Council and the majority of the UN membership. This was often difficult, even impossible, to achieve. The Geneva-based Human Rights Council was an alternative, but member states there were often either paralysed by disagreement or too likely to act in a politically one-sided way, as over Gaza in 2009.

I proposed at one point that in order to depoliticize proposals for independent investigations, there should be a special unit inside the UN Secretariat charged with *automatically* investigating any serious and plausible allegations of widespread abuses. There would be no need for any kind of political consensus or vote for such investigations to go ahead, although there would obviously have to be political backing for any follow-up action.

I continue to believe that something on these lines would be a good idea. However, the unfortunate reality is that the staff and resources for such a unit would need to be agreed and voted by UN members. This stands little chance of being endorsed by the majority as long as so many countries fear finding themselves on the wrong end of any investigations and subsequent calls for action, and prefer to retain a political veto.

It is also a sad truth that, without the full cooperation of the government of the country concerned and any non-state actors involved, getting to the real truth of what happened in any specific case is very difficult. This cooperation is rarely forthcoming, at least in the immediate aftermath of incidents. It may become easier when a future, less directly involved leadership takes over. That is why whatever evidence can be assembled should be preserved, as we saw over Sri Lanka.

The ICC

The major new weapon we now have is the International Criminal Court, agreed in principle in the late 1990s and finally established in 2002. Its remit is to investigate and prosecute individuals accused of genocide, crimes against humanity, and war crimes (and potentially in future the crime of aggression). It is a last resort, for use when national courts are unable or unwilling to deal with cases, and is only able to act when the accused is a member of a state party, the alleged offence took place on the territory of a state party, or the Security Council has referred a case to the Court.

The ICC statute has been signed and ratified by 121 countries as I write, and signed but not ratified by a further thirty-one. This may sound encouraging, but the reality behind the numbers is much less positive. Russia has signed, but not ratified. The US signed originally, but then indicated it was 'unsigning' and would not ratify, as did Israel and Sudan (an unlikely trio). The US, like Israel, has always been concerned that its soldiers might get caught up in 'unreasonable' cases brought for political reasons. China, India, and a number of other countries have not signed and seem unlikely to do so as things stand. Many African governments have not signed because of worries about the infringement of national sovereignty the ICC potentially represents.

The ICC is seen by its supporters as the tool which can, over time, end impunity and ensure accountability. However, its early years have brought mixed results. As I write, it has so far conducted investigations into seven conflict situations, all in Africa. Twenty-eight individuals have been indicted, five are in custody and one has been found guilty: a DRC militia leader called Lubanga, convicted in 2011 for recruiting and using child soldiers.

Because of the apparent focus on African countries the Court has been accused of bias by its detractors. This is unreasonable. The Court can only consider cases brought to its attention. Three of the seven situations have been referred to the Court by the country concerned itself – DRC, Uganda (for the LRA), and the Central African Republic. Moreover, one of the active and important forerunners of the Court, the ad hoc International Tribunal for Former Yugoslavia, has nothing to do with Africa, and has several convictions to its credit. Nevertheless, this accusation of selectivity has been used to good effect by opponents of the Court – Sudan, for one. It remains a problem for the ICC not only in attracting more African signatories to the statute, but also ensuring the countries of the region cooperate – for example, by handing over indictees if they turn up on their territory.

The Court also faces other challenges to its credibility. Its first prosecutor, with his human rights campaigning background and penchant for publicity, sometimes seemed to be acting politically as much as judicially in the way in which he handled sensitive situations, notably Darfur. His occasional reports to the Security Council were highly political and polemical. The question is not whether he was right about the individuals he was pursuing, but whether his campaigning approach was helpful for the wider credibility of the Court and its necessary reputation for judicial impartiality.

I also have doubts about the way in which the Security Council has sometimes used referral of situations to the ICC. Faced with intractable political problems and a lack of tools and collective political will to influence them, the Council has occasionally seemed tempted to reach for the ICC just as *something* to do, a way to express condemnation of a particular regime, without necessarily thinking through how this might affect political resolution of the problems. Again, the question is not whether the regimes concerned – for example, that of Colonel Gaddafi in Libya – merit indictment, but whether a referral might reduce further the possibility of a negotiated outcome to a conflict or civil war.

The point is that once the ICC is engaged, it is extremely difficult to turn off again. An individual leader faced with an ICC indictment can be left without a realistic option of going into exile peacefully, since all countries signed up to the Court will be obliged to hand him over and his travel will always be restricted at best. He or she may, therefore, be reinforced in the belief that there is no choice but to fight on and hang on to power at all costs. More lives may be lost as a result, and an opportunity for an early resolution can disappear.

The wider point is that peace and justice do not always go hand in hand, however much idealists may wish that they do. In many situations, there can be no lasting peace without justice, but in the short term the ICC's involvement may block off helpful possibilities. Would Colonel Gaddafi have fought to the bitter end if he could have been offered exile for himself and his family? Probably, in his case, but we will never know. Would the leader of the LRA, Joseph Kony, have come in from the bush and signed the peace agreement if he had not faced ICC charges which could be lifted only by the Security Council, which could not have been persuaded to do any such thing? Possibly not, but if he had signed and come in, tens of thousands of lives would not have been ruined in the years since. Would President Bashir of Sudan have been more amenable to a negotiated settlement in Darfur if he had not been indicted by the ICC and put beyond the pale by most of the international community in 2009? Probably not, but his indictment was certainly not helpful to the prospects of peace in Darfur, and did untold damage to the humanitarian operation and its beneficiaries in the process. Any hopes of the then prosecutor that the indictment would lead to Bashir's downfall were vain, and predictably so, since the reaction of the rest of the regime, even those who did not care much for Bashir, was to close ranks around him.

It is sometimes suggested that this is all a question of timing or sequencing – indictment need not hinder negotiation, and the legal issues can be returned to later, once the leader in question is out of power. This has merit in principle. But it is naive in practice: the leader concerned can see the likely sequence perfectly well too. In any case, the cover was blown from this idea by what happened to Charles Taylor, the former dictator from Liberia. He was indicted in 2003 by the Special Tribunal for Sierra Leone for his crimes in the civil war there; then offered asylum in Nigeria, apparently with promises of protection from the Tribunal; and then later, in 2006, handed over when the government of Liberia requested his extradition. Good for justice in one sense – like the others I have mentioned, he certainly deserved to be put on trial for his many crimes, and was duly convicted in mid-2012. But it demonstrated again to other dictators and people like Kony that once the ICC has you on its list there may be no escape: negotiation of a peaceful way out will lead nowhere for you personally.

A final concern is that indictments which do not lead to arrests and trials are not good for the credibility of the ICC. President Bashir of Sudan has been able to carry on with his official duties almost without interruption, and has travelled in the region and more widely with relative ease. Demonstrations that the ICC is a paper tiger, unless the person concerned travels to The Hague voluntarily, or goes to a country where he will be arrested, cannot be helpful from any point of view.

I share the wider view that ending impunity for leaders who do terrible things to their own people is crucial in the longer term. I see the argument that justice must be blind to where its conclusions might lead in the political short term. But I also see the injustice of millions of people who are suffering at the hands of terrible leaders having to go on doing so for longer than is necessary if the ICC is used without sufficient thought for the real-world consequences.

Moreover, it is not always true that there can be no peace without justice. The successful peace negotiation I know best, the 1998 Good Friday Agreement in Northern Ireland, involved a deal on early release for duly convicted prisoners from all illegal armed groups. This had nothing to do with justice and everything to do with the need for such a deal if the groups concerned and their communities were to accept the agreement and give up violence. It worked, even though all concerned had to hold their noses. Other countries in varying circumstances have decided that the interests of peace are best served by not opening up afresh all the wounds of painful civil wars. Sometimes they may just want to avoid painful realities, but sometimes they may be right.

The parallel between Northern Ireland and situations involving dictators with thousands of lives on their consciences is, of course, far from exact. Justice and truth-telling are often the only ways of healing profound divisions in societies. But we need to accept that peace and justice are not always easy bedfellows, rather than hoping, saying, and believing that they will always go together.

One other highly sensitive issue around the ICC is whether humanitarian organizations or their staff should help the Court in its work, for example by providing information about war crimes in the areas in which they are working. A distinction has to be made between UN organizations and NGOs. The ICC is not part of the UN family, but there is a Relationship Agreement which specifies mutual cooperation. Under certain conditions and on request, therefore, the UN has to furnish information and documents to the Court, although this does not override concerns about staff safety. NGOs have no formal relationship with the ICC and have complete freedom of choice about whether and, if so, how they help the ICC.

The choice is essentially between on the one hand assisting justice and preventing war crimes by governments or non-state actors, through reduction of impunity; and on the other risking the vital perception of impartiality and independence of humanitarian organizations by seeming to take sides. Different organizations have come to different conclusions about this dilemma. But if there is to be cooperation, there has to be confidentiality, for the sake of both the organization and any individual who decides to supply information. This is less easy than it may appear, since promises from the ICC about confidentiality may prove hard to keep. If the case comes to trial, the defence lawyers may well demand to know where the evidence came from, with the serious risk that the trial may collapse otherwise. This risk is not theoretical, as I know from experience.

The 'Responsibility to Protect'

The issue of humanitarian intervention is at once simple and immensely complex. The simplicity comes from the imperative felt by all of us to stop atrocities when we hear of them and see them on our televisions or YouTube. If we have the capability to do so, how can we not act? The question of what to do about terrible events in another country has come up many times in history. But the starting point for current thinking is the massacre of one community by another in Rwanda in 1994, when the international community wrung its collective hands, but effectively did nothing to stop what was happening. Some 800,000 people, mostly Tutsis, were killed by rival Hutus over a period of a hundred days, despite global condemnation and the presence of a UN force containing French and Belgian troops.

A strong and widespread reaction afterwards was 'never again' – the international community could henceforth not be allowed to stand idly by while a country's citizens were slaughtered. The 1995 horror of Srebrenica reinforced the sentiment that something new and more effective was needed: Bosnian Serbs massacred thousands of Bosnian Muslims despite the fact that the UN had declared the town a safe area, with a Dutch UN unit close by at the time.

However, many governments in the developing world, with the support of Russia and China, continued to take a more cautious view: while events like the Rwanda genocide clearly had to be condemned, and there had been a case for action, the key principles of the primacy of national sovereignty and the unacceptability of interference in the internal affairs of another country should not be prejudiced. Humanitarian concerns should not become an interveners' charter, providing an excuse for Western countries to invade other countries whenever they felt like it, without regard to international law or the role of the UN Security Council. The developing countries felt particularly strongly about this because they saw Western countries as operating double standards in their foreign policy, condemning and wanting to intervene in those countries they did not like for political or other reasons, and letting off lightly others they did support or where they had large commercial/security interests.

These arguments echo a wider, long-standing argument about

the universal applicability of human rights standards and the legitimacy of the international community in insisting on their relevance to the internal affairs of all countries. This debate is by no means resolved. But the norms of international behaviour have, in recent years, been codified in ways which assume that national sovereignty *is* limited and certainly does not just mean the right of the government of a state to do what it likes within its own borders. It is now generally – and rightly – assumed that the international community does have a legitimate interest in what is going on inside countries, not least because internal problems and abuses can often become threats to international peace and security.

As part of the debate which followed Rwanda and Srebrenica, former British prime minister Tony Blair, in a speech in Chicago in April 1999, set out what became known – at least for a while – as the Blair doctrine. The context was the NATO intervention in Kosovo and the bombing campaign against Serbia which was not, at the time, producing the hoped-for results. Mr Blair spent a lot of the speech defending the Kosovo operation as a just war against the evil of ethnic cleansing. But he also put it in the broader context of the pressing need for new rules for international action in a post-Cold War age of interdependence.

He emphasized that the principle of non-interference had to have its limits. Equally, we could not right every wrong in the world. We therefore had to decide what we could and should do. He set out five major considerations which, in his view, would have to be satisfied before 'we' (he meant the major pillars of the international community) intervened militarily:

1. Are we sure of our case?
2. Have we exhausted all the diplomatic alternatives and given peace every chance?

3. Are there military operations we can sensibly and prudently undertake?
4. Are we prepared for the long term?
5. Do we have national interests involved?

He added that while the UN had to remain central to this, new ways had to be found to make the UN and the Security Council work, to avoid Cold-War style deadlocks.

This speech helped prompt the establishment of an International Commission on Intervention and State Sovereignty. Their report in 2001 on 'The Responsibility to Protect' cleverly turned the sovereignty argument on its head. They argued that sovereignty should be seen not as giving governments freedom to act without check inside their borders, but as conferring responsibility for the welfare of the citizens of the state. Governments should be helped to exercise this responsibility wherever possible, but where they proved unable or unwilling to exercise their responsibility to protect their own population effectively, or were actually abusing their own people, the principle of non-intervention should yield to that of international responsibility. Four conditions were attached to any intervention, similar to the Blair criteria, but not quite the same:

- The intentions had to be right.
- It had to be a last resort.
- Only proportional means should be used.
- There should be reasonable prospects of success.

The report also emphasized the crucial role of the Security Council in authorizing any intervention.

After a long and difficult debate, the UN World Summit of 2005 unanimously adopted paragraphs 138 and 139 of the

Outcome Document on this Responsibility to Protect, or R2P, as it became more commonly known. Picking up where the International Commission had left off, these paragraphs spelled out that it was for each state to protect its population from genocide, war crimes, ethnic cleansing, and crimes against humanity, and that the international community should encourage and help states to fulfil this responsibility; but that if states had manifestly failed in this respect, the international community were obliged to use appropriate peaceful means to do so and, if all else failed, to intervene in other ways, through the Security Council.

This was a significant step – indeed, in many ways a break-through – in international readiness to establish when intervention might be justified. It was greeted with some jubilation by campaigners for humanitarian intervention. However, it quickly became clear that this was not the end of the argument. Many states which had agreed to the World Summit Outcome Document seemed to suffer almost immediately from buyers' remorse. They wanted to forget or ignore what they had signed up to because of their fear of how it might be used in the future. The context was, of course, the disastrous aftermath of the invasion of Iraq by a US-led coalition without specific Security Council authorization and the continuing military intervention in Afghanistan, even though neither of these was a humanitarian intervention as such. The latter *was* authorized by the UN in 2001 after 9/11, on counter-terrorism rather than humanitarian grounds, but was also proving increasingly difficult and controversial.

There has been a long and continuing discussion since 2005 about how R2P should be turned into reality. There is a strong group in favour of regular and robust intervention to make the world a better place. They include former Australian foreign minister Gareth Evans, who has written a powerful book on the subject. The UN General Assembly has since 2009 passed a series of resolutions noting, though not explicitly endorsing, plans to 'operationalize' R2P. The UN experts have tried to take some of the toxicity out of the debate by stressing that R2P is not just or even mainly about military intervention. The aim is, above all, to avoid the need for this by helping national governments fulfil their obligations and responsibilities, and by sounding the alarm early enough so that more peaceful means can be used. This has helped to calm the debate to some extent.

However, the objections based on the sacred principles of sovereignty and non-interference have certainly not gone away, as we have seen over Syria. And however valid the points may be about doing everything possible to avoid a situation where armed action comes on to the agenda, the issue of military intervention and when it is appropriate cannot be ducked.

So how confident can we now be that the international community would act to prevent another Rwandan genocide? Have we, in fact, gone backwards because of the toxic legacy of Iraq and Afghanistan? Or have we, on the contrary, unleashed in R2P a diplomatic monster which we cannot control and which may lead us back into more international adventures than we can deal with? It is worth highlighting some of the particular points of contention over humanitarian intervention.

First, what is meant by humanitarian? Obviously, this refers to avoidance of loss of civilian life and suffering. But how great does the threat have to be, and who is going to judge the extent and nature of this threat? It is useful to note that it is usually politicians, and sometimes human rights campaigners, not humanitarians or aid organizations, who press for military intervention on humanitarian grounds. The aid community itself is often not at all convinced, except in absolutely clear-cut and appalling cases like that of Rwanda, that military intervention is going to be the right answer. They fear, as do many others, the law of unintended consequences, which often seems to work particularly fiercely in cases of armed intervention in other countries. Military action designed to protect one group of civilians may well end up harming and killing, however inadvertently, another. The balance may be very hard to strike. They also observe that those who argue most strongly for humanitarian intervention in a particular case often seem to have political motives as well, be they domestic or international.

Second is the question of who should decide when a situation merits intervention. The obvious answer is the UN Security Council, which has the mandate and the legitimacy. This is the ideal scenario, to be sought at all times. But if the Security Council cannot agree, what then? The purists argue that in those circumstances there can be no legal intervention, by definition, and that there should therefore be no intervention at all. Others suggest that *legitimate* intervention can still be possible if agreement in the Security Council is unreasonably blocked – for example, by one or more states acting from motives of obvious self-interest or a close relationship with the country in question; if there is wide international support for the idea of action; and especially if there is support from within the country concerned, from its neighbours, and/or from the relevant regional organization. The intervention in Kosovo in 1999 was, for example, not approved by the Security Council because it was thought that the Russians would veto any resolution because of their close relationship with the Serbs. But because the case seemed strong, and the Kosovars were themselves pressing for intervention, and it had wide European and international support otherwise, it was widely seen as legitimate – even if not strictly legal.

Personally, I agree with the view that there can be cases where intervention is vital and justifiable even without Security Council authorization. However, the burden of proof has to be much higher in these cases, and the gap between legitimacy and legality remains an uncomfortable one. Military intervention should always be absolutely a last resort in any case, but without Security Council agreement, the case in humanitarian terms needs to be overwhelming, and widely recognized as such, and local and regional support particularly strong.

International law is far from fully developed in areas like this, and is constantly evolving. A purely legal view at any given moment therefore cannot be the end of the story. How, for example, are we supposed to deal with a pre-emptive intervention when the threat is even more a matter of judgment, not susceptible to any objective test or covered by international law as it stands?

The third related question, often ignored, is who is actually going to carry out the intervention, assuming one is agreed. Security Council authorization of military intervention may, in some circumstances, be the beginning of the argument, not the end. Some country or countries, or some organization, is going to have to agree to put their soldiers in harm's way; to bear the financial costs, which may be very considerable unless it is turned into a UN peacekeeping operation, where the burden can be shared; and to withstand all the undoubted political and other pressures which will be brought to bear. There is no UN or other international standing force which can be used, and little or no prospect of one being agreed or established, for a mixture of political and financial reasons, however good the idea might be in principle.

Even if all the alarm bells had been rung in time over Rwanda, and the Security Council had agreed to authorize a military intervention, who would have been willing to take this on, and could they have mobilized an effective force in time to do anything substantive on the ground? In addition, since Rwanda, the Iraq and Afghan operations have poisoned the well pretty thoroughly when it comes to willingness to put large numbers of troops into other countries for long periods, in anything but the most exceptional circumstances.

For the moment, the reality remains that if something is going to be done, it will usually have to be done by Western countries or organizations such as NATO – which naturally increases the suspicion in other parts of the world that the whole business is some kind of Western conspiracy to impose their own views and to deal with regimes they don't like, under the cloak of humanitarian concerns. Regional organizations are gradually becoming more active and vocal in this area, and their support for any intervention in their region is increasingly becoming a sine qua non. But they do not have the unity or capacity to do much in reality themselves, certainly not meaningful military intervention, without huge support.

Fourth, do we really understand the situation and all its local dynamics well enough to make a military intervention effective, and, just as important, sustain it over time? Can we really tell the good guys from the bad guys, and do we know how to build a nation back up after we have intervened? If the West decides to intervene, and can get together a force, it can usually get through the immediate military operation reasonably well and quickly because of its military capacity and technology. But the Western countries involved have proved singularly inept at the next step of creating a local political consensus, using local capacities, and establishing a sustainable economic, political, and social system. Moreover, the military capacity and technology are much less effective when it comes to holding territory in hostile circumstances, and to waging asymmetrical warfare against non-state armed resistance groups. The examples of both Iraq and Afghanistan are eloquent in this regard.

This is not because those concerned are stupid or incompetent, though bad mistakes were made in both cases. It is genuinely difficult to come in from the outside and to build a new system on the ruins of the old in a situation where the nuances – for example, of the existing economic and social networks – are hard to understand and even harder to work with successfully. This is tough even using the advice of the experts who know the country concerned well. If those experts are systematically ignored or belittled, as we have seen in some cases, it becomes almost impossible.

The colonial powers did not ignore local knowledge, were there for the long term, and could usually manage to impose their will and create functional systems in the end through a combination of brutality, with no outside media to watch, and cunning co-option of parts of the existing system. But Western countries have no desire to stay long enough to understand or change everything. It costs too much in blood and treasure apart from anything else. There is no colonial instinct at work. And the media are, rightly, watching very closely. So for good reasons, Western interveners are looking for quick wins and effective exit strategies from day one. They also tend to make the fatal mistake of assuming that they are building from scratch and can impose models – like Western-style democracy – in a few years. It is hardly surprising that they are not doing very well in this area. Nation-building is extremely hard even in the best of circumstances.

The UN sometimes has a better chance of success, using international peacekeeping forces and with consent from the host countries. It has a decent track record in some places – for example, in Timor and Liberia. There is a clear difference between coercive interventions and consensual ones, involving peacekeepers. The problems mainly arise where the intervention is against the wishes of the government in place at the time, and even directed at them. But even a consensual intervention is no guarantee of success, as we have seen in DRC.

We have also been guilty of attaching too much importance to the act of voting in elections, and not enough to the hard slog of building up the kind of civil society institutions and traditions which are the underpinnings of a genuine democracy. Elections are clearly important. It is hard to see how a new government can be given legitimacy in any other way. Watching people who have not voted before stand in line to do so with great enthusiasm is always a humbling and moving experience. But elections are only the start of the process, not the end, and the West have often seemed not to be as aware of that as they should have been.

These arguments do not undermine the case for humanitarian intervention in the right circumstances. They rather bring out some of the difficulties of the concept and the pitfalls in its practical implementation. I have already mentioned in the cases of Sri Lanka and Myanmar the extra complications in already difficult situations from the introduction of the possibility of military intervention on humanitarian grounds in circumstances where there was no real prospect of it happening.

This was the background to the debates reignited in earnest in 2011 and 2012 by the cases of first Libya, then Syria. Libya was, in many ways, the first action which was explicitly based on R2P principles since they were adopted. The immediate aim was clearly humanitarian: to save the population of Benghazi and other rebel-held cities from imminent attack and presumed – because specifically threatened – massacre by Colonel Gaddafi's forces. The air operation was explicitly approved by the Security Council in Resolution 1973, not least because of regional support, particularly from the Arab League. It was being called for by the rebel forces on the ground. It therefore had legitimacy as well as legality. And there were forces from Western and other countries willing to carry it out.

Although the campaign was not entirely straightforward, since the rebel forces were disorganized and ill-armed, to say the least, and not all supposedly surgical air attacks hit their targets, gradually it made the essential difference to the struggle. The rebels took over the country and the regime was defeated and destroyed. The immediate aim of saving the civilian populations of the threatened cities was certainly achieved. Few, if any, outside his immediate Libyan circle mourned for Colonel Gaddafi, or regretted his departure from power. So far, so good.

However, even in these apparently successful circumstances, significant questions still arose:

How deep was international support for the operation? The Arab League assistance was for the most part theoretical. Some of those who voted for the Security Council resolution, and even more so some of those who abstained, like Russia and China, afterwards seemed less sure of their vote or actively regretted it. They believed that they had been duped, since the aim of the operation quickly changed – in practice, if not in principle – from protection of civilians to regime change. Against that it is argued that they must have known what they were voting for, and that, given the attitude and actions of the regime, the only effective way of protecting civilians was to get rid of it. The fact remains that the resolution said one thing and the outcome was another.

How far did we know whom we were helping? The rebels were very diverse in their outlook and motives – political, tribal, regional, or religious – and had no coherent political or other platform. In one sense this did not matter if the civilian lives we set out to save were saved. But were we, in fact, doing little more than supporting one side in a civil war whose dynamics were lost on us? How could we be sure that those we were helping to install in power would be significantly better, including in behaviour towards civilians, than those they were trying to depose? Such doubts were not assuaged by the chaos and confusion in the months after the fall of the regime, with armed militias calling the shots and taking brutal revenge, in some cases on Gaddafi supporters.

Why were we intervening in Libya, but not interested in doing so elsewhere in the region? This argument can, of course, be extended to situations outside the region, such as Zimbabwe. Where is the consistency? This is in many ways the most difficult question. Naturally, each case is different. There are many reasons why Bahrain is a completely separate case from Libya, or why we should worry about the consequences of intervening in Syria and its immediate neighbourhood much more than in the Libyan case. From a military point of view, interventions elsewhere in the region would be much more difficult in many ways than in Libya, with its large geographic area and small population. It was already clear that the Security Council would not repeat its Libyan vote in the Syrian or indeed any other likely current case.

How far does this matter? Perfect consistency in foreign policy is certainly unattainable. But there is a requirement for a minimum of consistency and for the absence of too obvious double standards, without which the motives of interveners are going to be even more suspect than they would be otherwise. The main answer given to this charge of inconsistency is that the impossibility of intervening everywhere does not mean you should not intervene anywhere. Otherwise, you are condemned to impotence in all circumstances. This is indeed a powerful argument. But it is not powerful enough, to my mind, to still all doubts about why we choose one situation in which to intervene over others.

How far did the intervention in Libya match up to the tests set by Tony Blair and the International Commission?

Were we sure of our case? Gaddafi and his regime do not find many defenders, quite rightly, and saving Benghazi was easy to agree with. But the doubts about the endgame, and about the nature and motives of the rebels, meant that the case was not watertight.

Had we exhausted all diplomatic options? There may not have been many, given the nature of the Gaddafi regime and the threats they were making. And if Benghazi was to be saved, there was no time or opportunity to negotiate. But the truth is that we did not really want to negotiate with Gaddafi, and from an early stage stuck to the mantra that nothing was possible unless he went. So a not completely satisfactory answer here either.

Were there military operations we could sensibly and prudently undertake? Yes, in the sense that we could conduct an air campaign at little risk to ourselves – though not to those underneath – and to good effect on the ground. Ruling out a ground assault made achieving our military aims more difficult, but there were good reasons to avoid another Middle East quagmire.

Were we prepared for the long term? The fact that it was an air intervention meant we were less directly responsible for what happened on the ground, and could take the view that what followed was for the Libyans to decide, rather than get ourselves in an Iraq-style mess. An exit strategy was in this sense easy. But standing back from the aftermath in this way left awkward questions about whether we should have tried harder to ensure that what followed was satisfactory.

Were our intentions good, and did we have national interests involved? It is not obvious that we did follow national interests, at least in any narrow sense. Some have pointed to Libyan oil or other commercial interests. But if we had really wanted to keep the international oil price down or have access to Libyan oil in particular, a military campaign in Libya was far from the obvious way of achieving such aims – and easily the most expensive! It was certainly in our broad national interest that democracy spread in the region and that human rights were more universally respected. Those were reasons to support the Arab spring in general, as well as supporting change in Libya.

Was the use of force proportional to the aims? Here, the answer seems to me clearly yes.

Overall, therefore, the Libyan operation did seem to meet the R2P criteria reasonably well. So the question arises whether it presages other similar operations in the future. Was it the first of a new generation of coercive interventions, based on remote power, rather than foreign boots on the ground, much cheaper and easier (at least for the intervening powers) than Iraq-style invasions, and with no complex about 'we broke it, therefore we have to fix it'? Or was it the last hurrah of international intervention in rarely-to-be-repeated circumstances? The extreme reluctance to get involved militarily in Syria, as I write, seems to support the second hypothesis. But it is hard not to believe that other cases of intervention will come along, or that current remote methods of involvement, like drone strikes, will become and remain the preferred way of intervening in all circumstances. Meanwhile, the arguments about the legality, legitimacy, and effectiveness of international interventions are bound to continue.

My view is that humanitarian intervention must remain in the international community's toolbox as the last resort for unacceptable Rwanda-style situations. Each case will be sui generis and each must involve elements of political and other judgment at the time which cannot be over-specified or completely regulated in advance by pretending that international law is like national law and can cover every eventuality. But because coercive outside intervention raises so many short- and long-term problems, whenever this issue arises we must think through all the angles very carefully indeed, even where events are moving fast, before we intervene. We need to learn properly the lessons of past failures. On each occasion, we need to reflect on whether we really know what we are doing. Is the goal achievable, are we the right people to be trying to achieve it, and what are the broader consequences likely to be? Even once we have answered these questions satisfactorily, I would say we still need to reflect once again before we finally decide whether to go in.

CHAPTER FOURTEEN

Humanitarianism in the twenty-first century: rising needs and declining security

What will humanitarian needs be in the future and how should the system change to meet them? What are the political challenges which humanitarians will have to face?

Needs

It seems sadly clear that requirements for humanitarian aid will continue growing at a significant pace, even on reasonably optimistic scenarios. If more pessimistic projections are right, the explosion of suffering could leave the international community unable to meet many urgent life-saving needs.

As we have seen, the biggest single driver is likely to be climate change. More and more intense disasters are the predicted outcome of continued warming of the planet and greater weather unpredictability – global weirding, as it has been rightly called. Dry areas will be dryer and wet areas wetter. Drought could become the biggest single threat, since it can affect tens or even hundreds of millions of people simultaneously. Some parts of the Sahel could become effectively uninhabitable as the desert spreads south, with disastrous consequences in terms of movement of people.

More conflict is not inevitable as a result of these changes – historically, for example, water shortages have tended to produce agreements between neighbours, rather than the water wars one might have expected, such as between India and Pakistan, or Sudan and Egypt. But deadly disputes cannot be excluded, as the pressures on resources reach new levels, and populations continue to rise rapidly in the worst-affected areas. Resource battles and migration could well prove to be major sources of extra humanitarian need as the century advances. Meanwhile, major floods or earthquakes in vulnerable big cities become potentially more deadly with every year as their populations rise.

Even these risks could pale into insignificance compared to the scary consequences of sea-level rise – for example in the Bangladesh delta where around 60 million people live, in a country with no spare land; or the prospect, however distant, of glacier melt in the Himalayas, with potentially catastrophic consequences for the major river systems of the Ganges, Brahmaputra and Indus on which hundreds of millions of people depend. The political and security ramifications would be huge. But the humanitarian consequences could also dwarf anything we have seen so far.

Is the fear that international response may prove incapable of dealing with a plethora of simultaneous disasters just the result of the usual blind extrapolation of existing trends? Are we taking insufficient account of unpredictable factors and of human ingenuity in devising solutions to problems when they become pressing enough? Perhaps. But it would be unsafe, to say the least, to assume it cannot happen.

There is occasional interesting talk of other solutions. For example, insurance policies triggering automatic payments in the event of disasters – catastrophe bonds. There may be some value in this, particularly if the premiums are paid by donors, not by those most vulnerable, who cannot possibly afford them. The insurance and reinsurance companies are certainly interested. Some pilots already exist. The policies need to be designed to encourage disaster risk-reduction measures, not the reverse, in the same way that good household insurance policies promote better use of locks and alarms. The unavailability of insurance is already discouraging people in developed countries from building on flood plains, or living in places on the Florida coast frequently exposed to hurricanes. But I do not believe insurance can ever be more than a small part of the answer, as long as it is not a feature of daily life in so many of the worst-affected parts of the world.

At present most humanitarian relief goes to victims of man-made violence, not natural disasters. What are the prospects for conflict? There is no sign of the number of people affected declining, even if there are fewer interstate wars than at any stage in recent human history. The long-running internal conflicts which cause so many civilian victims, in Darfur, Somalia, DRC, Afghanistan and elsewhere, show few signs of ending. Political trends in these regions look more likely to spawn fresh disputes than bring the current ones to peaceful conclusions. And the risk that fighting over agricultural land, water rights, and living space will become the new norm cannot be discounted.

Resources

We must, therefore, be prepared to deal with bigger emergencies, and more of them at the same time. In 2010 two huge catastrophes almost coincided, in Haiti and Pakistan. Each one on its own brought the system close to breaking point. Together, they overwhelmed it for months. What more do we need to do, beyond the fundamental shift to more emphasis on disaster risk reduction and local-capacity building I have already discussed?

First, more money will have to be found. In recent years, though funding is never enough for all needs, the generous response from governments, the private sector, and individuals has just managed to cover the majority of the most pressing life-saving requirements. But this is increasingly less likely to be the case unless we can spread the burden more widely. Most money currently comes from governments, but the number of governments which contribute significantly is extremely limited – a dozen Western countries bear 90 per cent of the burden. They will not be able to increase their contributions much further, certainly not while existing economic crises continue and austerity is the name of the game.

Long-running efforts to draw in other countries have had limited results. The Gulf countries, despite oil revenues beyond imagining, continue to give little multilaterally and much less than they claim bilaterally, with a lot of it channelled through opaque government-to-government arrangements or between dubious Red Crescent offices too close to governments for comfort. The big emerging economies have so far not been persuaded to match their growing economic and political power with major responsibilities in the humanitarian field. There has been some progress with countries like China, India, Brazil, and Mexico, but the amounts so far are small. Of course, these countries have huge poor populations of their own, and are themselves prone to disasters. China and India rarely ask for outside help. All this justifies them paying less than rich, less disaster-prone industrialized countries, but not with such a huge gap as now. With great power status comes great power responsibility, including sharing the burden of disaster relief.

One possibility canvassed from time to time is a system of compulsory assessed contributions from all countries, on the principle of a mutual insurance fund into which everyone is obliged to pay according to their means. The contributions scale could be weighted to ensure that the richest countries paid more than their share, but every country would pay at least something, as a signal of shared responsibility. I believe this is worth exploring. One of my greatest satisfactions as ERC was persuading almost two thirds of the UN's 193 member countries to contribute to the UN Central Emergency Response Fund. Many poor recipient countries were ready to make a token contribution themselves, out of gratitude and recognition of a universal obligation to help. But even here, the vast bulk of CERF money still came from a few of the usual suspects.

We will also have to mobilize the private sector much more effectively than hitherto. I was keen to do this, but made little progress, partly because OCHA lacked the resources to engage with companies on a long-term basis. We need to move to another level of effort to overcome apparent company reluctance to devote significant resources to humanitarian relief. Commercial actors like to see something tangible for their money, like a school or clinic, rather than the temporary satisfaction of saving lives in an emergency. Many companies are generous in other ways. The enthusiasm of employees to make a contribution of some kind is striking. But it is currently unsystematic.

There are some effective partnerships between agencies/ NGOs and private companies – for example, in the field of logistics – and some efforts to create wider alliances. But these are only scratching the surface. Partnerships in areas such as water, health, and shelter would make a lot of sense, but have not really happened. A new effort to put together the private sector and the humanitarian community is urgently needed.

This will not be easy. Humanitarians tend to be suspicious of private companies, especially when some are looking to provide aid or services on a commercial basis. They ask how this can be compatible with humanitarian principles, and why we should think that companies will be more efficient and cost-effective than NGOs, when profits have to be factored in. Experiences with big contractors in Iraq and Afghanistan have reinforced these fears. They are therefore only prepared to engage with the private sector on their own principled terms and if companies are prepared to fit into their structures and ways of doing business. This will have to change if we really want the private sector's help.

Meanwhile, attempts to engage the big foundations in humanitarian work and giving – Gates and so on – have also, so far, come to little. They too seem to prefer more tangible outcomes, but again the humanitarian community has not put enough effort into engaging with them. I see no reason why the demonstrable benefits of emergency help should not be attractive to foundations, as they have been for government donors looking to prove to sceptical publics that their money is making a difference in the world.

For individuals, the challenge, even in generous countries like the UK, will be to overcome growing donor fatigue and cynicism at yet more appeals, often for repeated crises. We have to do a much better job at showing where the money goes, i.e. not into the pockets of middlemen or corrupt local governments, but straight to those who need the help most. We have not only to do much more to tackle the underlying causes of disasters such as those in the Horn of Africa, but also to show that we are doing so. The right balance has to be found between putting graphic images of dying babies on our TV screens to shock people, and not creating a counterproductive response. In countries where there is a less strong tradition of individual giving for distant causes, new ways to get the message across must be devised. Greater investment in professional help, much of which could be pro bono, is needed. Technology can also come to our rescue, through the use of innovative methods of donation, such as through text messaging, as was done to astonishingly successful effect by the American Red Cross after the Haiti earthquake.

Systemic change

More funds are a necessary, but not sufficient, condition for better response in the future. The other requirement is to get the organization, coordination, and leadership right at every level. The establishment of OCHA and its predecessor from 1991 onwards, designed to coordinate what was too often a patchy, fragmented, and unpredictable response, has helped a lot. Successive reforms, including after the Indian Ocean tsunami of 2004, have improved the system further. But the issue now is whether further incremental change, in the face of the rising needs I have described, can be enough to transform performance. The answer may well be no. However, it is much more difficult to agree on a radical new system, or on which big changes would make the necessary difference.

The response certainly remains too fragmented, with a wide variety of independent organizations still working in only loosely coordinated ways. The number of NGOs in particular is incompatible with efficient delivery of aid. But how can such independent organizations, so committed and so effective in their own fields, be convinced to give up their identity? How can we preserve valuable diversity and constructive emulation, while reducing duplication? Voluntary certification of capacity to help in major disasters, and mergers between similar NGOs will, in my view, have to be part of the answer. Some are already aware of this. The impetus has to come from them, and cannot be imposed.

Meanwhile, how can the UN agencies, which also have overlapping mandates and responsibilities, be brought together more without creating the risk of a single bureaucratic monster where the cure would risk being worse than the disease? Again, this will have to be driven from within over time. I do not believe there is a single or simple solution, and care must be taken not to disrupt to no good purpose the improvements which have been made. Further incremental change may still be better than a badly thought-out 'big-bang' reorganization of the system at one go, throwing out the good parts with the bad, possibly for no eventual gain.

The leadership of the system must also be improved. Should the ERC position be given more authority, since currently there is only limited persuasive power? The answer is yes. But it cannot come through any imposed ability to give orders, which would be resisted and, ultimately, ineffective. Greater authority has to be earned, through continued demonstration of the added value that better coordination can bring, and encouraged through continuing donor insistence that organizations which do not play the coordination game properly will suffer financial consequences.

Good leadership at country level is even more vital. Past arguments over whether development and humanitarian leadership responsibilities can be combined need to be resolved. The decision that any new major crisis needs to see the rapid appointment of an individual capable of taking on such a huge humanitarian task needs to be effectively implemented. And the quality of UN resident and humanitarian coordinators needs to be improved by making the jobs more attractive. At the moment they have huge responsibilities and little power over the rest of the UN system in the country. The remuneration and terms of service are inadequate, and the future rewards for those who take on these challenges are unclear. UNDP, which is in charge of the resident-coordinator system, has to do more to fix it, while OCHA does more to widen the recruitment pool for those who can become humanitarian coordinators.

Whatever the structure, two areas we have to improve urgently are reliable collective needs assessment, and genuine impact evaluation. Neither is easy but it is no longer acceptable, if it ever was, to dodge these challenges. Donors and others need to know not just what the individual technical agencies think is needed in their particular area, but also what the system as a whole considers to be the best assessment of the extent and nature of the needs in each crisis situation. They also need information which will enable them to make meaningful comparisons between crises. Progress has to be made here irrespective of unworthy agency and NGO concerns about either competition with other agencies or worries that if they give 'too much' information to donors or the media, their appeals for funds might be challenged.

Everyone also needs to have a better idea of what works and what doesn't in terms of emergency relief. There are already many evaluations of emergency responses, both after the fact, and in real time, and increasing efforts to understand how those in need themselves perceive, and benefit from, what they are given. But there is still a very long way to go before we understand these dynamics well enough.

The other big transformation, already discussed, is to break down the barriers more comprehensively between humanitarian and development work. These distinctions have always been artificial and meaningless to those in need. But they are still very much there in organizational structures, sources of funds, and attitudes. Even big agencies and NGOs which do both humanitarian and development work tend to split their efforts into self-contained units, with little communication between the two. This will no longer do as we gradually face more crises which have no obvious triggers or exit points and combine the characteristics of humanitarian emergencies with long-running development problems. The donors need to do their bit here too. A single pot of money for such crises would help, with the long-term help financed as generously as the short-term emergency aid.

A final area of change should come from technology, which has been slower than it should be to make a difference to humanitarian assistance. There are, of course, inventions which have helped, from the peanut-based nutritional supplement product Plumpy'Nut, to drinking straws which filter dirty water and fuel-efficient cooking stoves. But the full effect of modern internet and communications technology is yet to be felt or exploited. For example, communication to and from those affected by disaster using mobile messaging is in its infancy. The situation is similar over checking whether those supposed to receive aid have indeed done so, using social media, rather than vulnerable and expensive human monitors. Satellite imagery to show the extent of flooding or earthquake damage is increasingly available, but still little used. Haiti showed the way in the use of mobile phones to communicate both ways, but the possibilities of Twitter, Facebook and other social media remain largely untapped.

There is no lack of talented, creative, and self-questioning people in the humanitarian business, and academic study of humanitarian aid is burgeoning as never before. If we can invest more in DRR and local capacity and continue to improve delivery and coordination of response, and if the necessary resources can be mobilized, we have a reasonable chance of keeping pace with need, and averting the worst. Otherwise, the world may face huge catastrophes without the means to tackle them effectively. Every one of us will have to face the consequences, wherever we may be lucky enough to live.

Politics, security, and humanitarians

I have talked at different points in the book about the need for governments and international institutions to get their act together better to solve problems and indeed prevent them before they happen. I recognize from my own experience that this is an easy criticism to make from the outside. Better conflict prevention and mediation are constant cries from all sides. I have no silver bullet. But if there is one piece of advice I would offer, above all to Western governments, it is the need to understand much more profoundly the roots of conflict and political problems, in all their complexities, and not to fall prey to simplistic diagnoses and solutions. The nuances are important. The problem is that much media coverage is not interested in nuance, and the experts who do exist within our systems are not listened to because what they say is not black and white enough to conform to our prejudices or fit into the sound-bite mentality. Learning that lesson, as we should have done from Iraq and Afghanistan, would be truly valuable. Humanitarian insights can help with this because they are born of first-hand experiences on the ground, not desk analysis or ideology of any kind.

Meanwhile, humanitarians have to persuade governments, of both donor and recipient countries, that respect for humanitarian principles is fundamental to properly functioning emergency relief; and that abuses of the system, either by donor governments and military organizations trying to instrumentalize aid for their own political and security purposes, or by recipient governments or non-state actors trying to divert, direct, or restrict aid, are simply unacceptable, as well as ineffective. We will not do this without finding new ways of addressing governments and other actors which are less self-regarding and high-minded, and more practical and understandable.

The problem is that the humanitarian world, like other driven communities faced by constant challenges, tends to be impermeable to outsiders. Humanitarians talk to each other a good deal, in their own special language, and assume that when they address the outside world, they will automatically be understood. My experience tells me that this is simply wrong. As I have suggested, humanitarians talk a lot about concepts like protecting and expanding humanitarian space, for example, without realizing that this means little or nothing to those outside the magic circle. We should be explaining in simple language instead why we must, in strictly practical terms, operate only on the basis of need, without political interference, and talk to all the actors on the ground; and why humanitarian aid which is not clearly independent of political considerations is automatically undermined, and the safety of those delivering it fatally compromised. A reputation for independence and impartiality is long and hard to acquire, but easy and quick to lose.

A sustained effort to this effect is needed from all humanitarian organizations, and particularly from their leaders. We have to intensify the dialogue with politicians, generals, diplomats, and journalists. In particular, humanitarians and soldiers may make awkward bedfellows, but are often on the ground together and have a shared experience of reality. They will not always agree, but they need to talk to each other much more to minimize the frictions. Sharing more training in operating together and understanding each other's worlds would be a start.

Governments and humanitarians do not have to clash, but too

often do. Unless mutual understanding can be increased, the risks to humanitarians are bound to go on growing, and the possibilities of helping people where the needs are greatest will shrink further. I hope this book may make a modest contribution by explaining why the principles matter, and why they are subject to so many pressures from others, well- and ill-intentioned alike. The politics of humanity need to be understood, and shared.

Glossary

ACF Action Contre la Faim: France-based NGO specialising in food aid.

AMIS African Mission in Sudan: peacekeeping force in Darfur until 2006.

AMISOM African Union Mission in Somalia (peacekeeping force).

ASEAN Association of South East Asian Nations.

AU African Union.

CERF United Nations Central Emergency Response Fund.

CFA Comprehensive Framework for Action: drawn up in response to the 2008 food crisis.

cluster Sectoral unit of coordination for humanitarian assistance, e.g. health, water and shelter.

CPA Comprehensive Peace Agreement: signed between south Sudan and Khartoum in 2005

DfID UK Government Department for International Development

DPA Darfur Peace Agreement: signed in 2006 but not implemented.

DPA United Nations Department of Political Affairs.

DPKO United Nations Department of Peacekeeping Operations.

DRC Democratic Republic of Congo.

DRR Disaster Risk Reduction.

D/SRSG Deputy Special Representative of the UN Secretary-General (see SRSG).

ERC United Nations Emergency Relief Coordinator.

FAO United Nations Food and Agriculture Organisation.

FARDC Armed Forces of the Democratic Republic of Congo.

FCO UK Foreign and Commonwealth Office.

FDLR Democratic Forces for the Liberation of Rwanda, also known as the Interahamwe: a predominantly Hutu rebel group based in DRC.

HC United Nations Humanitarian Coordinator: a country-based official responsible for humanitarian coordination.

HFA Hyogo Framework for Action: a strategy on disaster risk reduction agreed in 2005.

HLTF High Level Task Force: a group of agency heads set up by the UN Secretary-General to deal with the 2008 food crisis.

IASC Inter-Agency Standing Committee: a body bringing together the main humanitarian agencies.

ICC International Criminal Court.

ICRC International Committee of the Red Cross.

IDP Internally Displaced Person.

IFRC International Federation of Red Cross and Red Crescent Societies.

IOM International Organisation for Migration.

IRC International Rescue Committee: US-based NGO.

ISAF International Security Assistance Force: NATO-led security mission in Afghanistan.

ISDR/UNISDR International Strategy for Disaster Reduction.

JEM Justice and Equality Movement: Darfur rebel movement led by Khalil Ibrahim until his death in 2011.

LRA Lord's Resistance Army: armed group originally from north Uganda but now operating in South Sudan, DRC and the Central African Republic.

LTTE Liberation Tigers of Tamil Eelam: Tamil separatist movement in Sri Lanka.

MONUC/MONUSCO United Nations (Stabilization) Mission in Congo (peacekeeping force).

MINURCAT UN Peacekeeping Mission to Central African Republic and Chad.

MINUSTAH United Nations Stabilization Mission in Haiti (peacekeeping force).

MSF Médecins Sans Frontières: NGO specialising in healthcare.

OCHA United Nations Office for the Coordination of Humanitarian Affairs.

ONLF Ogaden National Liberation Front: rebel separatist movement in the Somali region of eastern Ethiopia.

oPt occupied Palestinian territories (West Bank and Gaza).

PA Palestinian Authority: Fatah-dominated legitimate government of the occupied Palestinian territories.

POC Protection of Civilians: often shortened to 'protection'.

Quartet Group of US, EU, UN and Russia seeking to play a role in the Middle East peace process.

RC United Nations Resident Coordinator: country-based official responsible for overall coordination of UN activities.

RC/HC country-based UN official combining the Resident and Humanitarian Coordinator roles.

R2P Responsibility to Protect: a doctrine on protection of civilians agreed by the World Summit in 2005.

SLM/A Sudan Liberation Movement/Army: Darfur rebel movement led by Abdul Wahid.

SG/UNSG United Nations Secretary-General.

SPLM/A Sudan People's Liberation Movement/Army: group that led the south Sudanese rebellion against the north.

SRSG Special Representative of the UN Secretary-General: country-based leader of the UN effort in crisis countries.

TFG Transitional Federal Government: legitimate government authority in Somalia 2004–2012.

UNAMA United Nations Assistance Mission in Afghanistan.

UNAMID United Nations African Union Mission in Darfur (peacekeeping force).

UNDAC United Nations Disaster Assessment and Coordination: unit of OCHA responsible for immediate assessment of disasters.

UNDP United Nations Development Programme: agency responsible for development aid and coordination of the UN system in individual countries.

UNFPA United Nations Population Fund.

UNHCR United Nations High Commissioner for Refugees (an agency as well as a person).

UNICEF United Nations Children's Fund: agency primarily responsible for child welfare.

UNMIS/UNMISS United Nations Mission in (South) Sudan: peacekeeping force.

UNSC/UNSCR United Nations Security Council/Resolution.

UNRWA United Nations Relief and Works Agency: responsible for Palestinian refugees.

USG United Nations Under Secretary-General.

WFP World Food Programme: UN agency responsible for emergency food aid.

WHO World Health Organisation: UN agency responsible for health issues.

Index

'JH' indicates John
Holmes.

9/11 attacks
(September 11,
2001) 253, 380

Abdallah, Ahmed Ould
174, 180
Abdi Dhiblawe, Hawa
170–1
Abeche, Chad 38
Abuja, Nigeria: attack
on UN building
(2011) 272
Abyei, South Sudan 76,
77–8
ACF massacre (2006)
87, 89, 91
Action Contre la Faim
4, 46, 87, 321
Addis Ababa, Ethiopia
319
Afghanistan 173, 176,
177, 182, 186, 254–
63, 273, 275, 282,
385, 395, 403

Afghanistan (*cont.*)
Afghan refugee
returnees 257
big contractors in 398
civilian deaths 257–8
continuing military
intervention in 380
elections 134
International
Security Assistance
Force (ISAF) 253
NATO actions in
367
and OCHA 256–63
Soviet withdrawal
254
Taliban takeover
(1996) 254
toxic legacy of 381
US crimes against
civilians 125
wheat imports from
Pakistan 257
Afgooye Corridor,
Somalia 170–1, 182
Africa
drought 342

Africa (*cont.*)
expenditure on
agriculture 331
food transport 338
and ICC 372
poverty 314
productivity stagnates
331
so-called African
world war 140
weather forecasting
343
see also individual
countries
African Mission in
Sudan (AMIS) 30
African Union (AU)
29, 30, 32, 42, 48,
51, 165
Agok, South Sudan 77
'aid-dependency
syndrome' 42
Aidid, Mohamed 164
Akobo, South Sudan
75, 77
Al Arish, Egypt 238–9

Al Qaeda 160, 163,
164, 172, 177, 178,
186, 324
Al Shabaab (The
Youth) militia
group 164, 169,
177–81, 184, 185,
186
Al Shifah hospital,
Gaza city 235
Algiers: 2007 attack
271
American Red Cross
399
AMISOM (African
Union Mission to
Somalia) 165, 166,
173–4, 185
Amos, Valerie 280
Angola 133, 135
Annabi, Hedi 300, 301
Annan, Kofi 35
Arab League 48, 51,
387
Arab spring 26, 60, 81,
390
Arbour, Louise 121
Aristide, Jean-Bertrand
286, 310
Association of South
East Asian Nations
(ASEAN) 190, 191,
198–9, 200, 202,
203, 210, 212
Aung San Suu Kyi
(ASSK) see Suu
Kyi, Aung San

Bahrain 388
Baidoa, Somalia 163,
171
Baker, Dan 199, 302,
303

Balkans 151
Balochistan 277
Ban ki-Moon
and Afghanistan 260
appoints JH HLTF
coordinator 327
appraisal of 14–15
and Darfur 30, 31
and DRC 139
ERC as one of his
key advisers 13–14
and the FAO head
328
and food crisis (2008)
326, 327
and Gaza 236–7, 239,
242, 243, 246
and Haiti 298
JH reports after a
field trip 22
lack of contact with
Bashir after 2009
57
and Myanmar 190,
193–4, 200, 202–3,
205, 210, 213, 214
and Pakistan 271,
274, 279
Policy Committee
meetings 30
senior management
team 1–2
sets up HLTF 326
and Somalia 172
and Sri Lanka 92,
108, 111, 114, 115,
117, 118, 127
Bangladesh 189, 198,
211, 212, 348, 394
warning of tropical
cyclones 343–4

Bashir, President 43–7,
55, 56–7, 60, 373–4
BBC 34, 91, 321
World Service 21
Bedouins 220
Belgium, and DRC
139
Bellerive, Jean-Max 306
Benghazi, Libya 386,
389
'Black Hawk Down'
incident 164
Blair, Tony 1, 378–9,
389
Blair doctrine 378
Bogotá, Colombia 349
Boko Haram 272
Bolduc, Kim 301, 303
Bosnian Muslims 377
Bosnian Serbs 377
Bowden, Mark 171–2
Brazil 333, 396
British Red Cross 208
Buhne, Neil 92, 99
Bukavu, South Kivu
134, 140
Buner, Pakistan 268–9
Burundi 135

Canada, and Haiti 289,
292, 305
Care 4, 46, 52, 169
Central African
Republic 25, 135,
141, 372
Centre of Research on
the Epidemiology
of Disasters
(CRED) 349
CERF see UN Central
Emergency
Response Fund

CFA *see* Comprehensive Framework for Action
Chad 25, 27, 38, 39
  food insecurity 324–6
Channel Four television 128, 180
China
  and Cyclone Nargis disaster 198
  rarely asks for outside help 396
Chissano, Joaquim 158
Christmas massacres (DRC, 2008) 156
'Christmas tree' mandate 32
CIA 194
Clinton, Bill 304, 307
Clinton, Hillary 304
CNDP (Congrès National pour la Défense du Peuple) 134
CNN 291
Colvin, Marie 113
Comprehensive Framework for Action (CFA) 329, 333, 334–5
Comprehensive Peace Agreement (CPA) 65, 66
Concern 4, 169
Congo 15
Congo Free State 132
'consolidated appeals' 7
Côte d'Ivoire 139
Cox, Andrew 17
Cyclone Nargis *see under* Myanmar

Cyclone Sidr (2007) 344
Cyprus 244

Daadab camp, northern Kenya 184
Danish Refugee Council 169
Darfur crisis 8, 15, 25–60, 65, 66, 67, 131, 136, 324, 366, 372, 395
  the aftermath 55–7
  the background 25–30
  farewell to Darfur 57–60
  first visit 33–40
  and the ICC 44–55, 373–4
  Joint Communiqué 35–6
  lobby groups 59
  Moratorium (2004) 35
  NGO expulsions (2009) 45–50, 53, 354–5
  OCHA office 261
  returns 40–2
  stagnation and deterioration 43–4
  statistics 28
Darfur Peace Agreement (DPA) (Abuja, Nigeria, 2006) 29
Darusman, Marzuki 127
Democratic Republic of Congo (DRC) 65, 131–60, 176, 372, 386, 395

Democratic Republic of Congo (*cont.*)
  humanitarian needs and problems 136–9
  international failures and MONUC 139–44
  LRA nightmare 155–60
  OCHA office 261
  peacekeepers and humanitarians 144–8
  'the rape capital of the world' 148–55
  the tragic importance of minerals 135–6
  troubles in the east 134–5
  unavoidable history 132–4
Democrats (US) 51–2
Department for International Development (DfID) (UK) 2, 347
Deribat, Darfur 37–8
Diouf, Jacques 328
disaster preventative measures 341–60
  building disaster-management capacity 357–8
  building local capacity 350
  disaster risk reduction 341–7
  go local 356–7
  a new business model 358–60
  what we know, but don't do 347–50

disaster preventative measures (*cont.*)
white men in shorts 351–6
disaster risk reduction (DRR) 344–9, 358, 402
Djibouti 314
Dominican Republic 286, 287, 290, 291
Don Muang former airbase, Thailand 206–7
DRC *see* Democratic Republic of the Congo
DRR *see* disaster risk reduction
DSRG/RC/HC 261
Dungu, Haut Uele, DRC 156
Duvalier, Baby Doc 286, 310
Duvalier, Papa Doc 286

Egeland, Jan 2, 28, 33, 157, 321
Egypt
frontier with Israel 221
and Gaza 230, 239, 248, 249
Palestinian refugees 220
revolution in 248
and water shortages 394
Eide, Kai 260, 262
El Fasher, North Darfur 34
Eliasson, Jan 42

Emergency Relief Coordinator (ERC)
chairs Inter-Agency Standing Committee 7
controls UN Central Emergency Response Fund 9
JH's appointment 2–3
JH's field trips 9–10, 18–22, 37
JH's most testing challenge 85
a key advisor to the secretary-general 13–14
powers 8, 400
role of 9
Ensler, Eve 152
The Vagina Monologues 152
Eritrea 186
Ethiopia
and Eritrea 186
food insecurity 314–21
Ethiopian troops
in Somalia 165, 173, 185
in South Sudan 78
European Union (EU)
disposal of surplus food 338
troops in DRC 140
Evans, Gareth 380–1

Facebook 402
FARDC (Forces Armées du République

Démocratique du Congo) 134–5
Fatah 221, 223, 227, 238, 239, 249
FDLR (Forces Démocratiques pour la Libération du Rwanda; previously Interahamwe) 135, 149, 155
Fernandez, Gloria 157
First Geneva Convention (1863) 3
Fisher, Nigel 303
'flash appeals' 7, 193, 266
Florida
disaster warnings 343
hurricane-prone coastline 348, 395
Fonseka, General Sarath 93, 113, 123
Food and Agriculture Organization (FAO) 4, 13, 316, 326–9, 334, 335, 338
food insecurity 313–39
the 2008 food crisis 326–37
Chad 324–6
Ethiopia 314–21
food aid 337–9
Niger 321–4
Foreign and Commonwealth Office (FCO) 1, 3, 10, 224
Foundation for Human Rights and Freedoms

and Humanitarian
Relief 244
France
and DRC 139
and Myanmar 196
Friends of Democratic
Pakistan 272
Funant, Henri 3
Fur tribe 25

G8 Summit (L'Aquila,
Italy, 2009) 335
Gaddafi, Colonel
Muammar 373,
386–9
Gambari, Ibrahim 57,
192, 213
Gandhi, Rajiv 86
Garang, John 65, 66
Gates, Bill 398
Gaylard, Max 239
Gaza 219–50
accountability 245–8
the aftermath 236–41
the build-up to war
228–9
controversy 232–6
first visit 223–8
the future 248–50
Hamas takeover
221–3
and the Human
Rights Council
370
one year on 241–3
Operation Cast Lead
126, 229–31, 233,
235, 239, 240, 241,
245–8
the Turkish flotilla
243–5
what crisis? 219–21

Gaza Freedom Flotilla
243–4
Geldof, Bob 313
genetic modification
(GM) technology
333
Geneva 16, 18
Geneva Global
Platform on DRR
346
Germany: mediates
negotations over
Gilad Shalat 229,
242
Ging, John 231
Global Facility for
Disaster Reduction
and Recovery 348
Goldstone, Judge
Richard 245, 246
Goma, North Kivu
134, 140–1
Gonaïves, Haiti 285
Good Friday
Agreement
(Northern Ireland,
1998) 375
Gorbachev, Mikhail
214
Grande, Lise 79
Gration, General Scott
51, 52, 55
Greatest Silence: Rape
in the Congo, The
(film) 150
Guehenno, Jean-Marie
260
Gulf countries 396
Guterres, Antonio 260

Haiti 15, 274, 279,
285–311, 356,
395–6, 402
and American Red
Cross 399
building back better
306–8
cataclysm 287–9
cholera 308
the context 286–7
frustration 297–301
getting the basics
right 289–92
humanitarian
leadership 301–4
independence from
France (1804) 286
lessons 309–11
protection 296–7
sanitation 296
shelter 292–6
US occupation
(1915–34) 286
working with other
players 304–6
Haitian police 297
Hamas 221, 222, 223,
225–35, 237–43,
246–9
Haq, Ameerah 47
Haroun, Ahmed 44
Harris, Shani 17
Haut Uele, DRC 156
Heal Africa Hospital,
Goma 152
Hebron 225
Helmand province,
Afghanistan 259
High Level Task Force
(HLTF) 326–9, 335
Hispaniola 286
Hizbul-Islam extremist
militia group 170

Holbrooke, Dick 272
Holmes, John
 career in the Foreign
 Office 1, 3, 10, 224
 and CERF 397
 diplomatic adviser to
 Tony Blair 1
 field trip statistics
 9–10
 head of OCHA 2,
 16–17
 HLTF coordinator
 327, 335
 leaves OCHA 308
 and the media 17, 22,
 231
 most testing challenge
 as ERC 85
 succeeded as ERC by
 Valerie Amos 280
 supervises UNISDR
 345
 typical field visit
 18–22
 UN Executive
 Committee on
 Humanitarian
 Affairs 15–16
 USG for
 humanitarian affairs
 and Emergency
 Relief Coordinator
 (ERC) 2–3, 9–10
Horn of Africa 184,
 313, 314, 320, 321,
 398
Human Rights
 Council 370
Humanitarian Action
 Plan 263
humanitarian aid
 aim of 4–5

humanitarian aid (cont.)
 destination of 6
 statistics 5
humanitarian
 intervention
 363–91
 accountability 369–
 71
 the ICC 371–6
 POC and the
 Security Council
 366–9
 protection of civilians
 (POC) 363–6
 the 'Responsibility to
 Protect' 376–91
humanitarianism in
 the twenty-first
 century 393–405
 needs 393–5
 politics, security,
 and humanitarians
 403–5
 resources 395–9
 systemic change
 399–403
hunger, world 313, 314
Hurricane Katrina
 (2005) 349
Hussein, Nur Hassan
 171
Hutus 133, 155, 377
Hyogo Framework
 for Action (HFA)
 345–6

Ibrahim, Khalil 29, 38,
 60
ICC see International
 Criminal Court
India
 and Cyclone Nargis
 disaster 198

India (cont.)
 poverty 314
 rarely asks for outside
 help 396
 and water shortages
 394
Indian Ocean
 tsunami (2004) 2, 8,
 88, 345, 358, 399
 tsunami warning
 systems 343
Indonesia: disaster
 management
 institutions 357–8
Inter-Agency Standing
 Committee (IASC)
 7, 16
Interahamwe (later
 FDLR) 133, 135,
 149
internally displaced
 persons (IDPs)
 more numerous than
 refugees 365
 in Pakistan 43, 264,
 265, 269, 279
 in Somalia 167–8,
 170
 in Sri Lanka 43, 101,
 115, 116, 118–22
 in Sudan 39, 40–4
International
 Commission on
 Intervention and
 State Sovereignty
 379, 380, 389
 'The Responsibility
 to Protect' report
 (2001) 379
International
 Committee of the
 Red Cross (ICRC)
 3, 4, 50, 95, 97–8,

106, 119, 276–7, 347

International Court for the Former Republic of Yugoslavia 246

International Criminal Court (ICC) 363, 371–6

and Darfur 44–5, 55, 56, 57, 60

and DRC 132, 152, 155, 158–9

established (2002) 371

and Gaza 245

mixed results 371–2

role of 371

signing and ratifying of statute 371

and Sri Lanka 126

International Crisis Group report (2010) 95–6, 126

International Federation of the Red Cross/Red Crescent (IFRC) 4, 295

International Fund for Agricultural Development (IFAD) 327–8

International Organization for Migration (IOM) 294

International Rescue Committee 4, 28, 46, 72, 136

International Security Assistance Force

(ISAF) 253, 255, 258, 259, 262, 263

International Tribunal for Former Yugoslavia 372

Iran

and Hamas 221

regime hated by Israel 222, 249

Syria's main local supporter 248

Iraq 173, 385, 403

big contractors in 398

elections 134

invasion of 380

toxic legacy of 381

US crimes against civilians 125

Irrawaddy peninsula, Myanmar 189

Islamic Courts Union (ICU) 165, 173

Islamic Jihad 222, 226, 241

Islamic Relief 4

Israel

accountability for abuses 369

air strikes on Gaza 222, 226, 227, 229–30, 231, 241, 245, 246–7

allegations against 234–5

allegations by 235–6

attitude to Iran 222, 249

blockade on Gaza 221–2, 223

builds Barrier/Wall 223–4

Israel (cont.)

declares Gaza a hostile entity (2007) 222

denies humanitarian crisis in West Bank and Gaza 219–20

established (1948) 220

Goldstone attacked 246

and Haiti 289

Israeli forces enter Gaza (2009) 229

Israeli forces leave Gaza 230

Operation Cast Lead 126

and protection of civilians 369

rocket attacks on 222, 226, 228, 229, 230, 234, 235, 241, 245

six-month ceasefire with Gaza (2008) 228–9

Israel-Palestine 172

Israeli air force 229

Israeli army 235, 247–8

Ituri, DRC 140

Jackson, Lisa 150

Jaffna, Sri Lanka 89, 90, 93

janjaweed 26–7, 28, 33, 44

Japan tsunami (2011) 342

Jebel Marra region, Darfur 37, 57

Jerusalem 242

Israeli policies 243

OCHA office 223–4

Jerusalem (*cont.*)
  Palestinian population
    in 224–5
Joint Protection Teams
    146
Jonglei state, South
    Sudan 75
Jordan 220
Juba, South Sudan 63,
    66, 69, 72, 75, 79
Justice and Equality
    Movement (JEM)
    26, 29, 38

K50 airfield, Somalia
    169–70
Kabila, Joseph 134
Kabila, President
    Laurent-Desire
    132, 133, 134, 137,
    146, 152
Kabul, Afghanistan 259,
    262
Kaelin, Walter 121
Kakuma camp,
    northern Kenya 64,
    184
Kalma camp, South
    Darfur 39–40, 43–4
Karamoja, Kenya 73
Kashmir earthquake
    (2005) 264, 270
Katanga, DRC 133
Kenya
  drought 314
  food exports to Juba,
    south Sudan 72
  nomadic societies 73
  and Somalia 184, 185
  and South Sudanese
    oil 82
Kerem Shalom, Israel
    222

Khartoum, Sudan 26,
    78
Khyber region,
    Pakistan 281
Kiir, President Salva 66
Kilinochchi, Sri Lanka
    94, 95
Kinshasa, DRC 132,
    133, 140, 141
Kismayo, Somalia 163
Kobe, Hyogo Province,
    Japan: earthquake
    (1995) 345
Kony, Joseph 141, 155–
    60, 373, 374
Korean War 14
Kosovo 142, 378, 382
Kouchner, Bernard 195
Kunar province,
    Afghanistan 259
Kushayb, Ali 44

Laroche, Eric 171–2
Lebanon 220
Leopold II, King of
    Belgium 132–3
Lessons Learnt and
    Reconciliation
    Commission (Sri
    Lanka) 126–7
Liberation Tigers
    of Tamil Eelam
    (LTTE; Tamil
    Tigers) 85–91,
    92, 93–5, 97–113,
    115–16, 118–20,
    123–8, 370
Liberia 71, 374, 385
Libya 126, 386–90
Live Aid 313
Lord's Resistance Army
    (LRA) 65–6, 70,

132, 137, 141, 144,
    155–60, 372, 373
'Lost Boys' of south
    Sudan 64
LRA *see* Lord's
    Resistance Army
Lubanga (DRC militia
    leader) 372

M23 154–5
Machar, Riek 66
Mali 324
malnutrition statistics
    313–14
Mannar, Sri Lanka 93
Mao, Chad 325
Mardan province,
    Pakistan 265, 281
Mayi-Mayi 135
Médecins sans
    Frontières 4, 46,
    170, 276–7, 289,
    321
Menik Farm camp, Sri
    Lanka 100, 101,
    109, 111, 114–15,
    118
Mercy Malaysia 356–7
Mexico 396
Middle East 15
  peace process 155
MINURCAT UN
    peacekeeping force
    324–5
MINUSTAH 286, 292,
    297, 300, 301, 308
Misseriya tribe 76, 77
Mobutu, Colonel 133
Mogadishu, Somalia
    163, 165–71, 174,
    182
Mogwanja, Martin 273,
    274

Monitoring Group on
Somalia 180
MONUC (Mission
de l'Organisation
des Nations Unies
en République
Démocratique
du Congo; later
MONUSCO) 134,
138, 140–8, 153,
155, 156, 157
Mountain, Ross 148,
157
Mukwege, Dr Denis
151
Mullaitivu, Sri Lanka
94
Multilateral Trust Fund
for development
projects 70
Muslim Brotherhood
221, 248
Muttur, Sri Lanka 87
Myanmar 15, 189–216,
302, 386
Cyclone Nargis strikes
(2008) 189–90
death statistics during
Nargis 344
isolation and paranoia
190–2
local v. international
207–9
making it happen
210–12
Nay Pi Taw 204–6
opening up 198–200
political change 213–
14
Potemkin lives 200–3
reacting to
catastrophe 192–8

Myanmar (*cont.*)
referendum (2008)
190, 191
conclusions 214–16
Myanmar Red Cross
192, 208

Nabarro, David 335
Nadesan, Balasingham
112–13
Nairobi, Kenya 165,
180
Nambiar, Vijay 108–9,
111
Namibia 133
Nangahar province,
Afghanistan 259
National League for
Democracy (NLD)
191, 214
NATO 142, 255, 259,
367, 378, 384
Nay Pi Taw, Myanmar
202, 204–5, 206
New York 16, 17, 18,
22
main UN building
13
Ngok Dinkas 76, 77
Niger 325
food insecurity 321–4
Nkunda, General 134,
140, 141, 154
non-governmental
organizations
(NGOs) 261, 353,
398
in Afghanistan 254,
256, 257, 259, 262
and the CFA 334–5
Darfur 33, 35, 36,
45–50, 52–5
and DRC 146

NGOs (*cont.*)
and ERC field trips
18, 19
and Ethiopia 318,
319, 320–1
faith-based 355–6
and food crisis (2008)
327
funding 6
in Haiti 286–7, 288,
292, 294, 298, 300–
1
and Hamas 242
humanitarian and
development work
401–2
and the ICC 376
independence 8
and Inter-Agency
Standing
Committee 7, 16
Israeli NGOs 246
and JH's appointment
3
local and
international
NGOs 356–7
and malnutrition 314
merger of 399–400
in Myanmar 192–3,
197–200, 209, 211
and Niger 321, 322–
3
number of 4, 399
and OCHA staff 17
in Pakistan 276
perceptions of 45–6,
354–5
and private
companies 397
relationship with UN
9

NGOs (*cont.*)
  and sexual violence
    in DRC 152
  in Somalia 168, 170,
    178, 179, 180, 182,
    184, 187
  in South Sudan 67,
    74
  in Sri Lanka 87–8,
    95, 101, 110, 111
  staff 351, 352
  values issue 355
  visas 36
  and WFP 337–8
North Darfur 34, 53
Northern Ireland 375
Norwegian
  government 106
Norwegian Refugee
  Council 169
Ntaganda, Bosco 155

Obama, President
  Barack 51
Ocampo, Luis 45
OCHA *see* UN
  Office for the
  Coordination of
  Humanitarian
  Affairs
Ogaden, Somali
  Regional State,
  Ethiopia 165
Ogaden National
  Liberation Front
  (ONLF) 315,
  318–21
'One UN' initiative 68,
  175
Operation Cast Lead
  126, 229–31, 233,
  235, 239, 240, 241,
  245–8

Operation Lifeline
  Sudan 64
oPt (occupied
  Palestinian
  territories) 219,
  224
  see also Gaza; West
    Bank
Organization for
  Economic
  Cooperation and
  Development
  (OECD) 326
OXFAM 4, 46

Pakistan 182, 263–82,
  302, 395–6
  back to the future
    281–2
  crisis on the north-
    west frontier 264–6
  floods 228–31
  how to operate safely
    275–6
  internally displaced
    persons (IDPs) 43
  JH sees for himself
    268–70
  Pakistani sensitivities
    266–8
  programme criticality
    survey 271
  security threats 270–
    2
  talking to terrorists
    276–7
  UN leadership 272–4
  and US 253–4, 272–3,
    281
  and water shortages
    394
  wheat exports to
    Afghanistan 257

Pakistan army 265, 267,
  279
Palestinian Authority
  (PA) 221, 239, 240
Palestinian Ministry of
  Health 230, 232–3
Panel of Experts (Sri
  Lanka) 127
Panzi Hospital, near
  Bukavu, DRC 151,
  152
Pascoe, Lynn 114, 121,
  243
Pathmanathan,
  Selvarasa (KP)
  107–8, 123
Peshawar, Pakistan 269
Petrie, Charles 192
Pitsuan, Secretary-
  General Surin 199
PLO (Palestine
  Liberation
  Organization) 221,
  249
Plumpy'Nut 314, 402
POC *see* protection of
  civilians
Port Sudan 31, 82
Port-au-Prince, Haiti
  285–8, 292, 296,
  299, 305, 307, 308
Prabakharan, Villupai
  86, 93, 112, 113,
  114
Prendergast, Kieran 1
Préval, René 286, 306
Production Safety
  Nets Programme
  (PSNP) 315
protection of civilians
  (POC) 363–6
  and the Security
    Council 366–9

provincial
  reconstructions
  teams (PRTs) 256
Puntland 163, 186

Qatar: sponsors an
  initiative in Sudan
  58
Quartet (US, EU,
  Russia and the
  UN) 225, 243

Rajapaksa, Basil 93
Rajapaksa, Gothabaya
  93, 110
Rajapaksa, President
  Mahinda 89, 91–2,
  93, 100, 117, 123,
  126, 127
Red Crescent 4, 7, 16,
  171, 396
Red Cross 4, 6, 16, 91,
  152, 192, 289, 351
  independence of 8
Refugee Convention
  (1951) 365
Republic of Congo
  (Congo-
  Brazzaville) 135
Republicans (US) 51
Responsibility to
  Protect (R2P)
  doctrine 104–5,
  190, 195, 380, 381,
  386, 390
Reuters 91
Ripert, Jean-Maurice
  274
Rome food summit
  (2008) 329
Rome institutions 327
Rwanda 135, 139, 155

Rwanda (cont.)
  genocide 133, 150,
  151, 377, 378, 381,
  382, 383–4
Rwandan army 133,
  134, 135

Sahel 321, 324, 393–4
Salim, Salim 42
Sarassoro, Idelene 319
Save the Children 4, 46
Sderot, Israel 226
Serbia conflict (1999)
  142
Serry, Robert 239
Shalit, Corporal Gilad
  226, 229, 240, 242
Sheeran, Josette 328
Siad Barre, Mohamed
  164
Sichuan earthquake,
  China (2008) 206
Sierra Leone 71, 374
  British intervention
  (2000) 140
Solferino, Battle of
  (1859) 3
Somali Red Crescent
  Society 171
Somali region, Ethiopia
  315, 316, 318, 319
Somalia 163–87, 274,
  320, 395
  the battle over
  'integration' 175–8
  drought 314
  an explosive visit
  165–8
  getting aid through
  169–75
  military efforts and
  political solutions
  185–7

Somalia (cont.)
  outsiders beware
  164–5
  withdrawal 181–5
  working where the
  'terrorists' are 178–
  81
Somaliland 163, 187
South Sudan 63–83,
  135, 141
  accepting the
  inevitable 78–80
  arrested development
  74–8
  a better future 80–3
  the importance of
  agriculture 72–4
  the legacy of civil
  war 64–7
  LRA fighters in 159
  the transition gap
  67–71
South Sudan
  government 82
South/South-East Asia:
  tropical storms and
  floods 342
Southern Nations,
  Nationalities and
  Peoples Region
  (SNNPR),
  Ethiopia 315
Soviet Union:
  withdrawal from
  Afghanistan 254
special representative
  of the secretary-
  general (SRSG)
  174, 178, 179–80,
  191–2, 261, 272,
  273
Special Tribune for
  Sierra Leone 374

Srebrenica massacre (1995) 377, 378
Sri Lanka 85–128, 131, 195, 366, 370, 386
2008: the northern offensive 92–8
2009: bloody endgame 98–106
Ban ki-Moon flies in 114–18
internally displaced persons (IDPs) 43, 101, 115, 116
the last battles 108–14
No-Fire Zone 96, 105
post-war recovery 118–23
and protection of civilians 369
reflections 123–8
talking to the LTTE 106–8
the terrorist from the UN 92
Stern, Nick: report on climate change (2006) 347
Strohmeyer, Hans-Joerg 327
Sudan
and water shortages 394
see also Darfur crisis
Sudan Liberation Movement/Army (SLM/A) 26, 29, 40, 60
Sudan People's Liberation Movement/Army

(SPLM/A) 64, 65, 75, 80
Sudanese army 25
Sudanization 46, 50, 53
Sunday Times 113
Suu Kyi, Aung San (ASSK) 191, 196–7, 213, 214, 216
Swat valley, Pakistan 264, 268, 269, 281
Syria 381, 386, 388, 390
and Hamas 248
and Iran 248
mobile phones 126
Palestinian refugees 220

Taliban 186
in Afghanistan 254–9, 261–2, 263
in Pakistan 243, 264–70, 277, 278, 281
Tamil diaspora 86, 92, 104, 105, 107, 118, 119, 123
Tamil National Association (TNA) 100
Tan Shwe, Senior General 194, 201, 205
Tandja, President 321, 322
Tanzania 135
Taylor, Charles 374
Thailand, and Cyclone Nargis disaster 198
Thein Sein, General 202, 203, 206, 213–14
Timor 385
Tontons Macoutes 286

Transitional Federal Government (TFG) (Somalia) 165, 166, 167, 171–4, 176, 177, 179, 185
Turkish flotilla to Gaza 243–4
Tutsis 133, 134, 154, 377
Twitter 402

Uganda 135
drought 314
food exports to Juba, south Sudan 72
and LRA 70, 141, 156, 157, 158, 372
and Somalia 185
Ugandan army 133
UN see United Nations
UN agencies
in Darfur 50
dealing with individual issues 13
funding 6
and High Level Task Force 326
independence 8
and Inter-Agency Standing Committee 7
in Myanmar 192–3, 199–200, 209, 211
overlapping mandates and responsibilities 400
in Pakistan 271
and sexual violence in DRC 152
in Somalia 168, 182

UN agencies (*cont.*)
in South Sudan 68–9,
74
staff 351–2
UN Assistance Mission
in Afghanistan
(UNAMA) 254–8,
260, 262
UN Central
Emergency
Response Fund
(CERF) 9, 266, 397
UN Council on
Human Rights 245
UN Department of
Humanitarian
Affairs *see* UN
Office for the
Coordination of
Humanitarian
Affairs (OCHA)
UN Disaster
Coordination
and Assessment
(UNDAC) 193,
358
UN Executive
Committee on
Humanitarian
Affairs 15–16
UN Human Rights
Council 125, 128,
246
UN humanitarian
coordinators (HCs)
8, 19, 79, 157, 178,
273, 301, 302, 303,
319, 401
UN International
Secretariat for
Disaster Risk
Reduction

(UNISDR) 345,
346, 348, 349
UN Office for the
Coordination of
Humanitarian
Affairs (OCHA) 8
in Afghanistan 254,
256–63
country offices 8, 19
creation of 67, 399
and Darfur 39, 40, 47,
261
in DRC 138, 148,
261
and Ethiopia 319
funding 16
Gaza office hit 231
and Haiti 288, 299
humanitarian
coordinators 401
Jerusalem office
223–4
JH becomes head of
2
JH leaves 308
originally named
Department of
Humanitarian
Affairs 7
policy department
327
and private
companies 397
role of 7, 9
and Somalia 178,
182–3
and South Sudan
63–4, 67–8, 78
in Sri Lanka 88
staff 7, 10, 17, 351
and UNDAC 193,
358

UN Office for the
Coordination of
Humanitarian
Affairs (OCHA)/
Department of
Peacekeeping study
(2009) 368
UN Population Fund
(UNFPA) 4
UN Press Office 17
UN Relief and Works
Agency (UNRWA)
220, 222, 231, 235,
236, 237
UN resident
coordinators (RCs)
8, 19, 68, 273, 301,
302, 303, 319, 401
UN Secretariat 13, 16
and Somalia 172
USG for
humanitarian affairs
2
USG for political
affairs 1–2, 121
UN Security Council
377, 379, 388
and Afghanistan 255
and allegations
of violations of
human rights 370
Darfur 28, 30, 37, 45,
46
DRC 139, 140, 141,
157, 158, 159
Expert Working
Group on POC
368–9
and Gaza 228, 230,
245, 246, 250
and Haiti 286
and the ICC 371,
372–3

UN Security Council
(*cont.*)
intervention without
Security Council
agreement 382–3
JH reports to 22, 367
and Kosovo 382
Myanmar 195
and protection of
civilians 366–9
Resolution 1265
366–7
Resolution 1860 230
Resolution 1973 386,
387
and Somalia 180
Sri Lanka 103, 126
UN World Food
Programme (WFP)
4, 9, 13, 16, 73, 106,
169, 178–84, 203,
207, 209, 210, 222,
231, 258, 270, 271,
290, 291, 292, 316,
326, 327, 328, 334,
335, 337–8
UN World Summit
(2005) 104, 379–80
UNAMID 30, 31, 32,
54, 57–8, 141
UNICEF 169, 273,
316, 326
United Kingdom:
relationship with
Rwanda 139
United Nations (UN)
379
and Afghanistan 255,
256, 258, 259, 261,
262, 263, 271, 380
and the African
Union 29, 30, 32,
42

UN (*cont.*)
and ASEAN 190
Department of
Peacekeeping
Operations
(DPKO) 14, 174–5
Department of
Political Affairs
(DPA) 14, 174, 175,
177, 192
and DRC 137, 139,
140, 142, 143, 157,
158, 159
and Gaza 219, 227,
230–1, 232, 236–7,
239, 240, 243
General Assembly
381
and Haiti 288, 290,
291, 299, 300, 301,
303, 304, 308
and the ICC 376
and Myanmar 196,
199, 200, 202
opposes ransom
payments 54
and Pakistan 269,
270–1, 272–4
peace negotiators in
Darfur 28
peacekeeping forces
368, 385–6
shaping norms of
behaviour 367
and Somalia 163, 165,
166, 169, 171–8
and South Sudan 66,
76
and Sri Lanka 95, 96,
98, 99, 101, 104,
105, 107, 114, 115,
121, 125, 126

Taliban claim 270
and the World Bank
69–70, 329
and world hunger
313
United Nations
Children's Fund
(UNICEF) 4, 9, 15
United Nations
Development
Programme
(UNDP) 13, 68, 69,
302, 303, 307, 401
Human
Development
Index 321
United Nations High
Commissioner
for Refugees
(UNHCR) 4, 15,
43, 260, 270, 364–5
United States
and Afghanistan
255–6, 259
disposal of surplus
food 338
and Gaza 239, 240,
242, 243, 245–6,
250
Goldstone attacked
246
and Haiti 286, 289,
292, 297, 301–2,
304–6, 307
Hurricane Katrina
349
and Israel's
accountability for
abuses 369
major drought in 336
and Myanmar 196
offers military
advisers to track

down LRA members 159
and Pakistan 253–4, 272–3, 281
and Somalia 164, 165, 172, 173, 180–1, 184
subsidies for corn for ethanol 333
UNMIS 76, 77
UNOSOM (United Nations Operation in Somalia) 164
Urquhart, Brian 1
US Congress 126, 181, 182

Vanni, Sri Lanka 93–4
Vavuniya, Sri Lanka 100
Villa Somalia, Mogadishu 166, 174

Wade, President 324
Wahid, Abdul 40, 60
Wahlstrom, Margareta 345
Walikale, DRC 132
Wallstrom, Margot 152

Waziristan, Pakistan 268, 281
West Bank
Barrier/Wall 223–4
Bedouins 220
carved-up territory 225
future of the 250
Hamas in 221
Israeli policies 243
occupied territory 219
Palestinian refugees 220
settlements 224, 240
tightly controlled by Israel 227
two-state solution issue 243, 249
WFP see UN World Food Programme
World Bank 69–70, 307, 329, 331, 334, 336, 347–8
World Bank et al: 'Natural Hazards, Unnatural Disasters - The economics of effective prevention' 348–9

World Conference on Disaster Reduction (Kobe, Japan, 2005) 345
World Health Organization (WHO) 4, 8, 169, 199
World Vision 4

Yangon (Rangoon), Myanmar 189, 200, 204
airport 207
pledging conference 203, 206
Yemen 182
Yusuf, President 166, 167

Zaire 133
Zam Zam camp, North Darfur 53
Zambia 135
Zardari, President 268, 280
Zenawi, Prime Minister Meles 315, 316, 319
Zimbabwe 133, 388
Zoellick, Bob 329